I0796728

For Bruna, who doesn't even like Disney films that much

In loving memory of Julia, because I told her I would

Disney's Animated Classics

Disney's Animated Classics

A Comprehensive Guide

Stephen Rötzsch Thomas

First published in Great Britain in 2025 by
White Owl
An imprint of Pen & Sword Books Limited
Yorkshire – Philadelphia

ISBN 978 1 03612 055 9

A CIP catalogue record for this book is available from the British Library.

Typeset by Mac Style
Printed in the UK by CPI Group (UK) Ltd, Croydon, CR0 4YY.

The Publisher's authorised representative in the EU for product safety is Authorised Rep Compliance Ltd., Ground Floor, 71 Lower Baggot Street, Dublin D02 P593, Ireland.
www.arccompliance.com

For a complete list of Pen & Sword titles please contact

PEN & SWORD BOOKS LIMITED
47 Church Street, Barnsley, South Yorkshire, S70 2AS, England
E-mail: enquiries@pen-and-sword.co.uk
Website: www.pen-and-sword.co.uk
or
PEN AND SWORD BOOKS
1950 Lawrence Road, Havertown, PA 19083, USA
E-mail: uspen-and-sword@casematepublishers.com
Website: www.penandswordbooks.com

Contents

Introduction viii

The Golden Age 1

Chapter 1 Snow White and the Seven Dwarfs – Once Upon a Time… 3
Chapter 2 Pinocchio – Manifesting a Theme Song 9
Chapter 3 Fantasia – Fantasound and Vision 13
Chapter 4 Dumbo – Cheers, Big Ears 17
Chapter 5 Bambi – A Death in the Woods 21

The Package Era 25

Chapter 6 Saludos Amigos – A Few Goofy Men 27
Chapter 7 The Three Caballeros – What! No Mickey Mouse? 32
Chapter 8 Make Mine Music – Sinking with a Trace 36
Chapter 9 Fun & Fancy Free – RSVP (Really Suspect Ventriloquist's Party) 39
Chapter 10 Melody Time – Yippee-kay-nay 42
Chapter 11 The Adventures of Ichabod and Mr. Toad – Copy Paste Chase 46

The Silver Age 49

Chapter 12 Cinderella – A Rags-to-Riches Tale 51
Chapter 13 Alice in Wonderland – How Do You Get to Wonderland? 54
Chapter 14 Peter Pan – Ten Old Men and One Old Woman 58
Chapter 15 Lady and the Tramp – Barks and Recreation 65
Chapter 16 Sleeping Beauty – Beautiful Dreamer 68

The Transition Era 71

Chapter 17 One Hundred and One Dalmatians – Spot the Difference 73
Chapter 18 The Sword in the Stone – The King's Hand 76
Chapter 19 The Jungle Book – Marvelling at the Cinematic Universe 78

The Bronze Age 81

Chapter 20 The Aristocats – Cat's Got His Tongue 83
Chapter 21 Robin Hood – Hot in Nottingham 87
Chapter 22 The Many Adventures of Winnie the Pooh – Oh Bother, Where Are Thou? 90
Chapter 23 The Rescuers – Hide and Squeak 93
Chapter 24 The Fox and the Hound – Hounded Out and Hunted Down 96
Chapter 25 The Black Cauldron – Toil and Trouble 100
Chapter 26 The Great Mouse Detective – Big Cheese 103
Chapter 27 Oliver & Company – Cool Cats and Hot Dogs 107

The Disney Renaissance 111

Chapter 28 The Little Mermaid – Renaissance Men 113
Chapter 29 The Rescuers Down Under – Sloppy Seconds 116
Chapter 30 Beauty and the Beast – Something There 120
Chapter 31 Aladdin – When You Wish Upon a Corporate Entity 125
Chapter 32 The Lion King – Shakespeare on the Savannah 129
Chapter 33 Pocahontas – And They All Lived… 134
Chapter 34 The Hunchback of Notre Dame – French Horn 138
Chapter 35 Hercules – Drawing on the Classics 142
Chapter 36 Mulan – Exit, Propelled by a Firework 145
Chapter 37 Tarzan – Welcome to the Jungle, We Got Soft Rock Ballads 148

The Post-Renaissance Era 151

Chapter 38 Fantasia 2000 – Rhapsody Mk. 2 153
Chapter 39 Dinosaur – One of Our Disney Films is Missing 157
Chapter 40 The Emperor's New Groove – Llama Drama 161
Chapter 41 Atlantis: The Lost Empire – Mirror, Mirror 165
Chapter 42 Lilo & Stitch – Close Encounters of the Merch Kind 169
Chapter 43 Treasure Planet – 2002: A Space Odyssey 172
Chapter 44 Brother Bear – And the Winner is… 176
Chapter 45 Home on the Range – A Discouraging Herd 180
Chapter 46 Chicken Little – Clucking Hell 182
Chapter 47 Meet the Robinsons – The Bare Necessities are the Mother of Invention 187
Chapter 48 Bolt – His Bark is Worse Than His 'Good Morning! Oh, and in Case I Don't See You, Good Afternoon, Good Evening, and Goodnight." 190

The Revival Era 195

Chapter 49 The Princess and the Frog – In Black and White 197
Chapter 50 Tangled – Big Hair, Don't Care 202
Chapter 51 Winnie the Pooh – Hunny, I'm Home 205
Chapter 52 Wreck-It Ralph – Playing to the Crowd 208
Chapter 53 Frozen – Top of the Ice Pops 211
Chapter 54 Big Hero 6 – Parental Leave 215
Chapter 55 Zootopia – A Brave New World 219
Chapter 56 Moana – Miranda, Make Way! 222
Chapter 57 Ralph Breaks the Internet – The Princess Inquiries 225
Chapter 58 Frozen II – Do You Want to Build a Franchise? 229

The Streaming Era 233

Chapter 59 Raya and the Last Dragon – It's the End of Baloo as We Know Him (But He Feels Fine) 235
Chapter 60 Encanto – The First Rule of Bruno is… 238
Chapter 61 Strange World – Journey to the Self-Centred of the World 241
Chapter 62 Wish – Seeking Happily Ever After 245
Chapter 63 Moana 2 – A Waterlogged Epilogue 249

Acknowledgments 252
Bibliography 254
Index 258

Introduction

It is Christmas Day 1994, and I am on the living room floor of my family home in West Sussex. Various relatives have just arrived and, with only a little pressure from my younger sister and me, we have moved promptly on to the gift-giving part of the day. Jumpers have already been exchanged. Kneepads for weeding in the garden. My sister has been given a cuddly toy cat, its limbs and tail painstakingly wrapped individually so that everybody in the room knows exactly what it is the moment we set our eyes on it.

I am still watching my sister unwrap the cat when my Uncle Jim taps me on my shoulder and hands me a hard, rectangular package. I know right away that I am holding a VHS case.

I eagerly tear at the paper and, in that brief moment, my mind races through all the possible options. I know the video in my hands will be a Disney release, but which one will it be? In my heart, I hope it is *Aladdin*, easily the most popular film among the other kids at school, and also one that I have not yet seen. Maybe, though, it will be *The Fox and the Hound*, which I've seen on the shelves at my local supermarket. Surely, my uncle must know that my favourite animal in the world is the fox – not least because of Disney's *Robin Hood*, which we recorded from the TV a year or so earlier.

I've been so lost in thought that the video case now sits in my hands, shreds of paper on the floor below, as though I've begun making a nest for myself.

Snow White and the Seven Dwarfs.

I don't know what to say. I wanted adventure, or foxes – ideally a little of both. Instead I have been given a film that is older than my grandparents. A film about someone whose biggest claim to fame is that she's *pretty*. I turn the case over in my hands and wonder if perhaps I have been given a gift that was intended for my sister. Maybe there's another film amid the small pile of presents at my uncle's feet. Maybe it's all some sort of horrible mistake. I turn, confused, and look to Uncle Jim.

"A little birdy told me you wanted this," he says.

Someone in my inner circle has betrayed me. My eyes dart about the room – I am seven, and my inner circle consists more or less of my parents, my sister, and the less overtly aggressive of our two cats. I see no beads of sweat, guilty looks, or repressed laughter. Mustering all the faux sincerity I can, I thank my uncle for my present.

Over the coming years, *Snow White* will sit on the shelf among a few other Disney videos. *The Little Mermaid*, *Peter Pan* and *The Jungle Book* are all regularly watched in our household. So too, are *Beauty and the Beast*, *The Lion King* and *The Aristocats.*

But I watch *Snow White* only once or twice. And each time I do, I ask myself the same question: how did *this* lead to all those films I love so much?

That question has stuck with me ever since, even as my appreciation of that earliest Disney feature has grown significantly. Disney has entrenched itself in the collective consciousness with a remarkable run of unique animated features known by fans and film historians alike as 'the animated classics' or 'the animated canon.' These films, starting with *Snow White* in 1937, have played an immeasurable role in defining the childhoods of multiple generations; this book celebrates the extraordinary creativity that runs through them all.

I've separated the sixty-three films covered here into nine sections, each covering a different era within the canon. The first five films, from *Snow White* to *Bambi*, have been recognised retroactively as the studio's 'Golden Age.' After the United States entered the Second World War, Disney was forced to rethink his approach to filmmaking – the movies that followed are known as the 'Package Era' because they each consist of various shorts 'packaged' together into a longer feature. If you aren't a big old Disney nerd like me, it's very possible you won't be familiar with the films of this period at all. Fear not – all but one are available on Disney Plus, and you honestly aren't missing out if you never see *Make Mine Music*.

Disney's post-war return to form was led by *Cinderella*, which ushered in the so-called 'Silver Age.' Then, as Walt Disney's interests moved from animation to live-action features and theme parks, we have the 'Transition Era.' In 1966, Walt passed away, and the following two decades or so have been variously described as Disney's 'Dark Age' or 'Bronze Age.' I've gone for the latter in this book because the former feels a little hyperbolic and because *The Aristocats* deserves more credit than the former title is giving it.

In the late 1980s, a change of leadership at the studio brought about an unprecedented new run of critically revered classics, including *Beauty and the Beast*, *Aladdin* and *The Lion King*. Unfortunately for the teams involved at the time, Walt had already nabbed the 'Golden Age' title, and so this period became known as 'The Disney Renaissance,' which does have a nice ring to it. Since then, the studio has both floundered again (the 'Post-Renaissance Era') and flourished again (the 'Revival Era'). The last few years have ushered in another period of uncertainty for Disney as the studio moves into the global streaming wars, fending off competition from Netflix, Amazon and Apple. For now, fans refer to this period as the 'Streaming Era'. Time will only tell where popular opinion settles on the current run of Disney classics.

I urge you not to take this book too seriously. I have tried to capture both the individual moments that made these classic films what they are, and the broader trends and themes that we can see running through these otherwise very disparate stories. But I am also a fan of the Disney canon; like any fan, I have opinions that won't be universally shared among all of my readers. I apologise in advance to anyone who holds a special place in their heart for *The Black Cauldron*, and I know that my choice for the best song in *Frozen* will upset more than a few of you.

Hopefully, though, you'll find much to love in this book. It is, after all, a celebration of a studio that has played a role in the lives of billions. Whether you self-identify as a Disney Adult or are just a casual fan looking to better understand one of the most influential companies in motion picture history, there is so much to explore here.

And finally, I owe one person a belated apology. I'm sorry, Jim. I still don't know who told you to buy me *Snow White and the Seven Dwarfs* that Christmas. But by giving me that film, you set off a curiosity about Disney – and cinema itself – that has burned in me ever since. In a sense – in a very literal sense – you gave me a film I did not want and a video that I only watched twice (and even then, mostly out of guilt on both occasions). But you also gave me everything I needed to write this book. And my thanks for that is much, much more sincere than the one I gave you back in 1994.

The Golden Age

Chapter 1

Once Upon A Time…

Snow White and the Seven Dwarfs • *1937* • *David Hand*

The acclaimed artist sits on a stool, a table of prop art materials set out before him. The man's eyes – steely, determined – are focused somewhere just off camera. A thin moustache ensures he is instantly recognisable to fans of his work. Behind him is a poster for his latest cartoon – the first animated feature film the world has seen. The year is 1917, the artist's name is Quirino Cristiani, and his new feature, *El Ápostol*, is a landmark in cinema history.

Walt Disney was a pioneering force in the world of film, but he was very rarely the first to any particular milestone. From the late 19th century, and throughout much of the first half of the 20th, animation seemed like a new American gold rush. As new technologies tumbled out into the world, hundreds of ambitious young men and women sought to exploit their possibilities. As a result, it's often hard to pinpoint exactly who managed to do what first.

El Ápostol may be considered by many to be the first animated feature, but even this is in dispute. Cristiani's film – an Argentinian political satire whose lead character was the nation's then-president, Hipólito Yrigoyen – was only ever screened in Buenos Aires and was eventually banned for its subversive message. But it may not be the first full-length animated film. A year before *El Ápostol* debuted, an American named Pinto Colvig completed his own animated effort, *Creation.* Little is known about the film now, and only five 33mm frames survive. It's unclear exactly how long a feature film should be, or even how long Colvig's film was, but it remains frequently cited as the first past the post.

And here's the real kicker: *Snow White and the Seven Dwarfs* wasn't even the first animated feature released by Walt Disney Pictures. Earlier in 1937, the studio released the snappily titled *Academy Award Review of Walt Disney Cartoons.* The film is a bit of a cheat, though: a compilation of the winners of Best Animated Short Film from each of the five Academy Awards that had been held to date – all Disney productions, of course. But it served audiences as a reminder of just what Disney was capable of, whetting their appetite for the studio's first full-length film, which Walt had been promising for the previous three years.

* * *

Walt Disney had already been making cartoons for over a decade when he decided the time was right to move into features. He'd been just 19-years-old when he produced his first shorts for a local cinema in Kansas City, establishing his own studio to meet demands. He was still only 21 when the company went bankrupt.

His second company fared a little better. After two successful series, Walt and his close collaborator Ub Iwerks created Mickey Mouse. Mickey's third short offers up one of those few occasions where Walt really can claim a milestone in cinema – *Steamboat Willie* was the first cartoon to feature synchronised sound. From this point on, the Walt Disney Studio was a force to be reckoned with. Their cartoons were global successes, beloved by audiences and critically acclaimed to boot.

Walt's willingness to push boundaries and embrace new technologies often yielded fantastic results, but was also frequently responsible for his company's financial troubles. When Technicolor was looking to see how their new three-colour process might work with animation, Walt ordered his teams to re-do the black and white work already completed on a Silly Symphonies short named *Flowers and Trees*. The project ran so over budget that the company's very existence seemed to balance upon whether or not the film succeeded. *Flowers and Trees* became the first winner of the Academy Award for Animated Short Film and opened Disney's aforementioned compilation feature. It was also a roaring success among audiences in 1932, who, it turned out, had been simply *begging* to watch some vibrant trees cavort about. An exclusive contract with Technicolor was drawn up, and no other animator could use the three-colour process until 1936.

* * *

For all the acclaim, Walt's problem was this: it cost a lot of money to make the best cartoons in the world, but cinemas had very different pay scales for short and feature-length films and were unwilling to pay larger fees for a seven-minute-long animation.

Walt began to toy with the obvious solution: releasing his own feature-length films. He knew the project might be a hard sell, so started dropping the idea into conversations with colleagues around the studio to see how it was received. There was plenty of enthusiasm, and after considering a number of stories (including a contemporary novel by Felix Salten named *Bambi, a Life in the Woods*), the studio settled on an old Brothers Grimm fairy tale, *Snow White*. Walt knew that the story could make for a captivating film – one of his very first experiences with cinema had been a free screening of a silent film version in 1916.

Even as they began production on the film, though, Walt and his animators worried about the public's willingness to commit to a feature length animation. They weren't alone: leading figures throughout the film industry were dismissive of the endeavour. Before long, the film was being discussed around Hollywood as 'Disney's Folly', which is the sort of phrase that might seem pretty tame now, but in the 1930s was an absolutely *devastating* burn. It wasn't until the summer of 1935, when Walt stumbled across a cinema in Paris that was running a programme consisting entirely of his cartoons and not featuring a full-length film at all that he realised the audience appetite was there. Now Walt was all in.

* * *

When watching *Snow White* today, perhaps the most striking aspect of the film is just how gorgeous it remains. Every scene is exquisite – from Snow White's reflection shimmering in the water of the wishing well to the thunderous cliffside climax.

This is some feat for the studio's first true feature, and all the more impressive given that Disney needed to meet the continued demand for shorts that would help ensure they'd make it through production without going bust.

In order to deliver the amount of art needed for these competing projects, Disney brought in a glut of new artists. Walt had already surrounded himself with some of the brightest talent in the business – the prestige that Disney had built up meant that animators like Bill Tytla, who helped to define the personalities of the dwarfs in *Snow White*, would willingly take pay cuts in order to join the team at Hyperion Studios. Art classes were held at the studio in order to bring everybody up to Walt's exacting standards, and the impact is seen clearly in the film.[1] There would be many attempts, but no Disney film would look as good as *Snow White* for at least fifty years.

* * *

Disney had spent the years leading up to *Snow White* honing the concept of character in animation. Though there had been successful recurring stars of the genre, from Felix the Cat to the studio's own Oswald the Lucky Rabbit and Mickey Mouse, these characters had often been fairly shallow – devoid of anything more than a penchant for troublemaking, or a determination to continue against the odds.

1933's *Three Little Pigs*, the second short to win the Oscar for Disney, marked a turning point. The classic story lends itself to animation – singing pigs and wolves with the lung capacity to blow away wooden houses generally being pretty hard to come by in the real world. But the three little pigs look essentially the same as one another, and so Disney's animators worked to differentiate them through their personalities. The short was groundbreaking, and soon animators were finding new ways to define the characteristics of their biggest stars, allowing Mickey, Donald and Goofy to move closer to the versions we know today.

---

1. These art classes had actually been started by one of Walt's top animators, Art Babbitt, a few years earlier. Initially Babbitt had held an impromptu life-drawing class in his own home, inviting only the seven animators he shared an office with. As word spread of the evenings, which generally featured models in various states of undress as the subjects, more and more animators turned up. Eventually news reached Walt, who acknowledged both the value of the activity *and* how it might look for the company image if news got out about his animators gathering in somebody's living room to look at naked women. He offered to pay for a bigger space, and brought in professional art teacher Don Graham, who applied his broader understanding to the animator's work, and enabled the staff at Disney to make technical leaps and bounds in the coming years. As far as I can tell, naked women remained among the subjects on the curriculum.

These developments were also key to *Snow White*'s success. Although there are only twelve talking parts in the entire film, they would need to carry the story for over eighty minutes.

Of course, nowhere is the development of distinct personalities more obvious than in the dwarfs. The seven that made the final film – Doc, Bashful, Sneezy, Dopey, Sleepy, Dopey, Dopey and Grumpy[2] – were finalised fairly late in the process. The last of the gang to make the cut was Sneezy, who was settled on in early 1936, less than two years before the film premiered.

Sneezy was brought in to replace a dwarf named Deafy, whose presence might have very heavily impacted how well the film has aged in the years since. Early lists of proposed dwarfs reveal that many of the defining traits considered were physical – Chubby, Baldy and Shorty among them. Others, like Wheezy, Burpy and Sniffy, are more malady-based. Also considered were Lazy, Jumpy, Thrifty, Weepy and Graceful. One poor dwarf named Awful seemed to exist solely as the victim of the dwarfs' bullying. He would have been constantly lectured regarding how worthless he was, despite not really doing much to warrant it. The only characteristic animators ever seemed to settle on Awful having was a deep connection with animals. I know this depends heavily on *exactly* how deep that connection went, but it hardly seems worthy of the name. Elsewhere, dwarf names defy clear explanation altogether: Hotsy and Neurtsy leap to mind. My favourite of the rejected dwarfs is also – by some way – the one with the worst name. Biggo-Ego. Also considered under the name Biggy-Wiggy, there is a charming laziness to both choices. Sometimes a creative idea strikes you like lightning, out of the blue. This was clearly not the case for Biggo-Ego, who we can only assume was pitched out of sheer desperation at 3 am after a long night of brainstorming.

It feels, ultimately, as though the right little men made the cut.[3] Every other name suggested feels either too cruel or too dull. And the dwarfs are anything but dull. Though Happy tends to fade into the background a little, each of them adds something to the final film. Bashful is sweet without becoming tiresome. Doc's malapropisms would have been particularly hilarious to contemporary audiences – comedians like Joe Twerp and Roy Atwell were famous for their mispronunciations. It was Atwell who delivered Doc's lines here, stumbling happily over his words.

Though Dopey remains an absolute joy to watch – so clearly influenced by the likes of Harpo Marx – the dwarf with the most defined story arc is Grumpy. Among the first of the dwarfs to be chosen for the final line-up, Grumpy's immediate (and, let's face it, misogynistic) disdain for Snow White is among the biggest hurdles the princess faces in the film.[4] Walt was keen not to solve this tension too early – it

2. I am, of course, missing Happy here. This is the order in which Snow White kisses the dwarfs before they head off to work in the mines.
3. 'Little men' is how the dwarfs are described throughout the film – were it not for the title itself, it might have been how we think of them today, too.
4. You could argue the *only* one given that the animals and dwarfs save her from homelessness in the woods, and the Prince saves her from eternity in an entirely solar-powered tanning bed.

is only in Snow White's last meaningful interaction with the dwarfs, kissing their little bald heads on the doorstep, that Grumpy comes around.

That Grumpy remains a likeable character is down both to Tytla's animation in key scenes (including his response to the kiss) and to the actor behind the role – one Pinto Colvig. After directing *Creation*, Colvig's career seemed to draw him closer and closer to Disney. First, after Universal booted Walt and his animators off of the Oswald the Lucky Rabbit series, the studio sought to replicate the success of the new sound cartoons featuring Mickey. Colvig worked on the post-Disney Oswald cartoons as an animator and writer, and in 1930 he became the voice of Walt's creation on film. That same year, Colvig followed so many other animators at the time and defected to Disney. By 1932 he was the voice of both Goofy and Pluto. He would continue to voice the former until shortly before his death in 1967. Colvig was an invaluable part of those early Disney days, making the mark on animation history that his own feature film had struggled to do. Not only does he voice Grumpy in *Snow White*, but he plays Sleepy too.

* * *

Snow White herself, in comparison to the dwarfs, can come across a little plain. Much effort was made to find the right balance in portraying the more traditional-looking princess, the Queen and Prince. Early drafts of Snow White proposed a much more stylised approach that left her looking a little like a Bratz doll. In the end the team turned to rotoscoping – a method of animating over filmed footage that we'll explore more in a later chapter. The result is character movements that feel more realistic, but at the cost of some of their charm.

The Queen comes in two distinct forms. Initially, she is tall and sublime, with a sinister air that would inform many Disney villains to come. Later, she transitions into the crooked witch – a change that so startled Walt's young daughter Diane that she had to be removed from an early screening. Both versions of the Queen were voiced by Lucille La Verne in what would turn out to be her final role. 68-years-old at the time of recording, there were concerns La Verne's voice was too aged for the Queen, but too 'smooth' for the Witch. For the latter, she found a handy trick that enabled her to deliver her lines perfectly: she removed her false teeth.

Though the Prince, the Woodsman and the Mirror all feature too, perhaps some of the most charming and impactful characters in the whole film are the forest animals who frequently come to Snow White's aid, whether she's lost in the woods, breaking and entering (and cleaning), or falling prey to an incredibly obvious con job involving a terrible apple.[5]

---

5. Poisoned, not Granny Smith. Though offer me both, and I'll still think twice before taking the Granny Smith.

Five supervisors were given the task of bringing the animals of the forest to life: James Algar,[6] Bernard Garbutt, Milt Kahl, Eric Larson, and Louie Schmitt. Their work, and that of the units they ran, give *Snow White* so much of its undeniable charm. The scenes around 'Whistle While You Work' feel like the connecting point with Disney animated shorts – as the animals clean the dwarfs' house, the audience, for a brief moment, could be fooled into thinking they were watching a classic Silly Symphony.

* * *

As late as September 1937, the film's completion remained in the air. *Snow White* was running wildly over budget, and the studio needed $250,000 to finish the film. Walt turned to Joe Rosenberg of the Bank of America for the financial push over the line, inviting him to come to the studio and watch the unfinished film. Rosenberg, being relatively new to the film business, spoke in advance to senior figures around Hollywood. They once again poured scorn on 'Disney's folly', convinced this was a further sign that the film was doomed. Rosenberg attended a private screening that even Roy Disney didn't turn up for. Rosenberg and Walt sat beside each other for the whole film, with Walt attempting to describe how the missing segments and unfinished art would come together. The banker said nothing throughout the screening, but as he got in his car to leave, turned to Walt and told him that the film would be a wild success. The loan was given, and the film was completed.

* * *

It's hard today to understand exactly how big a hit *Snow White* was upon its release. Audiences, it turned out, had no problem paying to see an animated feature, and they would continue to do so for a long time. The film became the most successful sound picture to date and made $7,846,000 internationally over the course of its run. It could have made more: two years after the film debuted, Disney removed it from the market. It was the first glimpse at the savvy art of scarcity that the studio would pull for years to come. By taking it out of circulation, Walt ensured his work wouldn't be shown in discount cinemas, retaining its status as a prestige piece of art.

This sort of thinking epitomises Walt Disney's approach to his work and is the reason why *Snow White* is still miscredited by so many as the first animated feature. Walt didn't do it first, but he did it *best*. By creating a culture where his artists could become the best in the business and by pouring all his resources into delivering the finest quality picture that he could, he created a first all of his own. *Snow White and the Seven Dwarfs*: the first film to show audiences the true potential of animated cinema.

---

6. Jim Algar has a long and storied history with Disney, and would go on to claim a director's credit in three future animated classics, peaking with *The Sorcerer's Apprentice* segment of *Fantasia*. But he also had a hand in one of Disney's darkest moments, as director of the 1958 documentary *White Wilderness*. It was this film that popularised the belief that lemmings jump from cliffs. In 1982 a CBC documentary revealed that the scene had been faked (albeit not directly by Algar). It makes for an interesting section on Wikipedia, and for a classic 1990s video game.

Chapter 2

Manifesting a Theme Song

Pinocchio • *1940* • *Hamilton Luske, Ben Sharpsteen*

While his animators had laboured away on *Snow White*, Walt had been harbouring grander ambitions. He believed that the studio, once settled into the practice of animating feature-length movies, would be capable of delivering no less than two new projects each year. Perhaps, had he had access to a wishing star, he might have been right.

Alas, the lengthy production of his second feature, *Pinocchio*, put paid to such lofty expectations. Walt was, after all, something of a perfectionist – several months' worth of early work on this new feature was thrown out as he attempted to mould the film into what he believed it could be.

There was much to shape, too. *Pinocchio* is based on a novel by Carlo Collodi. Though it offered more pre-existing plot and structure than *Snow White*'s source material had provided, it brought its own problems. For one, the literary Pinocchio is an obnoxious and frequently unlikeable character. As soon as Geppetto has taught the little wooden boy to walk, he runs away and, in doing so, manages to get Geppetto arrested. The first time Pinocchio is addressed by the (unnamed) talking cricket in Collodi's novel, he throws a hammer at it, killing the poor fellow.

Not that the puppet has an easy time of things himself. Over the course of the book, he is robbed, scammed, sent to prison, and hanged from a tree. He watches his adoptive father get eaten by a dogfish and is then made to go to school like nothing happened. He is, of course, turned into a donkey – and then sold to the circus, and then again, this time to a man who wishes to skin him. He is thrown into the sea to drown, where fish actually *do* skin him alive, turning him back into a puppet.

Walt clearly thought all of this was a bit much for a ninety-minute-long family film. He dropped large sections of the original novel (a relatively easy task, given that it was written for serialisation) and heavily adapted that which remained. His changes were so significant that he infuriated Collodi's nephew Paolo Lorenzini, who attempted (unsuccessfully) to have the Italian government sue Disney for libel, claiming they had presented the Italian icon as American. It's a bold claim given how distinctly Alpine the film's setting is. Lorenzini was himself an author, and it's very likely that his frustrations were simply that Disney's adaptation was distracting from his own cynical sequels to his uncle's book, which he had begun to churn out after an entirely original idea of his, *The Adventures of Pipetto: Story of a Puppet* had failed to grab the public's imagination.

Walt's willingness to diverge from the source material gives the film a distinct boost, as does his commitment to the artistic quality viewers had seen in *Snow White*. As a technical achievement, *Pinocchio* outperforms its predecessor at every opportunity. Take, for example, the groundbreaking shot of morning in the town, which pans in on the streets from afar using the studio's multiplane technology until it's close enough for townsfolk to wander into the shot.[1] It's a precursor to similar shots in *Beauty and the Beast* and *The Hunchback of Notre Dame*, both films that wouldn't be released for another half a century. The scene looks every bit as impressive, too. And then, just as you think the camera has settled, it drifts down to the right and through an archway, revealing another expansive vista.

Later, Pinocchio and his conscience, Jiminy Cricket, traverse the ocean floor on a hunt for the whale that ate Geppetto. The techniques used by the Disney animators to create a subtle watery effect over the scene would later provide a key reference point for *The Little Mermaid*. Walt's team weren't just delivering groundbreaking effects for the 1940s – they were setting the bar for the animation industry for decades to come.

Having been pulled from a serialised novel, Disney's *Pinocchio* does suffer a little from its episodic nature. Where most Disney films have just one central villain, and perhaps a henchman or two for added thrills, our brave puppet hero comes up against no less than five. There are, perhaps, too many, and by the end, it is only the final boss, Monstro the whale, who lingers with the audience.

Two of the film's supporting cast have retained a place in the public consciousness – though not without a little help. Jiminy Cricket remains the most famous figure in the movie beyond its star. But then he always was falling backwards into success. Here, he manages to wrangle a medal for his work as a conscience despite:

1. Frequently getting ignored while delivering the role.
2. Repeatedly giving up on his charge just because he wasn't getting through and
3. Only getting the job in the first place because he *literally broke into a house* twelve minutes before a fairy magically bestowed life upon a wooden puppet.

Jiminy Cricket – whose name had been used as a euphemistic exclamation in place of 'Jesus Christ' for well over a century by this point – has found numerous other gigs across Disney's output over the years. In fact, this isn't even the only time within the animated canon that we watch him trespass into a stranger's home.

You may also recognise Gepetto's cat, Figaro, from elsewhere. The character was Walt's favourite from the film's cast, and quite rightfully so. The little kitten offers most of the film's biggest laughs, with his grouchy dinner table performance a particular highlight. After *Pinocchio*'s release, Walt had Figaro replace a pomeranian as Minnie Mouse's pet in a number of short films, as well as giving him a brief series of his own.

1. We'll touch more on the groundbreaking multiplane technology in the *Meet the Robinsons* chapter.

But both of these characters have become a part of the collective consciousness as much through their post-*Pinocchio* careers as anything else.

Instead, it is those individual iconic moments that stick with us – so much so that we amplify their actual significance within the film. Take, for example, the common memory that Pinocchio's nose grows when he lies. It does – but we only see this happen in a single scene within the film, when the wooden boy is interrogated by the Blue Fairy as to how he came to be locked inside a small cage in a strange man's wagon.

The film's stand-out song, 'When You Wish Upon a Star' is probably the element of *Pinocchio* that has enjoyed the most cultural longevity. It bookends the story and features throughout the film as a theme within the wider score.

The song was written by composer Leigh Harline, a frequent collaborator with Disney on their Silly Symphonies shorts and *Snow White*, and Ned Washington, who would go on to write a number of title tracks for Western movies in the 1950s. The pair were talented musicians and immediately recognised that they had a hit on their hands. How big a hit they had was another matter entirely.

'When You Wish Upon a Star' has become the emblematic anthem of everything that Disney has come to stand for. It is, at its heart, an ahead of its time ode to the concept of manifestation, and though they'd never put it like that, this is more or less the message that Disney hopes to put across whenever they open a film with a twilight castle and the familiar melody of the song's chorus. The power – and indeed magic – of hope is a theme that is returned to time and time again over the course of the animated canon. For Cinderella 'a dream is a wish your heart makes', and faith and trust are two of the key ingredients to successful flight in *Peter Pan*.[2] Not for nothing is the release that marked a century of Disney animation simply titled *Wish*.

And so, 'When You Wish Upon a Star' is – as well as one of the very best numbers in the Disney songbook – the most culturally pervasive. The company, of course, uses it everywhere it can. It is the closest thing the studio had to a theme song. Those opening notes even appear as the signal horns on the ships in Disney's cruise liner fleet.

It's been covered by dozens of artists, too. Many are drawn in by the temptation to deliver big, sweeping versions that end up a little overblown. Both Cynthia Erivo and Sara Bareilles have lost their way in this manner in recent years. The best takes always reflect the quiet hope of the song. Olivia Newton-John just about holds herself back on a 1989 version. Gene Simmons offers up a surprisingly straightforward take as the closing track on his debut solo album. For me, the two definitive versions come from equally unexpected quarters. In 1991, Billy Joel recorded a lightly jazzy version for an official Disney compilation album called *Simply Mad About The Mouse*. His vocal – a little grizzled by his usual standards – is filled with more yearning

2. The final ingredient is, of course, pixie dust – which you suspect is doing most of the lifting (literal and metaphorical) in this particular recipe.

than any other recording of the track. It touches upon grandeur, but even as the strings swell, it never feels like it belongs anywhere bigger than a smoky piano bar.

The version recorded by mid-century doo-wop group Dion and the Belmonts is the other great take on the theme. It is gorgeous and pristinely arranged – Disney, re-imagined for the 1950s high school prom. The cover also acted as a major inspiration for The Beach Boys' early hit 'Surfer Girl' – an unexpected legacy for Disney's second film. A welcome legacy, too, given its resonance elsewhere. The song was such a universal success that it was bound to attract notoriety in some form. Indeed, the Nazi minister Albert Speer once reported that Hitler, having captured Paris, stood upon the Palais de Chaillot and whistled the tune to himself as he overlooked the Eiffel Tower and the occupied city beyond.[3]

Perhaps the most striking thing about the optimism of 'When You Wish Upon a Star', though, is how starkly contrasted it is by the themes of the film itself. Walt may have excluded many of the darkest elements of Collodi's original novel, but there's still plenty to fear in *Pinocchio*, which remains among the most grim of films in the Disney canon.

There's a distinct sense that the entire story is an allegory for life itself – or perhaps the very history of man, as seen through a Christian lens. Pinocchio is born naïve, though not inherently innocent. His instincts are towards sin, and only through external guidance (and his own mistakes) does he learn not to stray from the path (to school, in this case). If Stromboli is a warning against vanity, and Pleasure Island a very blatant lesson in not being idle, then perhaps Monstro the whale is simply a caution that, ultimately, the sheer natural forces of existence are going to come for us and do their best to swallow us whole. Though while we're leaning in on the theology, I'm sure Jonah would have something to say about the sequence, too.

Perhaps, then, we could read 'When You Wish Upon a Star' as a call to prayer. Maybe it becomes an anthem for the 'everything happens for a reason' folks – after all, Geppetto's wish does come true – but there's an awful lot of suffering along the way.

At the very beginning of the film, as Jiminy Cricket finishes singing the song, the character breaks the fourth wall and addresses the audience directly. A lot of you don't believe that, he says, and I didn't either. The entire film that follows is simply an account of how once upon a time, and not without a great deal of hardship, a wish did come true. It is an account that attempts to keep the audience's belief in wishes alive for a little bit longer. And that's what the song is about – at least in my preferred reading. Not the fulfilment of the wish, nor even the wishing action itself. Just the hope that it takes to believe that things might get better somewhere, someday, for someone.

---

3. Depressingly, this news may have thrilled the grotesquely named Christian Rub, who voiced Geppetto in the film. During production, he was a notorious supporter of Hitler, often espousing the Nazi leader's supposed qualities to the crew. Thankfully, it seems that nobody else present shared this view – when Rub was required to film a scene on a rocking boat to create live action reference footage for Geppetto's time inside Monstro's belly, the rest of the crew apparently revelled in the opportunity to shake the living daylights out of their resident Nazi sympathiser.

Chapter 3

Fantasound and Vision

Fantasia • 1940 • Samuel Armstrong, James Algar, Ford Beebe, Norman Ferguson, David Hand, Jim Handley, T. Hee,[1] Wilfred Jackson, Hamilton Luske, Bill Roberts, Paul Satterfield, Ben Sharpsteen

Walt Disney was a master of looking back in order to move forward. In *Snow White,* he took a century-old fairy tale and used it to deliver a landmark in animated cinema. His third film would draw on music by Bach and Beethoven and toy with some of the most ambitious and experimental filmmaking of his career.

But it didn't start like that. In the beginning, there was a simple ambition: to revive the fortunes of Mickey Mouse. By the late 1930s, audiences were more engaged with the studio's dynamic newer characters – Donald Duck and Goofy – than with Mickey. Some of the blame came down to redesigns that had made the mouse cuter as a character but less versatile as an animated performer. Many animators would have been content to let Mickey's fame fade, especially given the wild success the studio was seeing in all of its other endeavours. But Mickey was particularly close to Walt's heart – he was still personally delivering voice performances for him at this point.

And so, a special animated short called *The Sorcerer's Apprentice* was conceived to help revive his reputation.[2] Basing the short on Goethe's poem, Disney had also secured the rights to Paul Dukas' composition of the same name. At a chance meeting with Leopold Stokowski, conductor of the Philadelphia Orchestra, Walt spoke excitedly of the piece. Stokowski keenly offered to conduct the music for free.

Production began on the short with Stokowski holding midnight recording sessions with a hand-picked symphony orchestra. His hope was that the musicians, hopped up by coffee to fuel the unusually late sessions, would be at their most alert.

1. There was no over-arching supervising director on *Fantasia* – hence this absolutely massive list of segment directors. My favourite, of course, is the wonderfully named T. Hee (whose full name, Thornton Hee, really did allow for such a fun abbreviation). Hee worked on a number of early classics as a writer and sequence director. He was also the model for the design of Stromboli in *Pinocchio.*
2. Or Mickey was made the star of the short, which may have already been in development. It's unclear exactly what order this happened in, as *Snow White*'s Dopey was apparently also an early contender for the apprenticeship. Whatever the chronology, *The Sorceror's Apprentice* came to be seen as Mickey's big comeback.

In order to breathe new life into the character, Mickey went through another redesign – his appearance in *The Sorcerer's Apprentice* is much the same as it would remain for another seventy years. The biggest change is perhaps the simplest – for the first time, Mickey has eyeballs instead of indistinct black eyes. Suddenly Walt's favourite mouse can express all the emotions the film requires of him, from wonder to glee to shame. The final film remains Mickey's most iconic moment. He has never been more likeable than during his harried attempts to make right what he has already made so wrong.

But, as with so many of Walt's pet projects, costs quickly grew out of control. It would be impossible for the short film to make the money back. And so Walt conceived of '*The Concert Feature*', a chance to showcase *The Sorcerer's Apprentice* among other musical shorts.

Stowkowski's initial offer to work on the Mickey short paid off fantastically now – Walt signed him up to conduct the entire film, and to play an integral role in its conception. The two worked closely together to identify the right pieces and envision how the music might be brought to life onscreen. Together, the two men identified the need for a host who could give context to each segment and act as a palate cleanser between the disparate themes at play. Deems Taylor, a critic and commentator, came on board as the narrator of the film. Taylor offered further input to the music selection and was instrumental in identifying Stravinsky's 'The Rite of Spring' as a fit for the only piece in which the story was conceived first.

Initially planned to cover all of existence from the dawn of the cosmos to man's discovery of fire, the segment eventually soundtracked by 'The Rite of Spring' evolved to protect creationists who might take offence at the god-free history lesson. It's still a thrilling section, with the Earth erupting into shape and hundreds of millions of years drawn into a tight twenty-two-minute sequence. Dinosaurs rage and battle and then fade to nothing. Generations of children were thrilled. Some were so scared they gave up on the film altogether. A smart choice – if they couldn't handle the dinosaurs, they would stand no chance against Chernabog.

The ancient Slavic deity plays a central role in the film's harrowing final sequence, set to Modest Mussorgsky's 'Night on Bald Mountain'. Even as an adult, it is an incredibly dark and unnerving watch – ghostly skeletons rise from the earth, and writhing demons dance among flames; in some cases, they *are* the flames. The arrival of a gentle parade of Christians at the end is too little, too late. The children won't be sleeping tonight – Chernabog awaits.[3]

The early planning stages let loose Walt's most outlandish and experimental ideas. *Snow White* had given him a taste of what cinema could do, and with *Fantasia,* he

3. Early attempts to realise Chernabog saw horror icon Bela Legosi visit the studio to act as a reference. Even he could not adequately capture the role, and animator Bill Tytla ended up having the director of the segment take his shirt off and pose for drawings. To be fair, if there's one thing more unnerving than angry Slavic gods, it's being alone in a room with your topless boss.

sought to push these boundaries even further. His vision for the medium knew no bounds, but his pockets had much more distinct limits.

Among the ideas Walt explored were early versions of gimmicks that still exist in cinema today. He considered presenting a short section of the film in 3D, using stereoscopic glasses that audience members would find in their programmes. There was talk of 4D experiences, too – a sort of smell-o-vision approach that would have wafted scents into the theatre at appropriate moments in the film. At one point, Walt even considered a panoptic projector that would enable the film to be screened around the entire room.

In the end, only one of Walt's visionary ideas was followed through. After hearing rich playbacks of *The Sorcerer's Apprentice* at the recording studio, Walt had been disappointed at the flatness conventional cinema sound systems offered. He put his teams to work developing new methods that could replicate the concert experience for audiences watching *Fantasia*. In collaboration with electronics company RCA, an early surround sound system was created: Fantasound.

Though Fantasound offered unprecedented quality for the replication of the film's soundtrack, it was also incredibly expensive both to create and then to replicate in cinemas. Walt's determination not to deliver a half-hearted version of the film all but guaranteed that it would not be able to enjoy a widespread cinema run in its final form. The biggest barrier was the pioneering new sound system: because nowhere was equipped to deliver it, Disney paid to have Fantasound installed in theatres at a tremendous cost – different sources cite between $30,000 and $85,000 per screen[4]. Disney's distributor RKO had already been put off by the length and theme of the film. These costs meant that if *Fantasia* was going to reach the public, Disney would have to distribute it themselves.

The studio opted for a 'roadshow' approach to release – selecting thirteen cinemas across the country that would be equipped with Fantasound and chosen to screen the film at reservation-only performances charged at a premium. The result was mixed – while the New York roadshow, which premiered the film in November 1940, ran for over a year, other runs varied greatly. Some cities screened *Fantasia* for most of 1941 – others for less than two months. With the high cost of installing the sound equipment, the added burden of renting out the theatres for these exclusive runs, and the onset of World War II eliminating plans for European roadshows, the film didn't come close to returning on its budget.

By 1942, the financial situation at the studio was dire enough that Disney allowed RKO to distribute *Fantasia* for a wide release, even allowing for sweeping cuts to be made that removed around forty-five minutes of the film. By the mid-1950s, re-releases could be made that included some element of the audio ambition Walt had dreamed of for the film, and in 1963 another version – still edited down by almost ten minutes – became the only wide release in full stereo that would reach the public in Walt's lifetime.

---

4. This amounts to around $650,000-$1,900,000 today.

Eventually, these re-releases would earn back the $2.28 million that the studio had spent on *Fantasia*, but the film didn't begin to make a profit until three years after Walt's death. As with *Snow White*, money was a factor in the original conceit behind *Fantasia* – a way to justify the cost of reviving a floundering cartoon mouse. But as with so many of Walt's biggest dreams, it quickly became about the opportunity to deliver something that the world hadn't believed was possible. That *Fantasia* still stands out today as an unmatched landmark in cinema speaks to how successful that endeavour was.

Chapter 4

Cheers, Big Ears

Dumbo • *1941* • *Ben Sharpsteen*

The first five films of Disney's animated canon – the studio's Golden Age – marked not only the birth of a new motion picture format but also a period of bold experimentation that would define how exactly that format would work for the decades – for the *century* – that followed. For all of the innovations that Disney and its competitors would share with the world in the coming years, there is no period of creative discovery so interesting and fruitful for animated cinema as this initial run of classics.

And yet, *Dumbo* has always stood out among its contemporaries. While *Snow White* and *Pinocchio* are technical marvels, and *Fantasia* and *Bambi* are each innovative and experimental films that pushed the boundaries of animation as an art form, *Dumbo* is an anomaly. It is simply animated, with few special effects and, on occasion, some genuinely quite ugly animation.[1] It lacks the refinement of its Golden Age partners, with characters and action each being best described with a word that feels almost derogatory for the period: *cartoonish*.

Yet the film is widely adored. Of these five early releases, it is the one that is most enjoyable to return to time and time again.

* * *

The first person at Disney to come across the story of *Dumbo* was not Walt, nor any of the creative team at the studio, but rather Kay Kamen, the head of merchandise licensing. Kamen had been in a meeting with a publishing company, who were trying to pitch Disney on their new product, the Roll-A-Book – essentially a short children's story that was printed onto a long sheet of paper and put into a display box. Rather than turn the pages, young readers could scroll down through the entire story. Think Instagram, except every photo of somebody else's dinner is a bowl of porridge, and the other users are the three bears.

Kamen wasn't particularly interested in the product, presumably because somebody had already invented 'the book', and the public was still broadly onboard with the

1. The first circus stunt that Dumbo performs, in which the elephants form a tower, is a mess of inconsistencies and awkward, lumpy artwork. The elephants' outfits – do elephants wear outfits? – keep changing colour. Their grand collapse resembles mine during almost any activity at sports day: ungainly, unnatural and, ultimately, a little uncomfortable for those watching.

concept in its current form. He did, however, take an interest in the short story that was featured in the particular Roll-A-Book that he had been shown. Kamen took the story to Walt, who was quick to secure the rights.

The original *Dumbo* story ran to barely 4,500 words, which meant that there was relatively little source material for Disney to build their film upon. Walt handed the project over to two of his best story artists, Joe Grant and Dick Huemer.[2] Their approach to outlining the film was novel – in fact, it almost *was* a novel, as they delivered the treatment to Walt a chapter at a time, building up his anticipation and enthusiasm for the project as they went.

Everybody at the studio seemed to immediately grasp the appeal of *Dumbo*. The story was simple, unpretentious and deeply charming. There was a strong sense of moral justice to it, though nobody ever really came to any harm. Even the awful child who mocks Dumbo and incurs the wrath of his mother gets away with only a light spanking – and being spanked by an elephant isn't really a punishment at all, but rather an immediate candidate for the best 'one interesting fact about you' at any company retreat, or the birth of a niche later-life interest that is ideally kept between you and your internet browsing history.

The straightforward nature of the story was perhaps the biggest selling point for Walt. With minimal need for effects, and relatively few main characters, it would be possible to turn the film around in record time and within a much smaller budget than the studio had been operating on for its other projects. In the years that followed, animators would speak about the sheer speed at which they were expected to work on the project. The result is a film that looks less like *Snow White* or *Pinocchio*, and more like the Silly Symphonies toons.

Despite this, there was still time for experimentation within the film, with a sequence that is so boldly abstract and undeniably haunting that it must surely rank alongside the tunnel scene in *Willy Wonka & the Chocolate Factory* as being among the most unnerving in all of children's cinema.

I've always found it fascinating how frequently alcohol makes its way into films and television that are ostensibly made for children. And, of course, very rarely is alcohol seen in this context without the dual appearance of drunkenness. There's no fun in showing Bugs Bunny quietly having a nightcap after a long day of evading being shot in the face by a small man with a big hat (or a small man with a big 'tache – Bugs really had a type). Where is the comedy in Goofy enjoying a craft beer with his friends? No. In animation, alcohol and drunkenness are intertwined with one another.

Inebriation is usually played for laughs within the Disney canon. Take the appearance of Uncle Waldo, the goose in *The Aristocats* who hasn't just been basted in white wine by the chef of a Parisian restaurant – 'he's been marinated'. Waldo's drunkenness is a masterclass in character animation – the old goose sways and

---

2. Dick Huemer's name is pronounced *exactly* as you'd hope it would be.

stumbles and chuckles jovially. He is an amiable old lush, who would easily break the top ten in a list of Disney characters who would be good on a night out.[3]

There is little in the way of alcohol's darkest effects in the family-oriented world of Disney, though the practice of drinking is generally portrayed as something to avoid. Alcohol, more than anything else, will turn you into a fool – at least as far as the animated canon is concerned. It's a useful tool that usually brings some comic relief into a serious scene. In *Peter Pan*, Smee quietly gets hammered while Captain Hook manipulates Tinker Bell into giving away the Lost Boys' hideout. He misunderstands almost everything that is happening around him and gets his finger stuck in the neck of his rum bottle. In *Sleeping Beauty*, the castle's bard sneaks a luteful of the king's vintage red wine and ends up asleep under the banquet table.

In the 1980s, the United States tightened restrictions around what is and is not appropriate in films and television intended for younger viewers. As a result, animation sobered up considerably. Nowadays, audiences must settle for metaphorical drunkenness in their Disney classics. After an early chase scene in *Big Hero 6*, the inflatable robot Baymax finds himself punctured and low on battery – with both his body and energy depleted, Baymax's movements begin to echo those of Uncle Waldo. He staggers and slumps, slurs his words and struggles to make it up the stairs. Eventually we find Baymax sitting on the floor, stroking the cat while calling it a 'hairy baby'. This is, I think it's entirely fair to say, how most of my biggest nights out finish up.[4]

With all this in mind, *Dumbo* represents a starkly different approach to the representation of inebriation in Disney's films. When Dumbo and his hype man Timothy Q. Mouse accidentally get wasted in water that's been spiked with champagne, we aren't simply shown the exploits of two amiable drunkards. We are shown their elaborate and haunting joint hallucination.

Now I've never watered down my champagne, and all previous experiences with alcohol suggest that it would be unlikely to trigger a phantasmagoria quite like that shown in *Dumbo*. But, given how freaky the pair's trip is, I don't intend on finding out.

The 'Pink Elephants' sequence remains one of the most unexpected turns taken by any of Disney's films. It draws on an old euphemism for hallucinations that were brought on either by alcohol or by its withdrawal. The phrase had been in use since

---

3. Meg from *Hercules* would also be high up the list, as would Robin Hood and Little John. The joint winners, though, assuming you could convince them to all get along, would be the entire principal animal cast of *The Jungle Book*. Baloo is the life of the party, of course, and would encourage everyone to get in their rounds. Shere Khan would be filled with catty little stories, if you'll excuse the pun – it'd be like spending an evening at the pub with Richard E. Grant. King Louis would be telling jokes, and Kaa would be happy to laugh along. And at the end of the night, who better than Bagheera to sit up front in the Uber, chatting politely with the driver and making sure that everybody gets home in one piece?
4. In my defence, I have taken my cat, Joni Mitchell, to numerous vets and the diagnosis is universally agreed: she is a hairy baby, and should be treated accordingly.

the late 1890s, and so the scene was a more direct manifestation of the public's view of drunkenness when *Dumbo* was released less than half a century later.

In the midst of a sweet and emotionally direct film like *Dumbo*, the surreal sequence is a genuine shock. Of course, it doesn't help that the entire scene seems to have the sole purpose of making the viewer afraid of what is happening. The accompanying song warns the audience to 'look out', and the dark, empty eyes of the elephants themselves are fairly unnerving even today. In one shot, a body formed solely of multi-coloured elephant heads marches directly towards the viewer. Moments later, a purple cobra morphs into a belly-dancing pachyderm, which itself turns into a lone eyeball, staring back at the audience.

As well as being the sole moment of experimentation within the film (albeit, at five minutes long, one that takes up roughly a twelfth of the movie's entire runtime), the sequence also demanded the only real innovation on display here. Towards the end of the scene, two elephants ice skate with one another in the darkness. They are formed only of abstract strokes of colour, as though drawn by an animator who had been given only three Sharpies with which to create his art. The crew had difficulty filming the section, finding that the light of their camera was washing out the stark black surroundings. As a result, the scene is the only one in the Disney canon in which the background is actually a piece of velvet – the only material that could adequately soak up the camera's light.

* * *

I suspect that the reason *Dumbo* remains so popular over eighty years after its initial release is, indirectly, the same reason it stands apart from the other films of the Golden Age. In creating a smaller movie that was less interested in pushing boundaries and more concerned with telling a simple and emotionally relatable story, Disney accidentally created the film that would most reflect those that the studio would become famous for in the years ahead.

Dumbo might not push the boundaries of cinema in the way that its contemporaries at the studio did, but it did finally prove to Walt that it was possible to create cartoon features that would strike a chord with audiences, and do so without breaking the bank. *Snow White* might have launched Disney's animated features, but it was *Dumbo* that demonstrated their long-term viability. And, for what it's worth, it's also gentle enough a film to enjoy on a quiet Sunday morning, the night after you've seen a few pink elephants of your own.

Chapter 5

A Death in the Woods

Bambi • 1942 • David Hand

We all remember how it goes, don't we? It's a warm autumnal day, and Bambi and his mother are in the great meadow that stretches along the edge of the forest. The young prince has just been introduced to other deer for the first time, frolicking about with another fawn, Faline, and looking on with reverence as his father – a majestic stag – watches over the meadow from afar.

The call of crows can be heard in the distance. The stag wastes no time and rushes to alert the deer below. Man has entered the forest. A flurry of birds take to the sky, and the herd disperse, panicked. In the chaos, Bambi and his mother have been separated. She calls for him but is too far away. Bambi is exposed, out in the middle of the meadow, the unseen hunter closing in. Suddenly the great stag appears – his father – and ushers him to run for cover. As they sprint towards safety, Bambi's mother appears. But a gunshot rings out, and then the frantic noise of birds. And then… nothing. Bambi's mum emerges from the undergrowth, her child in tow, and all is fine.

Such is the collective awareness around *Bambi*'s most traumatic moment that most of us remember only *that* his mother dies. Very few of us remember the exact details of how and when. Partly, that's because the death of Bambi's mother has transcended the rest of the film. Like the paternity of Luke Skywalker, or the meaning of 'Rosebud', the fact that Bambi's mother dies has become an intrinsic part of Western culture. At the same time, though, none of us have actually seen Bambi's mother die. For all the trauma we hold Disney's killing of a sacrificial deer accountable for, the murder of Bambi's mother happens off-screen and is referred to only in the most oblique of terms. His father stops by briefly to tell the young deer that his mother can't be with him anymore. He doesn't specify why, but the way Bambi's head drops suggests he is not so naïve that he cannot join the dots himself.

And so, upon revisiting, this pivotal scene can't help but lose some of its impact. We have, after all, been expecting it. That earlier encounter with Man, a conceptual evil so strong that the American Film Institute once ranked Bambi's off-screen nemesis among the top twenty cinematic villains of all time, serves as a false start. We know Bambi's mother will die, so surely this will be the moment? Instead, an entire season must pass (Bambi inexplicably remains a diminutive fawn for at least the first nine months of his life) before, at the tail end of winter, Man returns to the forest.

But in many ways, the real impact of the film's central death has been to dampen its own emotional impact. Because, while Walt had already toyed with deeply melancholic themes in *Dumbo*, this is the film that set an early precedent for animated features that require follow-up conversations with the kids on the way home from the cinema.

Disney's longtime collaborators Pixar have perhaps the most skin in the ever-popular game of making pre-teens (and, frankly, post-teens) cry. As early as *Toy Story 2*, the studio was breaking audience members' hearts with the backstory of Jessie the cowgirl, whose trust issues stemmed from being abandoned by her owner and forced to listen to Sarah McLachlan on loop. Over the years that followed, the studio continued to pursue emotional moments with such vigour that one might be tempted to check if they had Kleenex stock options. *Finding Nemo* starts by wiping out all but one of its hero's family. *Inside Out* infuses the very act of growing up with grief, leaving Riley's imaginary friend to fade from memory. *Coco* made my wife cry four times in the cinema.[1] *Toy Story 3* threatened to kill off the entire cast by literally burning them all to death, a conclusion that somehow in the moment, felt entirely inevitable, despite the many, many reasons why it simply could not be. Now, with the advent of generative AI, I'm afraid it probably *is* inevitable. You might want to be careful which *Toy Story* clips you load up for the kids to watch on YouTube for the next decade or so.

Among the Pixar downers, though, surely nothing competes with the first ten minutes of *Up*. This phenomenally well-made sequence essentially distils the emotional heart of *Bambi* into a single montage – the meeting of two strangers, the blossoming of a friendship, and the evolution of a romance, the building of a home. The attempts at building a family, the heartbreak of infertility. The rediscovery of ambition, the overdue gesture that comes a little too late. The loss of a loved one. Though not all of these elements can be found in *Bambi*, they each represent the legacy of a film that was unafraid to delve into the more difficult truths of life.

Disney's own animated canon would touch upon these areas again, too. Almost forty years after *Bambi*, *The Fox and the Hound* would return to the heartbreaking lives of animals torn apart by mankind's violence. *Lilo & Stitch* might not kill off any characters during the film, but its nuanced understanding of family and loss is informed in some small way by the foundations laid here.

And then, of course, there's *The Lion King* – a film that, on closer look, treads very familiar ground to *Bambi*. Both movies open and close with scenes in which the myriad animals of an ecosystem come together to celebrate the birth of royalty. Both films feature climactic fires that offer their protagonists a chance for a new start. And both films have gone down in cinema history for introducing children not only to the concept of mortality but to the concept of their *parents'* mortality.

The death of Mufasa hits a lot harder than that of Bambi's mother. It is, for a start, much more explicit. Though we are not shown the precise moment Simba's

1. Not me, though. I'm a big, brave man with full control over his emotions. I only cried *three* times.

father dies, we do see the action that triggers it. We do see the aftermath, and the lifeless body, nudged with impotent hope by a lion cub who is only now discovering the true meaning of death.

The Lion King benefits, too, from the sharp tonal shift that death brings to the film. Until this point there have been moments of peril, yes, but also moments of levity. Only recently had the audience been watching a multi-coloured animal jamboree as Simba sang joyfully about his bright future as king. The question of what might need to happen in order for succession to take place has thus far only been alluded to. *Bambi*, by comparison, is almost entirely understated, even when the young prince prances about with another fawn. We have already heard the hunter's gun, and have watched the two deer struggle to survive a harsh winter. We might not be ready for Bambi's mother to die, but it feels unsurprising amid the troubles of forest life.

It's worth remembering that *Bambi* is based on a book by Austro-Hungarian writer Felix Salten.[2] *Bambi, a Life in the Woods* was not written for children, but for adults. It was never intended as a light animal story to be told by America's most magical animation studio. Some critics have gone so far as to view it as an allegory for the treatment of Jews in Europe at the start of the twentieth century. Even the Nazis agreed with this reading, and despite Salten being a vocal advocate for their appeasement, most early copies of his novel were lost to their book burnings.

Salten was seventy-two years old when *Bambi* was released. He was living in Zürich, having left Austria when the Germans had annexed it barely four years previously. We know that he saw the film and that he professed to have enjoyed it, but it's hard to say how he viewed the various changes that Disney had made to his original text. It's a shame, because while his book had, for a while, been incredibly famous, its success was completely eclipsed by the film. Regardless of whether or not *Bambi, a Life in the Woods* is or is not meant as a parable for the Jewish experience at the time, we do know that it was very much a book about the evils of hunting (whether the author meant animals or humans is up to the reader to decide). In that sense, Disney's *Bambi* simultaneously echoes Salten's message and ignores it. Hunting animals is bad, it seems to suggest. Unless their death furthers the plot – in which case, everything is fair game.

2. Salten wrote a number of other books. Some of these are deeply problematic, including a popular erotic novel in which the protagonist is under the age of thirteen for the overwhelming majority of the story. Others return, repeatedly, to the world of animals: *Perri* is a sequel of sorts to *Bambi, a Life in the Woods*, which follows the story of a red squirrel. *Djibi, the Kitten* is a more realistic parable for man's interactions with animals. And *The Hound of Florence* is an absolutely unhinged story about a teenage boy in Vienna who must spend every other day of his life in the form of a dog. Specifically, the pet dog of the Archduke of Austria. The novel ends with the dog attempting to save the courtesan he loves, and being stabbed to death by the Archduke. This sounds like the direct opposite of *Bambi*, a story that Disney would not touch with a one-hundred-foot barge pole – and yet. *The Shaggy Dog* is a 1959 live-action comedy that is (very) loosely based on the story. The studio even found time for numerous remakes – most recently in a 2006 version that unsurprisingly did *not* end with star Tim Allen being murdered while in dog form during an attempt to save a high-end escort.

The Package Era

Chapter 6

A Few Goofy Men

Saludos Amigos • 1942 • Norman Ferguson

I'd be useless in a war. For a start, I doubt I'd make it through boot camp. I was always terrible at PE, two laps of the field behind the rest of the cross-country runners, and the recipient of patronising applause when I crossed a finish line or scored a goal in a penalty shootout. I peaked in Year 5 when I took part in a standing jump competition. Our entire class stood facing a wall, and took turns to jump as high as we could, stretching our arms to tap the wall, trying to achieve the loftiest point of contact. To this day, I suspect our teacher only engaged us in this competition – not one you'll see at the Olympics anytime soon – because she felt sorry for my lack of aptitude elsewhere in the physical world. Here, though, I would have an advantage. I had shot up that year and was now the tallest boy in class. A competition skewed in favour of someone with three inches of fresh, aching height would be ideal.

I came in second.

If there were a war, I've always hoped that any sensible leadership would be content to take advantage of my other skills. My *actual* skills. I imagine myself a useful asset in any government press department, able to utilise the best synonyms in order to instil a sense of patriotism and, you know, willingness to die. This is, I think, the ultimate goal for a writer: to be so adept with words that you can convince people that your silly little sentences are as valuable as the work they do in the real world. *You* go fight the war, I'll workshop this 'Keep Calm and Carry On' poster a little longer. *We're both equally useful, honest.*

The Second World War broke out on European shores long before it reached the United States. Nevertheless, the early stages of the war were acutely felt by the American government and businesses alike.

The Good Neighbor Policy, an approach to international diplomacy first initiated by Herbert Hoover during his presidency, became more relevant than ever. A move against the interventionism that had so far defined the US approach to nations in Central and South America, the policy sought instead to strengthen relationships through reciprocal exchanges and trade agreements.

South America, in particular, was home to large numbers of immigrants from Axis powers, including Germany and Italy, and this was concerning to the US government. The fear of fascist ideology spreading across South America fuelled a new wave of initiatives, and Disney was to play a key role in these efforts.

In 1941, a US government official, John Hay Whitney, reached out to Walt Disney to propose a goodwill tour of South America. The response he received was less than enthusiastic; Walt did not see himself as a diplomat. Whitney pitched another idea that would appeal to Walt the filmmaker. What if he and a group of his animators were to make a trip across the continent with the specific goal of creating some animated shorts? This was much more appealing – not simply because of the creative appeal of the cultures that they would be exploring, but also because it offered a sense of financial stability when the company most needed it.

The studio was in significant debt by 1941. An ambitious film-making schedule in the wake of *Snow White*'s success had been curtailed by the early days of the war – it had taken Disney two years to release their second film, *Pinocchio*, and the European and Asian audiences had been cut off, depriving the studio of key secondary markets.

A deal with the US government represented some security at a desperate moment – Walt was reportedly offered expenses of up to $70,000 to cover the cost of the trip, and an additional $50,000 each for a small number of films to be produced as a result of the expedition. It was not an outright gift, though – if the films made a profit for the company, the money would be paid back.

On 17 August 1941, seventeen representatives of the Disney studios left Los Angeles for a two-month-long trip that would take in seven of South America's countries. Much of this time was spent in Brazil and Argentina, two nations in which Disney's earliest characters (and in particular, Donald Duck) enjoyed enormous fame.[1]

Almost exactly a year after that trip began, *Saludos Amigos* premiered in Rio de Janeiro, Brazil. The film is far and away the shortest of the animated canon, running to just 42 minutes. By comparison, the next shortest are 2011's *Winnie the Pooh* (63 minutes) and *Dumbo* (64 minutes).

The first film of the Package Era, *Saludos Amigos* offers a fairly good representation of the output from the years ahead. Rather than deliver a singular narrative, it collects four short stories and compiles them under a loose theme. Frankly, 'Here, have a look at South America' is one of the stronger overarching ideas of the era. Films like *Melody Time* and *Make Mine Music* would later be content to simply say, 'Here are some things that all have a soundtrack'. So, for now, at least, we'll enjoy the relatively consistent themes offered up here.

Fittingly, given his local popularity at the time, Donald Duck takes the lead on two segments – a piece on Bolivia and Peru's Lake Titicaca, and an exploration of

1. Donald's popularity in South America may continue to this day, but it has not always been welcome. Ariel Dorfman and Armand Mattelart's searing essay *Para leer al Pato Donald* (*How to Read Donald Duck*) tore into the cultural colonisation that the authors believed Disney's comics were unleashing upon South American nations. Their arguments are occasionally built upon misunderstandings of the way Disney operated at the time, but nevertheless highlight how impactful America's pop culture has been spreading the nation's capitalist politics across the globe.

Brazilian culture called *Aquarela do Brasil* – which translates from Portuguese to "Watercolour of Brazil." Elsewhere, Goofy runs amuck among the gauchos of the Argentinean pampas and an original character – Pedro the little aeroplane – must traverse the Andes to deliver the mail to the people of Chile.

The animators revel in their role both offscreen and on – between each segment, we are shown glimpses of the trip, and sketches made by the artists as they are shown around the cities of South America.[2] As a result, the film is among the most beautiful of the period, filled with lush colours and engaging characters. Many of the stars of the film proved very popular – the green parrot José Carioca would appear in two more Disney features in the coming years, and would later become the star of a Brazilian comic book series that ran for over fifty years. Others were more divisive – Chilean cartoonist René Ríos Boettiger took such offence at what he took to be the portrayal of incompetence in his fellow countryman (country-plane?) Pedro that he created his own character that might better represent the nation. An anthropomorphic condor prone to the broadest of comedy pratfalls, Condorito may have had the last laugh; his comics have outperformed even José Carioca's and, in 2024, celebrated 75 years in print.

Upon release, *Saludos Amigos* and its spiritual sequel, *The Three Caballeros*, were modest successes in both the States and South America – enough so that Disney eventually paid back all the money initially fronted by the US government. But the studio's close working relationship with the Roosevelt administration was far from over. In fact, by the time *Saludos Amigos* was in cinemas, Disney's properties in California had been partially transformed into military facilities and the company was deep into production on a series of far more overt propaganda films.

Disney's first direct contract with a branch of the US military was signed the day after Pearl Harbor and concerned a series of technical videos to be made for the Navy. The US Army was quick to follow, and Canada's National Film Board got in on the action too. Perhaps the best example of these videos is a particularly gripping classic made for the latter in 1942: *Four Methods of Flush Riveting*. The film sits at complete odds with everything Disney had come to be known for. Plain images of sheet metal on a textured blue background, the closest the short comes to a classic cartoon are occasional glimpses of an illustrated human hand operating a tool.

Other shorts felt much closer to the lighter comic films of the day. In 1943, Disney released their first take on the classic children's story *Chicken Little* – a full sixty-two years ahead of their computer-animated feature film of the same name. In the short, the dopey Chicken Little and his neighbours are tricked by a wily fox into believing that the sky is falling. They are guided to shelter in a nearby cave

2. An early segment showing the expedition as they board their plane was actually mocked up and filmed at a later date due to a lack of footage taken during the initial flight. The travelling party probably considered this a relief, though, as the journey from L.A. had proven less than comfortable. Their plane, not being equipped with air conditioning, had to be pumped full of cold air at each stop en route. It was a long and often uncomfortable journey, taking 24 hours simply to make it so far as Miami.

and, despite the narrator's reassurances to the audience, promptly eaten. The final message is laid out on a platter by the fattened fox: "Don't believe everything you read, brother." It's a propaganda film specifically warning against paying too much attention to propaganda.

Elsewhere, these films delivered even more overt messages. *Education for Death* (1943) was subtitled '*The Making of the Nazi*' and told the story of a young boy called Hans, born to an Aryan couple under Hitler's rule. An incredibly dark film, it shows the indoctrination of Hans into the Nazi way of life – his kinder instincts derided until he "sees no more than the party wants him to, says nothing but what the party wants him to say, and he does nothing but what the party wants him to do". The film ends with a wide landscape of graves belonging to Hans and all those who, like him, had been given 'an education for death'.

Perhaps the most iconic of these propaganda films, though, is the far more comical *Der Fuehrer's Face*; a cartoon in which Donald Duck struggles with the daily grind of existing in Hitler's Germany.

The first half of the short features caricatures of major Axis figures as members of a marching band. Himmler, Goering and Goebbels all take part, with Mussolini on the bass drum and, on sousaphone, a particularly racist portrayal of Japanese prime minister Hideko Tojo.

The second half riffs rather lazily on Charlie Chaplin's 1936 classic *Modern Times*, as Donald struggles to keep pace in a munitions factory. The film ends with Donald waking – I bet you never thought you'd see the 'it was all a dream' trope applied to a Nazi Donald Duck – and tightly embracing the miniature Statue of Liberty that all good Americans keep on their bedside table. As though fearing that the film had, until this point, been a little too subtle in its meaning, he proclaims, "Oh boy, am I glad to be a citizen of the United States of America!" before the final shot throws a big red tomato at the stern face of Hitler himself.

By almost any measure, *Der Fuehrer's Face* is among the most dizzying watches in all of Disney's output. It is genuinely unnerving to watch Donald Duck in full Nazi regalia,[3] reading Mein Kampf – however reluctantly. But Donald Duck was a savvy choice to star in this film – as well as others encouraging the prompt payment of taxes or promoting the role of civilian aircraft spotters. Donald's tremendous popularity reached far beyond Brazil and Argentina.

Nowhere was this clearer than in the work carried out by a unit of Disney artists who dedicated much of their war to designing custom military insignia for members of the Allied forces. The group, headed by Hank Porter,[4] created over 1,300 such insignia over the course of the war. Military units and occasionally individual soldiers would write into the studio with requests for designs and Porter's team

3. Well, not exactly *full* regalia – even with the strict regulations of military uniform, Donald refuses to wear trousers.
4. Porter's time at Disney was relatively short but immensely impactful – it is believed that the iconic flourish on the 'looping D' of the Disney logo was his creation.

would deliver them original artwork that could be replicated on aeroplanes, tanks, or anything else they saw fit. Curiously, Mickey Mouse was not among the most requested characters in these insignia. Pluto, Goofy and *Pinocchio*'s Jiminy Cricket were popular choices, but no character was in demand more than the irascible Donald Duck.

Before the war broke out, animators at the Disney studio had averaged 30,000 feet of completed film each year. At their peak during the war, they managed ten times this amount. The work carried out by Disney was deemed so important that military leaders occupying parts of the studio in preparation for a potential land invasion of California brought draft board officers to the grounds. Though around a third of Disney's artists had been drafted into the war effort, they were returned to carry out their work at the studio – adorned now in their military uniforms.

And so we return to the dream of anyone in a creative profession. Walt Disney's animators had so much to offer the war effort as artists that they were deemed more useful at their desks, pen in hand, creating the latest Donald Duck short. Their work – ensuring the proper construction of military aircraft, informing ground troops of camouflage best practices, and occasionally pelting Adolf Hitler with a ripe cartoon tomato, helped save the lives of Allied soldiers – or at least kept them entertained for a little while amid the horrors of war.

Chapter 7

What! No Mickey Mouse?

The Three Caballeros • 1944 • Norman Ferguson

The problem with professional storytellers is that their tendency to create fictional tales often seeps into their everyday lives, too. Walt Disney had a habit of elaborating and exaggerating, and much of the true history of the early Disney company is now irrevocably intertwined with these embellishments.

The story of Mickey Mouse's origin is a perfect example of this. We know that Walt was caught off guard in 1928 when Charles Mintz, who had been distributing Disney's cartoon shorts for several years, effectively nabbed his business out from underneath his nose. Walt had been expecting a fairly routine contract renegotiation – but Mintz revealed that he had recruited the company's best animators and that his star character, Oswald the Lucky Rabbit, was technically the property of Universal Pictures.

We also know that Mickey Mouse was created as a direct response to this crisis. Walt would have us believe that he got straight to work on the character – leaving the talks in New York by train, and arriving back in Missouri with a fully formed hero to replace his stolen Oswald. The character had even experienced a name change already, Walt having been convinced by his wife to drop his first choice, Mortimer.

Back at his offices, and surrounded by a team of turncoat animators, Walt pressed on with the development of Mickey. While the artists worked on the final cartoons of the existing Oswald contract, Walt's close friend Ub Iwerks locked himself away in his office, drawing up the artwork for the first Mickey Mouse film, *Plane Crazy*. The animation itself was completed offsite. The Disney brothers' wives and sister-in-law took charge of the inking and painting, and Walt would secretly film the project back in the studio in the dead of night.

Despite their efforts, no distributor was found for the short. Faced with dwindling resources, Walt turned his attention to the new burgeoning trend for talking pictures. Terrific effort and expense were put into the second Mickey short that the team worked on, *Steamboat Willie*. Even so, Walt struggled to find a distributor for this groundbreaking cartoon. It eventually fell to a publicist named Harry Reichenbach, who paid to show the short in one single cinema across the country in New York. Reichenbach knew that industry veterans were conservative around new ideas, and needed to be confident an innovation would work before they invested. The Colony Theater run of *Steamboat Willie* would do just that. Audiences were enraptured by the film; distributors were enraptured by the audiences. As offers came in to support the wider release of the short, Walt was able to revisit *Plane Crazy*, adding a score for good measure, while also completing further Mickey shorts.

From the start, Mickey became a phenomenal success among audiences. *Steamboat Willie* debuted in November 1928. A fan club was launched thirteen months later, in January 1930. By 1932, the club had over a million members. That same year saw the release of 'What! No Mickey Mouse?', a song written by composer Irving Caesar and recorded by bandleader Ben Bernie. The title was a refrain often heard among disappointed cinema-goers across the country, faced with a program that didn't feature a Disney short.

It's also a complaint you can feel free to yell at the screen during *The Three Caballeros*. Like *Saludos Amigos* before it, the film is part of the 'Good Neighbor' policy that the US was engaging in at the time of release. And like *Saludos Amigos*, the biggest star of the production is Mickey's temperamental pal, Donald.

As Mickey's popularity grew, the studio felt more and more penned in with regards to what their leading character could do. With millions of children hooked on Mickey Mouse cartoons, it was important to Walt that the character – who he personally voiced – was a good role model. But the problem with good role models is that they aren't nearly as funny as bad ones. And so, the introduction of Donald Duck in 1934 represented a real boost for the company.

Donald's debut appearance in the Silly Symphony *The Wise Little Hen* pitches him as a cheeky miscreant – a role he'd return to in the exquisitely daft short *The Band Concert*. While Mickey attempts to conduct an orchestra in the park, Donald repeatedly hijacks the performance with his spritely flute playing. Whenever one flute is taken from him, another appears. As the source of Mickey's frustrations (and, by my count, roughly thirty wind instruments), Donald is the true star of the short.

Goofy took a much longer journey to success – initially appearing under a different name entirely. As 'Dippy Dawg', the character first appears in the 1932 short *Mickey's Revue*, before establishing himself under his own name a few months later. Still, Goofy wasn't afforded his own series for another seven years.

In the meantime, Goofy was regularly teamed up with Mickey and Donald. This arrangement suited Walt well, allowing him to keep his favourite mouse in the public eye while his friends did the heavy comedy lifting.

By the time *Snow White* was released, Mickey had appeared in almost one hundred short films. Donald and Goofy each had over twenty appearances to their names. It's surprising, then, that the trio have featured in so few of Disney's features themselves.

Mickey's first appearance in the canon comes in *Fantasia*, though the film was actually the third full-length feature he'd turned up in. For the first, we turn to 1934's *Hollywood Party*, a self-congratulatory musical in which Jimmy Durante explores a wild soiree filled with stars like Laurel and Hardy and The Three Stooges. Mickey charms in a short cameo where he is briefly mistaken for common vermin, and then gets in a fight with the leading man (who, in a testament to the film's overall quality, later realises it was all a dream).

He popped up again later that same year in a Laurel and Hardy feature entitled *Babes in Toyland.* Mickey is not likeable here as much as he is irredeemably terrifying. Instead of appearing in his usual cartoon form, he has a live-action cameo opposite a full-grown adult dressed as a cat. In order to maintain some sense of scale, the actor playing Mickey was not an adult. Nor even human. The first actor ever to portray Mickey in live-action was a monkey wearing a ghoulish mask that appears to have inspired Tim Burton's entire vibe. It is baffling how Walt ever came to approve the film, which at one point has Mickey dropping bombs from a tiny blimp.

After *Fantasia,* Mickey has only two further significant appearances among the animated classics – in a segment of Package Era film *Fun and Fancy Free,* and in the musical sequel *Fantasia 2000,* where his *Sorcerer's Apprentice* short is replayed in full.

Mickey made it to cinemas on a few other occasions in the intervening years, buddying up to his Looney Tunes rival Bugs Bunny in *Who Framed Roger Rabbit* and in a short film based on Dickens' *Christmas Carol,* which was released alongside repertory screenings of *The Jungle Book* and *The Rescuers* in 1983.

By comparison, Donald is the actual star of the trio. His first feature appearance was his extended role in *Saludos Amigos,* which led to a return to South America for *The Three Caballeros.* Here, Donald is the outright star of the film, which is built around the premise of his opening birthday presents.

Unlike his frequent co-stars, Donald exists in a wider world of friends and family. Jose Carioca returns here, alongside a debut appearance by Mexican rooster Panchito Pistoles. These three caballeros would reunite throughout the following decades, mostly in comic books. The 2017 revival of the classic cartoon series *Duck Tales* brought the three together on screen once again before a full-fledged show titled *Legend of the Three Caballeros* came out the following year. You do not need to watch this show.

As a film, *The Three Caballeros* doesn't bring anything new to the table. It is as vibrant as *Saludos Amigos* and yet, despite something more closely resembling an actual plot, somehow less coherent. Donald once again engages with samba dancers and local folk celebrations. He also reveals an unexpected sexual attraction to human women, engaging in blindfolded games of kiss chase and becoming inexplicably jealous when they opt instead for men of their own species.

Donald would turn up in the animated canon again, joining Mickey in *Fun and Fancy Free,* returning to Brazil once more in *Melody Time,* and getting a musical segment of his own in *Fantasia 2000.* But perhaps his most loved role was in 1959's featurette *Donald in Mathmagic Land,* which was as popular with bored schoolchildren as it was with overwhelmed teachers and, why not, tripping college students.

Goofy is the most under-used of the trio within the Disney classics (though not nearly as much as Daisy Duck, who has just one appearance, and Minnie, who has none whatsoever). His roles are limited to *Saludos Amigos* and *Fun and Fancy Free,* as well as brief cameos in *The Little Mermaid* (in an underwater crowd alongside Mickey and Donald) and as Disneyland merchandise at the end of *Aladdin.*

But of all the figures from Disney's early shorts, it is Goofy who has perhaps made the biggest direct impact on cinema, albeit not through his (non-animated canon) feature *A Goofy Movie* – an underrated film from Disney's international satellite studios that, being about the inherent embarrassment of having a parent, remains one of the most relatable films of the 1990s.

Goofy's legacy in cinema has instead been cemented by his distinct yelp – the Goofy holler. Like its more famous counterpart, the Wilhelm scream, the Goofy holler is a distinct vocal effect that has been used across films, television shows and more for over seventy years. It stems from the 1941 short *The Art of Skiing* – an unmistakable 'YAAAH-HOO-HOO-HOOEY!' that once recognised is impossible not to pick out in other media.

The Goofy holler turns up in animated classics, including *Cinderella*, *The Rescuers* and *Home on the Range*. It features in other Disney properties: *Bedknobs and Broomsticks*, *Pete's Dragon* and *Enchanted*, to name just a few. But it has also achieved immortality by finding its way – occasionally in edited forms – into some of cinema's most iconic films. *Indiana Jones and the Last Crusade*. *Streetfighter*. *Ernest Goes to Camp*.

Alright, it's not the most dignified of lists. But this is the strange thing about Disney's earliest stars. Mickey, Donald and Goofy had an incredible impact – on early animated cinema, on the very development of character animation as an art form, and on the childhood of millions. So films like *The Three Caballeros* might not be among the best in the Disney canon, but they're still important in their own right. They offer a big screen home to the three gentlemen who helped start it all.

Chapter 8

Sinking with a Trace

Make Mine Music • *1946* • *Bob Cormack, Clyde Geronimi, Jack Kinney, Hamilton Luske, Josh Meador*

After two rather on-the-nose propaganda efforts, *Make Mine Music* saw Disney's first attempt at delivering a straight package film devoid (almost) of any blatant political pandering. Their approach was to collate a number of ideas into a single film. We have a feud between warring mountain families, a lively jazz number that is seemingly illustrated live before our eyes, a recitation of a poem about baseball,[1] a tiresome retelling of Prokofiev's Peter and the Wolf,[2] a love story between two hats, and a story about an opera-singing whale that has a surprising twist.[3]

There are also a number of segments that betray an ambition to replicate the wonders of Fantasia. Among these, we see anthropomorphic instruments, a funereal trip to the Florida Everglades[4], and an Andy Russell ballad that can barely be described on paper. Not because it's beyond explanation, but because almost nothing of any consequence happens.

The segment titled *Two Silhouettes* falls into this *Fantasia*-aping category – the title figures being two ballet dancers who move gracefully among the scenery. These silhouetted dancers appear almost lifelike in their movements, a feat achieved through the process of rotoscoping.

---

1. Precisely as dull as this sounds.
2. This short is narrated by Sterling Holloway, who is making his debut for Disney here ahead of a career that will see him voice, among others, Winnie the Pooh and the Cheshire Cat. The story itself offers a distinctly positive portrayal of Russia, which makes sense given their status at the time as the United States' allies in war.
3. If you haven't any intention to watch *Make Mine Music* – and quite apart from the fact that it's the only film in the canon not available on Disney Plus, this really is one for the completists only – Willie the whale has dreams of singing at the opera. We are shown extensive scenes of him achieving this goal, appearing in operas including *The Barber of Seville* and *Lucia di Lammermoor*. I don't know if M. Night Shyamalan saw this film when he was growing up, but it would account for some things. These performances turn out to be hypothetical. Willie is instead harpooned by a delusional theatre producer and instead finishes the film playing to sold-out audiences in heaven. Somehow, this segment isn't nearly as interesting as I've made it sound.
4. The 'Blue Bayou' section is actually a direct off-cut from *Fantasia*. It was dropped from the original film due to running length, and the original music (a recording of Debussy's 'Clair de Lune') was switched out in favour of a significantly duller piece.

Max Fleischer, the man behind the invention of the rotoscope, is perhaps the only person who can claim to have had more of an impact on animation than Walt Disney. His studios introduced the world to Betty Boop and gave Popeye and Superman their first screen outings.[5] His *Out of the Inkwell* series had an immeasurable influence on the first Disney Studios cartoons. Fans of the Disney gateway drugs of the 1980s and 90s – Sing-Along Songs – also have Fleischer to thank for the creation of the bouncing ball that would lead audiences through the lyrics.

But no Fleischer achievement came close to having the impact that his rotoscope did. Developed by Fleischer and his brothers and patented in 1917, the rotoscope allowed animators to project images onto a glass panel so that they could be traced onto paper.

Early animation often appeared jerky and disjointed, as artists attempted to create natural movements in their characters with little reference to work from. The rotoscope was a revelation – now, live-action film could be drawn over, frame by frame, to create characters that moved like real humans. As well as creating a greater sense of realism in animation, it also sped the process up significantly.

Disney first used the technique in the 1934 short *The Goddess of Spring*; until that point, Fleischer's patent on the technology had given his studio a distinct advantage in the field. Walt's team of animators already represented some of the very best in the business, and their cartoons had been winning Academy Awards without the added realism the rotoscope offered.

Rotoscoping wasn't universally popular, either. The legendary animator Shamus Culhane, who had spells at both Fleischer and Disney's studios, echoed sentiments from that era when he wrote, in 1988, that 'imitation of real life is not art'.[6] After all, the argument went (primarily among those not yet legally able to use it thanks to Fleischer's patent), where is the art in tracing? In many ways the arguments against the process sound very much like those we hear today around the use of art generated using artificial intelligence. Don Graham, the art instructor Walt bought in ahead of the production of *Snow White*, told his classes in 1937 that they must always keep developing, lest a machine work them out of their profession.

Nevertheless, Walt could see the potential benefits of rotoscoping for both the delivery of quality work and the cost savings it might enable. Graham's passionate speeches on the subject would have been heavily influenced by the Disney Studio's own usage of the rotoscope in bringing the several characters in *Snow White* to the screen.

Walt may have looked to the dwarfs for comic relief, and the transformed witch for another worldly form, but Snow White herself needed to be the definition of elegance and grace. The Queen needed to move with a considered gravitas. The

5. Superman's screen debut, a 1942 animated short called *Japoteurs*, is somehow not quite as racist as you'd expect from a mid-war effort with that title. But don't get me wrong, it is still pretty damn racist.
6. *Animation: From Script to Screen*, St. Martin's Griffin, 1988

Prince... well, the Prince just needed to show up and look roughly like a human. For all three characters rotoscoping provided an answer. Though the process allowed for animators to take some liberties – Snow White's head appears to be roughly the size and shape of a basketball – it also enabled smooth, naturalistic movements. Watch the Prince's flirtations with Snow White by the wishing well, and it's impossible not to notice just how human their movements are.

The process would be used in many more Disney classics, giving a touch of realism to characters in *Pinocchio*, *Alice in Wonderland*, *One Hundred and One Dalmatians* and *Pocahontas*, to name just a few.

So the rotoscoping of ballet dancers in *Make Mine Music* represents a relatively early use of the technology. Unfortunately, it's also a rather poor example. The dancers, David Lichine and Tania Riabouchinska,[7] perform beautifully, but the animation around them does little justice. Though their silhouettes shift between colours, they ultimately remain simple silhouettes. From an artistic perspective, the short offers nothing up that Max Fleischer hadn't done in his earliest experimentations with the rotoscope over twenty years earlier.

Walt was never the biggest fan of rotoscoping himself, and among the earlier examples of its use in cinema, Disney's are usually the less obvious, with animators encouraged to give characters more typically cartoonish features. For a long time, it seemed that Walt favoured video referencing to direct tracing via the rotoscope – only after his death do we see the most obvious examples, as the studio took the technique to new extremes to save money.

Rotoscoping has turned up throughout cinema history, and in opposition to the views of Culhane and Graham, has frequently empowered artists to break new ground. The 2006 Richard Linklater film *A Scanner Darkly* is entirely rotoscoped, and the 2017 film *Loving Vincent* uses a form of the technique to deliver a story told using over 65,000 oil paintings. The original *Star Wars* lightsabers would have appeared on screen as drab metal poles had post-production not used the process to add their coloured glow. Even the Marvel Cinematic Universe has made use of rotoscoping, tying some animations of *Guardians of the Galaxy*'s Rocket Raccoon to a real raccoon named Oreo.[8]

Like its obvious successor, motion capture, and the emergence of AI technology today, rotoscoping has regularly represented some level of threat to the work of talented artists working in the film industry. Too often, these advances are not used to further the art, but rather to shrink the budget. There's little doubt that the relatively drab use of rotoscoping in *Make Mine Music* falls more into the latter category than the former. But since its inception, there have always been creative and innovative ways to make dazzling, unexpected art using a rotoscope. Part of the artist's job is simply to find them.

---

7. Lichine and Riabouchinska were a married couple who had worked with Disney before, acting as reference models for the dancing alligator and hippo in *Fantasia*.
8. You did not need me to tell you the raccoon's name, but admit it: you're glad I did.

Chapter 9

RSVP (Really Suspect Ventriloquist's Party)

Fun & Fancy Free • *1947* •
Jack Kinney, Hamilton Luske, William Morgan

What was the worst party you've ever been to? Once, in the summer of 2015, my partner and I were invited to a barbeque in a distant corner of east London. We suspected we might be in trouble when, as we began the twenty-minute walk from the nearest bus stop to our friend's flat, it started to rain. By the time we reached our destination, the entire city was engulfed by a thunderstorm. We stood, drenched, in the living room and watched lightning splinter behind Canary Wharf. And then, it came time for the guests to reveal what they had brought for the barbecue.

Everybody had been told our host would provide the drinks, and guests would bring everything else. My partner and I watched with horror as others reached into their bags and revealed a gross misunderstanding of what ingredients one might need in order to hold a successful barbeque. One person had provided a single small loaf of sourdough bread. Another took one pot of hummus out of their bag, before sorrowfully realising they'd left their other purchase – a tub of stuffed olives – at home. My partner and I were beginning to realise the entire meal would rely on the eighteen sausages we had brought with us.

We sat, sodden, for another hour – the now-indoor barbecue on hold until a fourth couple arrived, hopefully with some more meat. By the time they turned up, as late as they were annoyingly chipper, everybody was starving. At this point, the final couple revealed that they had not bought any meat. They had, instead, bought the ingredients for a mango salad, as yet unprepared. I sat miserably for another forty minutes as the salad-bringer slowly compiled his dish while guffawing through tales of the summer he'd just spent in Thailand, and I asked myself two questions:

How did I find myself surrounded by such unbearably clueless people?

and

Has there ever been a worse party than this?

Fun and Fancy Free might not be able to answer the former of those two questions, but it certainly has something to say about the latter. There is no party in the history of cinema more inherently suspect than the one Jiminy Cricket crashes during the second half of this film. But let's not get ahead of ourselves.

The feature opens with a song that had been dropped from *Pinocchio*, in which Jiminy sings about his happy-go-lucky life. The song fits neatly among the opening numbers of the Package Era films, in that it is lyrically vague to the point of meaninglessness. 'Smile', the song seems to say, as Jiminy skips across books with gloomy titles like 'Misery for the Masses' and 'The Anatomy of Melancholy',[1] 'it might never happen'. It's the live, laugh, love of Disney songs.

The film's two main narrative sections were each originally intended to be standalone features – though it's hard to imagine either maintaining interest levels over a full hour or more. The story of *Bongo*, which Jiminy plays for us via a record player, has barely enough material to cover a ten-minute short. It runs for *thirty minutes* here and is welcome for very few of them. Perhaps the strangest thing about *Bongo* for modern viewers is the curious conclusion of the short, in which the young circus bear learns that the only way to find love is to slap your romantic partner around the face. It's a silly gag, of course, but one that would never make it into a contemporary film.

Once *Bongo* is out of the way, Disney's favourite cricket goes back to roaming around the house. Off the back of this film, it's a wonder that the Blue Fairy ever saw Jiminy as a suitable candidate for the role of Pinocchio's conscience: he's a veritable felon here, breaking and entering, and rummaging through people's mail. The letter in question is an invite for Miss Luana Patten – one of the Disney studio's first two contracted actors, who had appeared the previous year in *Song of the South*. She's been invited to a party at the house across the way, and there are three signatories on the letter – it sounds like it'll be a busy and vibrant event! Jiminy is quick to hop out of one home and into another, gatecrashing the event with the audience in tow.

If viewers in the twenty-first century are prone to find *Bongo*'s spousal abuse jarring, then surely the guestlist at Edgar Bergen's house is a red flag too. Obviously – *obviously* – this is a family film from a simpler time, and we aren't meant to respond as though this party is actually happening. And a good thing, too, for this is the stuff that true crime podcasts are made of.

"When Luana Patten received a party invite from her celebrity neighbour Edgar Bergen," the narrator might begin, in a sinister tone, *"she finally thought she'd made it in Hollywood. But when Patten was greeted at the door, there were only three others present. "I thought that I must be early," she later told police, "but I was wrong. It was just me, Edgar Bergen, and two ventriloquist dolls." All this and more on this season of* No Strings Attached.*"*

---

1. *The Anatomy of Melancholy* is, in fact, a real book. It's a sprawling 17th-century tome that covers clinical depression, but also goblins, digestion, kissing and the geography of America. It was compiled in order to scrutinise all of human thought and emotion, and as such is a hugely important volume within literary history, broadly comparable in importance to the book you are reading now.

Because honestly, what an absolute nightmare. When you're a child, and you're invited to a party, you're usually thrilled. You're also well within your rights to assume that there'll be at least one other child present. All *Fun and Fancy Free* offers is a middle-aged man and his two seemingly sentient ventriloquist dolls. Yes, the dolls are roughly the same size as Luana – but goodness knows how old they're meant to be. The dumbest of the two is Mortimer Snerd (because, *of course*, one is a wise-cracking smart guy, and the other has all of the comprehension skills of a Tesla auto-driving car). He's certainly got the intelligence of a toddler – but he also has the appearance of a sozzled Richard Kind.

Perhaps the worst part of all for poor Luana Patten: Bergen isn't even a very good ventriloquist. He provides the voices for both puppets, even when they're on the other side of the room and clearly operated by someone else. But every time Bergen shares a screen with one of his two popular characters, it is very, very obvious that his lips are moving. There's a reason for this: though he was a nationally renowned ventriloquist, his work took place almost entirely on the radio. No, it doesn't make any sense to me either.

Bergen was a star of *The Chase and Sanborn Hour* from 1937 to 1956, and, away from the prying eyes of audiences, had become lazy. Seeing himself in *Fun and Fancy Free*, the ventriloquist realised he needed to get back on track with the fundamentals.

Of all the Package Era films, *Fun and Fancy Free* is at least broadly watchable – if only because it has some unexpected takeaways for modern audiences. In keeping with the rest of her party experience, though, there appears to be no such thing for Luana Patten. If Bergen forgot to invite other guests, I'm betting he forgot the party bags, too. All Patten will go home with is strange memories, and perhaps a little asbestos in her hair from when Willie the Giant pulled the roof off of the house at the end of the night.

Chapter 10

Yippee-ki-nay

Melody Time • 1948 • Clyde Geronimi, Wilfred Jackson, Hamilton Luske, Jack Kinney

By the late 1940s, one sensed that Disney was running out of ideas for its Package Era films. *Melody Time* feels like it's retreading familiar ground, a faint echo of what *Make Mine Music* did two years earlier.

Here we have another collection of animated musical shorts with no real connecting theme. There are two American folk heroes, a poem about trees, an aggressively preachy song about a tugboat, the physical assault of a bumblebee by the very *concept* of jazz, a welcome return for Donald Duck and Jose Carioca, and an opening segment so devoid of charm that it's entirely possible to forget it by the time the film's seventy-five-minute runtime rounds up.

Perhaps knowing that neither the stories nor the animation were up to scratch, Disney took what appears now to be a rather cynical decision, and overloaded the cast with some of the biggest celebrities of the day. These stars – mostly musical, occasionally equine – sing the songs, narrate the interludes, and appear on camera themselves. Though the Package Era had seen a few forays into live-action interludes (none more memorably so than *Fun and Fancy Free*), this remains a rare occurrence within the animated canon. The only film to feature actual humans after *Melody Time* is 1999's *Fantasia 2000* (and, I suppose, *Lilo & Stitch* and *Chicken Little* if you want to include photos of Elvis and brief clips of Indiana Jones, respectively).

The stars at the centre of *Melody Time* would have proven a big draw when the film was released – ironic, given that the feature's very existence is down to Walt Disney's wish for the studio to draw as little as possible while his animators were enlisted in the army. Today, the call sheet for the movie features a few names that linger in the popular consciousness and several that have faded away entirely. Once, though, this roster of artists represented the crème de la crème of American celebrity, so let's explore the names that Disney relied on to keep audiences flocking to their late-Package Era film.

* * *

When Melody Time was released, Buddy Clark was the epitome of the late 1940s All-American star. The singer, who had already had some success in the 1930s, served in World War II and dove straight back into show business upon his return.

In March 1947 Clark finally found fame with 'Linda', a saccharine song he'd released the previous year that slowly climbed the *Billboard* charts in the States until it peaked at number two. The song is notable for two reasons: first because songwriter Jack Lawrence had made the unusual decision to name the track after his attorney's 1-year-old daughter. And second, adding to the song's curious legacy, is the future career path of its namesake. Buddy Clark's breakthrough hit is named after the future Linda McCartney, wife of a Beatle, member of Wings, and purveyor of vegetarian sausages.

Following 'Linda' with a string of hits, Clark was a rising star when he took the Master of Ceremonies role in *Melody Time*. It's a thankless gig that mostly has him reading rhyming sentences that fall into the same poetry category as that found in adverts for McDonald's or the Post Office. His lines here are drab and vague at best, and at worst outright inane.

Unfortunately, just a year after the release of this breakthrough film role, Clark's life was cut short by a plane crash on Beverly Boulevard in Los Angeles.

I'm not going to lie – very few of the stories of *Melody Time*'s celebrity cast end happily. This is the nature of things when you're looking at a film made in 1948. It's like reading 'Where Are They Now?' clickbait articles about the animals from your favourite 1990s family films. Every story begins the same and is destined to have the same ending.

Sometimes the middle of the story plays out a little happier, though – the second segment of *Melody Time* is a relative oddity in the animated canon, narrated by actor and comedian Dennis Day. Another veteran of the war who found fame upon his return, his roles as both Johnny Appleseed and Appleseed's own guardian angel were early successes in a long and varied career. As well as starring across radio, film and television, Day was an accomplished impressionist – his take on James Stewart remains, well, almost exactly the same as every other impression of James Stewart that has come since. But it went down a storm on the wireless.

His involvement in *The Legend of Johnny Appleseed* places him at the heart of a rare example of outright Christian messaging in a Disney film. The short is very much a product of its time – though it moralises less than one might expect. That role is left to the following segment, *Little Toot*. This tale of sentient tugboats is based on a popular picture book from 1939. Its underlying message – children are awful and should grow up as quickly as possible – feels like a collab between Roald Dahl and Jordan Peterson.

Little Toot features one of the film's biggest name draws – The Andrews Sisters. More than any other act featured in *Melody Time*, The Andrews Sisters are perhaps the most recognisable to modern audiences. The close harmony songs of the trio still regularly pop up in film and television today and were a direct influence of Christina Aguilera's fourth best song, 'Candyman'.[1]

1. 1. Ain't No Other Man
   2. Genie In A Bottle
   3. Lady Marmalade (alongside P!nk, Mya and Lil' Kim)

The sisters' story is – I did warn you – a sad one. Already huge stars by the time World War II began, their extensive performances for Allied forces and a raft of military-themed hits (including their best-known song, 'Boogie Woogie Bugle Boy') forever tied them to the era in the public consciousness. They'd already appeared in over a dozen films throughout the 1940s, including *Make Mine Music*, when Disney approached them to narrate *Little Toot*. It was to be their last film as a trio.

Patty, the youngest of the sisters, and the de facto leader of the group, was the first to cause ruptures. Her husband became the band's manager and immediately demanded more money for his wife. Just a few years after *Melody Time*'s release, Patty decided to leave the group to become a soloist – but neglected to tell her sisters, who found out from newspaper gossip columns. By the time the three reunited, the charts were dominated by early rock-and-roll, and the group had lost their footing in the cultural zeitgeist. LaVerne, the eldest of the sisters, died of cancer. She had been the glue that held Patty and middle sister Maxene together. There would be one final flourish for the group in the early 1970s when frequent Disney collaborators, the Sherman Brothers, wrote a musical specifically for Patty and Maxene. After that, Patty pushed her remaining sister away, offering no reason for the estrangement either to the press or Maxene herself. Maxene died in 1995, and Patty lived a further eighteen years, finally free of the sisters she had inexplicably been desperate to be rid of for decades.

And that story is exactly what was told to Donald Duck and José Carioca to make them so sad when they first wander into Cafe do Samba in the film's penultimate section. Thankfully, organist Ethel Smith – competing with Engelbert Humperdinck for the least glamorous name in the history of popular music – is on hand to teach them the ways of samba and brighten things up again.

Smith is far and away my favourite of the famous figures to pop up in *Melody Time*. From the minute she appears in the midst of a gigantic cocktail, the screen is filled with effervescent joy. For a moment, nothing can stop the party. Even when the mischievous Aracuan Bird blows the organ up with dynamite, Smith finds a way to continue playing.

This determination carried through to Smith's real life, too. Wholly dedicated to her music, she was already touring with prestigious productions when, in 1935, Hammond released their first electric organ. It was love at first sight for Smith, who soon found herself touring with the instrument, playing Latin-influenced rhythms she'd picked up on trips across Central and South America. Before long, her gigs were marketed as featuring the 'Empress of the Hammond'.

Melody Time was far from Smith's first appearance in film, and it would not be her last. For a while, she was the only name you'd turn to when you needed a talented organ player to liven up your film. And this was the 1940s. Lively organists were the height of entertainment in cinema, like parkour chase scenes in 2008, or unexpected Matt Damon cameos in any film since 1999.

Iconic in every aspect of her life, in 1947, Smith divorced her husband of two years because he was intimidated by how successful she was. Sure, the court papers claimed 'abandonment' on the part of the actor Ralph Bellamy, but the popular understanding was that Bellamy simply couldn't handle the acclaim his wife was receiving. After the divorce, Smith happily lived out the rest of her life performing in off-Broadway productions, playing golf, and entertaining celebrity friends. If you want a happy ending, this is the best the cast of *Melody Time* will offer you.

The final segment of the film features a glut of cameos, from *Song of the South*'s Bobby Driscoll and Luana Patten to Western vocal group Sons of the Pioneers. But two of the stars present were famous enough to top the bill in the film's opening credits: Roy Rogers and Trigger.

Like The Andrews Sisters, Roy Rogers' name still means a little to contemporary audiences. From the mid-1930s, he had been synonymous with Western films, almost exclusively playing characters who were also called Roy Rogers. Before his appearance in *Melody Time* he had already featured in around *ninety* films.

His frequent co-star, Trigger, was dubbed 'The Smartest Horse in the Movies', which is a bit like calling Alan Sugar 'The Most Likeable Host of *The Apprentice*'. It's quite possibly true, but honestly, look at the competition.

Rogers and Trigger were inseparable, and the two appeared together in many films, as well as in *The Roy Rogers Show* on television, which ran for five years and 100 episodes in the 1950s. Rogers taught Trigger over 150 tricks, including how to walk on his hind legs, sign his name and sit in a chair. He was even housebroken – a useful skill when travelling, or on set. *Melody Time* doesn't offer many opportunities for the horse to show these tricks off – a few whinnies and a couple of nods – but Rogers makes the most of his narrating the story of Pecos Bill.

Trigger died in 1965, and Rogers made only one more film appearance afterwards before his death in 1998. But the feelings their adventures instilled in audiences linger on – Elton John's classic song 'Roy Rogers' is about escapism through television adventures, and the actor is referenced in *Die Hard*, which has reappropriated his catchphrase 'Yippee-ki-yay, kids' in a way that you suspect Rogers – and his clean-cut all-American image – might not have approved of.

Melody Time offers us a glimpse at a moment in the history of American celebrity. It doesn't necessarily offer much else, though – you'll be hard-pressed to picture the faces of the characters in your mind the next day. Still, the film represents a moment in Disney's history – the lowest ebb of creative water in the drought of the Package Era. From here on in, things begin to pick up significantly.

Chapter 11

Copy Paste Chase

The Adventures of Ichabod and Mr. Toad • *1949* •
James Algar, Clyde Geronimi, Jack Kinney

Are you Team Ichabod, or Team Mr. Toad? The two halves of this final film in the Package Era feel miles apart from one another. In the first half, we visit the river banks of Kenneth Grahame's *The Wind in the Willows* and meet the irrepressible Toad as he galivants about the countryside indulging in his latest hyperfixation. The second portion of the film severely tones down the gothic horror of Washington Irving's *The Legend of Sleepy Hollow*. The gangly Ichabod Crane – surely the Disney protagonist most likely to awake one morning from uneasy dreams to find himself transformed into a gigantic stick insect – is a local school teacher in post-revolutionary New York State. The story follows his battles with the brutish Brom as they compete for the heart (and family wealth) of the beautiful Katrina. It also deals with a headless horseman, but honestly, that barely seems to come into it.

The movie attempts to hold itself together by claiming each of the titular characters to be among the greatest their respective nations have yet produced. In the case of Ichabod Crane, it's a pretty fair shout; *The Legend of Sleepy Hollow* was one of the first pieces of fiction to overturn snobbish claims that the young American nation could not create great literature. To claim that Mr Toad represents the same for Britain's literary legacy does feel a little bold – can he really compete with David Copperfield, Othello, or even Bertie Wooster? Toad is, after all, essentially a slightly more likeable Jeremy Clarkson, always barrelling off to play with some new vehicle while his two staid friends watch in bewilderment.

The film was even originally going to be titled *Two Fabulous Characters*, which feels a bit on the nose, and not entirely truthful. *Two Characters Who You Would Hesitate to Invite to Your Wedding Even if They Were Blood Relatives* might have been more accurate.

Still, the wavering tone of the film means there's something for everyone here. Fans are often split between which half they prefer: Toad's busy, brash opening, or Ichabod's understated and very, very, *very* mildly spooky closer.

Personally, I lean very strongly towards the *Wind in the Willows* segment. It manages to jog briskly through a number of genres in its short runtime, from comedy to courtroom drama to escape adventure to heist movie. It is in this latter sequence that the film shines brightest, with an exciting chase scene in which the characters try to escape Toad Hall with a vital piece of evidence. The document at the heart of it all – the deed to the property – passes back and forth, from hero to villain. Characters duck and dive, and try to avoid the several hundred daggers that the evil weasels seem to keep on themselves even during a restful evening in front of the fireplace.

The sequence is so enjoyable, in fact, that much of the animation reappears almost twenty years later in *The Jungle Book*, as Baloo and Bagheera attempt to rescue Mowgli from King Louie's temple. It can be hard to spot initially – the paper sheet of the property deed has, after all, been replaced by a small boy in a red loincloth. But the movements are all there, traced over to save time and money during production. Where Mole escaped the swinging club of a weasel, King Louie slips beneath a swinging club wielded by Baloo. Where the Water Rat slides in to steal the deed from a weasel, only to be hit sharply on the head, King Louie attempts the exact same manoeuvre.

The practice of recycling old animation was already in place by the release of *Ichabod and Mr Toad*. *Saludos Amigos* appears to be the first feature to engage in the process, drawing on animation for an old Goofy short and reappropriating it for, perhaps unsurprisingly, a segment featuring Goofy.

But the later films released during the studio's Transition and Bronze eras would stretch the operation to breaking point, with Wolfgang Reitherman, one of the key figures in the studio from the early 1930s until his retirement in 1981, being a major proponent.[1] As a frequent director of films during the mid-century years, Reitherman would encourage animators to draw over sequences from earlier Disney productions. He would also freely loot from these newer films too.

Immediately before the *Jungle Book* chase scene that so closely replicates the Toad Hall battle, audiences are treated to an iconic song: 'I Wan'na Be Like You'. This sequence was one of many that would turn up in *Robin Hood*, as the outlaws celebrate in Sherwood Forest. Of all the scenes across all the films in the Disney canon, none steals so shamelessly as this. While Maid Marian dances with Robin and friends to 'The Phony King of England', eagle-eyed viewers will catch sequences lifted directly from *Snow White*, *The Jungle Book*, *The Aristocats* and even, with almost impressive cheek, an earlier scene from *Robin Hood*.

Thankfully, the result is barely noticeable unless you're actively looking for it. The forest dancing loses none of its joy for (literally) drawing on other artists' animation. Another prolific thief, *The Many Adventures of Winnie the Pooh* is no less charming when you realise that many of Christopher Robin's movements echo those of Mowgli.

Ichabod and Mr Toad plays a bigger role in this corner of Disney animation than most films – the headless rider's horse reappears in *Sleeping Beauty* and *The Sword in the Stone*. But even at this early stage of the studio's history, it still finds

1. Reitherman's work on *Ichabod and Mr Toad* can be seen in the grand finale of the *Sleepy Hollow* section, where he animated the headless horseman.

opportunities to steal some scenes itself. A short film called *The Old Mill* offers up two rural scenes during the latter half of the movie, and the dogs that chase Toad during his prison breakout had previously appeared in *Bambi*.[2]

The film might not have been one of the many sampled by *Robin Hood*, but it does share one of the titular character's primary beliefs – sometimes the best thing to do is to rob from the rich.

2. *Bambi* may be the most prolific influence of all. Its gentle bucolic scenes were ripe for the picking, and as a result also turn up in *The Three Caballeros, Make Mine Music, Fun and Fancy Free, Alice in Wonderland, The Sword in the Stone, The Jungle Book, The Rescuers, The Fox and the Hound, Beauty and the Beast* and even *The Princess and the Frog*.

The Silver Age

Chapter 12

A Rags-to-Riches Tale

Cinderella • 1950 • Clyde Geronimi, Wilfred Jackson, Hamilton Luske

In 1929, a young delivery boy named Joseph Barbera became mesmerised by the world of animation after a screening of Disney's first Silly Symphony cartoon, *The Skeleton Dance*. Drawn by Ub Iwerks, the five-minute short is almost entirely devoid of plot, but filled with spooky charm. Four skeletons gambol about in a moonlit graveyard; the film plays about with the human body, the audience's expectations, and the very form of animation itself. It is, in all honesty, among the top five things Walt Disney ever produced.[1]

Barbera spent much of the Great Depression attempting to break into animation, working at a bank to support himself as he submitted cartoons for publication. He even wrote to Walt himself, asking for advice, though a promised meeting never came to be. Eventually he began work in a number of New York animation studios before, in 1937, the opportunity arose to join MGM's cartoon studio in California.

Barbera found himself working opposite another talented animator, William Hanna. The two hit it off and spent a couple of years honing their skills together, frequently working alongside the legendary Tex Avery.

In 1940, Hanna and Barbera co-directed a short film about a cat called Jasper and his rival, an unnamed mouse. *Puss Gets The Boot* may not have been popular with the pair's boss, producer Fred Quimby, but audiences loved it, and the film even earned an Academy Award nomination for best cartoon short. A series was commissioned, and the cat and mouse were renamed Tom and Jerry.

Now, I know what you're thinking. What sort of fool starts the story of *Cinderella* with an unrelated tangent about a cat and a mouse? Well, Walt Disney, for one.

Though our titular character has a little screen time at the beginning of her own film, singing the classic 'A Dream Is A Wish Your Heart Makes' to an adoring audience of small birds and critters, much of the opening twenty minutes of the movie are dedicated to the battle between Cinderella's mouse friends and a portly cat who has unsubtly been named Lucifer.

---

1. Barbera was not the only young animator to have been inspired by *The Skeleton Dance*. Art Babbitt, too, was blown away by the short, and decided on the spot that his place in animation was on Disney's staff. It was Babbitt who, just a few years later, played an integral role in turning Goofy into the well-meaning klutz that he is today.

The biggest problem is this: Tom and Jerry had already been battling it out for a decade by the time *Cinderella* hit the big screen – and they were having a lot more fun, too. Gus and Jaq's prolonged escapades with Lucifer seem positively tame in comparison to the bolder antics of Hanna and Barbera's duo.

The choice to commit so heavily to this bit has dated fairly poorly – not in the same way that other Disney classics of the era have, with their pre-screening warnings on streaming services highlighting racist caricatures or the prominent use of tobacco. Rather, contemporary audiences may struggle to connect with a film where the actual storyline – and the title character herself – is mostly ignored for the first quarter of the runtime.

It's symptomatic of a film with a plot so slight it can be accurately summed up in just a few sentences. Cinderella, a young orphan, is treated as a house slave by her stepmother and step-siblings. When a ball is announced to find a partner for the prince, this adoptive family contrives to stop Cinderella from joining. A fairy godmother intervenes, and at the ball, the prince and Cinderella fall in love. But at midnight, the spell falls apart, and the prince is left with only a glass slipper as a souvenir of the evening. A search begins across the land to find the rightful owner, and though Cinderella's step-family intervenes once more, the couple are reunited and live happily ever after.

It's an incredibly straightforward plot, and one that was instantly familiar to audiences even at the time of the film's initial release. Widely believed to be an adaptation of a 2000-year-old Ancient Greek story, the version of Cinderella that is most recognised today comes to us through retellings by Giambattista Basile and Charles Perrault in the 1600s and the Brothers Grimm in their fairy tale collection of 1812.

The first half of the 20th century was rife with interpretations, too, from Pauline García-Viardot's 1904 operetta to Sergei Prokofiev's ballet, first performed just two years before storyboarding started on the Disney production.

Animation had already seen plenty of Cinderella, too. In 1938's *Cinderella Meets Fella*, the princess met an early version of Looney Tunes character Elmer Fudd. The previous year, Chevrolet had released two animated shorts that acted as adverts for the company's cars; gnome-like figures create a production line to build Cinderella's coach so that she might attend the ball. In fact, the story wasn't even new to Disney – Walt's early business Laugh-O-Gram had been responsible for the second animated version to reach screens.

But Walt did not see this slight plot and the familiarity audiences would have with it as detrimental to the success of his feature-length version. In fact, he was counting on them to help bring audiences back after a rough decade of moviemaking.

Disney had been exploring ways to bring *Cinderella* to the screen since 1933. Originally, it was envisioned as a Silly Symphony short before being considered for expansion into a feature-length film in the wake of *Snow White*'s success four years later. There were various treatments in the years that followed, but production didn't begin in earnest until 1947.

It had been a full decade since the triumphant release of *Snow White and the Seven Dwarfs*, and no film had come close to matching its success. The films of the Package Era had been made cheaply, but had brought in relatively low box office revenue to match. *Fantasia* was still on the long road to profitability. The other Golden Age films, each considered classics now, had all been hit by World War II, which had decimated the lucrative overseas market for its duration. Now, eleven years and eleven films into the animated classics story, Disney was $4 million in debt, and the studio's survival was a genuine concern.

Cinderella was Walt's great hope. He had picked it out from the titles in development at the studio, favouring it over *Alice in Wonderland* and *Peter Pan* precisely because it held so many of the same qualities that *Snow White* did. It was a classic fairy tale, with a prince and a princess (at least by the end). What better way to bring audiences back to Disney films than to return to the formula that won them over in the first place?

Walt threw himself into the work being done on the film – he insisted on careful planning. The scenes featuring human characters were filmed in live-action first in order to minimise mistakes and save money. The various animals in the movie escaped this process, though Lucifer was based on one animator's particularly belligerent cat. Walt argued his case on a number of key decisions but knew when to withdraw. If he'd had his way, the fairy godmother would have appeared more slender and ethereal, like the Blue Fairy in *Pinocchio*. Instead, she ended up looking like God's earliest drafts for Angela Lansbury.

As production wore on, though, Walt's energies were drawn elsewhere. In the aftermath of the war, Britain had frozen payments leaving the country for American studios, and in an effort to make the most of the not-inconsiderable amount of money stuck in the country, Walt had decided to film a live-action version of Treasure Island at Denham Film Studios in Buckinghamshire and on location across the southwest of the country.

As a result, the final leg of production was done mostly without Walt's direct supervision – theoretically a boost for the creative freedom of the three directors, but in practice, a costly endeavour. On those occasions when Walt did have an opinion to share, it was usually too late, and scenes would need to be reanimated to meet his expectations.

On 15 February 1950, the film was finally released into cinemas. It was the first full feature telling a single story that the animation department had put out since *Bambi*, almost eight years earlier. Critics and audiences fell for the padded-out tale of a hard-working gal done good, and though *Cinderella* did not reach the box office heights that *Snow White* had, it comfortably became the studio's second-biggest success to date. Finally, the company had a little financial breathing space – enough to fuel the flurry of Silver Age films that were to follow in the coming decade. Disney's labour after years of creative and box office poverty had brought about the magic that would finally cement their place in Hollywood.

Chapter 13

How Do You Get to Wonderland?

Alice in Wonderland • *1951* • *Clyde Geronimi, Wilfred Jackson, Hamilton Luske*

It's 1923, and Laugh-O-Gram Studios is struggling. Walt Disney's second attempt at making a business from cartooning had significantly outperformed his first, earning a few contracts and allowing his team to create a number of fairy-tale-inspired shorts. But now, a potentially lucrative deal has collapsed due to another company's bankruptcy, and Walt is in dire straits. He has managed to bring in a $500 payment for a short film about dental hygiene, and, rather than paying off some of Laugh-O-Gram's creditors, he invests the money into an ambitious new short.

Max Fleischer's popular *Out of the Inkwell* series combined live-action and animation, with cartoonists' illustrations coming alive on the page and interacting with the real world. What if a film were to reverse this phenomenon?

In *Alice's Wonderland*, a curious young girl visits a fictional animation studio. As in Fleischer's cartoons, illustrations come to life and entertain both young Alice and the studio's staff. That night, Alice dreams of a train journey to 'Cartoonland', where she is greeted by a menagerie of animals, before being chased off of a cliff by four lions.

The film bears little relation to the 1865 book *Alice's Adventures in Wonderland*, though it has clearly influenced Walt, who had read it during his school days.

* * *

Four years later, things have turned around for Walt and his close friend and best animator Ub Iwerks. Laugh-O-Gram had gone out of business immediately after the company had completed *Alice's Wonderland*, but the film was shopped around as a pilot of sorts for a potential *Alice* series.

Winkler Pictures, the distributors of *Felix the Cat*, had fallen out with the character's creator and, looking for a new series, made a deal with Walt and his new company. The second instalment of the Alice Comedies, *Alice's Day at Sea*, became the first production by the nascent Walt Disney Company (known for now as Disney Brothers Studio).

Over the course of four years, the studio releases fifty-six new Alice shorts. They mark Walt's first real success in the animation business, and allow for investment in a physical studio space.

It is 1927, and Winkler Pictures has had a management reshuffle. Charles Mintz, who is now in charge of distribution, is looking for something fresh. He proposes replacing the Alice Comedies with a plucky new character who can compete with their former star, Felix the Cat. Disney offers up Oswald the Lucky Rabbit.

* * *

Six years have passed. It's 1933. Last year, Walt's brother and business partner, Roy, looked into what it would take to secure the rights to Lewis Carroll's two *Alice* titles. It turned out they were in the public domain. Now, one of Hollywood's biggest stars, Mary Pickford, is proposing a feature-length project in which she would star as a live-action Alice among Disney's animations. Talks get so far that Pickford shares the news with the press, but it's premature: Paramount have a live-action adaptation of their own in the works. Walt abandons the project. That December, Paramount's film bombs at the box office. *Variety* magazine's review suggests that *Alice's Adventures in Wonderland* is too episodic to adapt into a film: "A series of scattered, unrelated incidents definitely won't do to hold interest for an hour and a quarter."

* * *

In the wake of *Snow White and the Seven Dwarfs*, Walt once again turns his eyes to *Alice*. He acquires the rights to John Tenniel's iconic illustrations, and asks storyboard artist Al Perkins to work on developing the project. Perkins compiles a 161-page breakdown of the original book and makes suggestions regarding how best to translate it to the screen. Among these suggestions is the expansion of the Cheshire Cat's role. He also proposes giving the White Rabbit glasses – though Tenniel's illustrations show him without, Lewis Carroll had once suggested that this was how he pictured the character.

Progress is made, but Walt doesn't like early concept art, and his enthusiasm begins to waver. In 1941 the project is shelved in response to a warning from the Bank of America regarding the studio's mid-war finances.

* * *

It is 7 December 1945, and the acclaimed novelist Aldous Huxley is meeting with Walt and his staff to discuss the first draft of his script for a film entitled *Alice and the Mysterious Mr. Carroll.* The author had been approached by Walt a few months earlier and asked to deliver a treatment for a live-action/animation hybrid feature film.

Aldous has presented a script that focuses as heavily on the real world as it does Wonderland. Like *The Wizard of Oz* before it, characters from each realm relate closely to one another. The plot fictionalises the lives of both Charles Dodgson (the real name of Lewis Carroll) and Alice Liddell, the girl who is commonly believed to have been the inspiration for the book's hero.

In their story meeting, Walt has plenty of notes – on a villainous guardian figure, and a cruel punishment in which Alice is locked in a summer house. He attempts to find a cleaner, happier ending for the film.

Walt is impressed with early concept artwork created by one of the studio's background artists, Mary Blair. Her vivid colours framed with dark, foreboding woodlands seem to help him realise that only animation can do *Alice* justice. Huxley's work is put aside, and work begins in earnest on a fully animated film adaptation of *Alice in Wonderland.*

* * *

It is 1951, and *Alice in Wonderland* is released in cinemas, a mere 28 years after Walt's first loose adaptation of the story. The film is a technicolour marvel that skips through the kaleidoscope of Wonderland with glee. It draws on work from the many past attempts to bring Carroll's book to the screen – elements of Al Perkins' 1938 treatment remain, and Mary Blair's lush concept art defines the world around Alice.

Nevertheless, initial reviews are tepid. It seems that *Variety*'s concerns about Paramount's 1933 version still ring true almost two decades later. In the *Chicago Tribune*, film critic Mae Tinee writes that the film's characters "abound in energy but are utterly lacking in enchantment", a review that seems baffling today. It is such a commercial failure that just three years later, it is screened – drastically edited – on television as part of the new *Walt Disney's Disneyland* series.

* * *

It is 1974, and Disney is returning *Alice in Wonderland* to cinemas for the first time since its release. For the past few years, the film has been a sell-out success on college campuses across the United States. It's almost as if teenagers in the 1970s have some sort of way to appreciate the hallucinatory visuals and trippy plot of Disney's hitherto unloved classic. Disney are an incredibly wholesome company, and certainly have no idea what this success could be at least in part attributed to. In completely unrelated news, radio adverts for the film's rerelease are soundtracked not by any track from the film itself, but instead by the song 'White Rabbit', by psychedelic rock band Jefferson Airplane.[1]

* * *

It's easy to recognise nowadays just how strange and magical *Alice in Wonderland* is. It's also easy to see how far it stands apart from the other films of its era – and,

1. A similar approach to marketing had been made five years earlier for a rerelease of *Fantasia*.

indeed, anything Disney has released since. But few films hold up so well on repeat watches as *Alice* does. Each character has become an icon in their own right, from Alice (played as the impeccable straight man of the film by a then pre-teen Kathryn Beaumont) to the White Rabbit, Mad Hatter and, of course, the Cheshire Cat.

The songs – of which there are more than in any other animated classic – have taken on lives of their own. None more so than the woozy title track, which has become a jazz standard under the influence of Dave Brubeck. Even those that didn't make the final film found a chance for a new life elsewhere; the dream-like 'Beyond the Laughing Sky' was dropped as Alice's opening song for being too slow, but the melody can still be heard today, adapted into Peter Pan's 'The Second Star to the Right'.

It took *Alice in Wonderland* almost three decades to make it to our screens, and then it took audiences two decades more to begin to appreciate it for what it was. Now it finally seems to be understood as one of the greatest achievements among the studio's animated classics. We might be a little late to do so, but if we've learnt anything, it's that somebody is always late in Wonderland.

Chapter 14

Ten Old Men and One Old Woman

Peter Pan • 1953 • Clyde Geronimi, Wilfred Jackson, Hamilton Luske

It's easy to see what drew Walt Disney to *Peter Pan*, J.M. Barrie's tale of the boy who wouldn't grow up. He had played the character in his school play as a child and had attended a touring production in 1913. But both Pan and Walt shared a certain spirit, too. Walt spent most of his adult life chasing the wonder of childhood – releasing his classic animations, and plotting a theme park that one could adventure in for days. Even his downtime was decidedly child-like, with many evenings and weekends spent pottering about on a one-eighth-scale railway that ran around the back of his house in Holmby Hills, Los Angeles.[1]

Walt was, more than most of his contemporary public figures, a boy who refused to grow up. He was also surrounded by friends and colleagues who shared his desire for wonder and joy. By the early 1950s, Walt had formed a tight-knit group within the studio; nine long-standing animators who had worked with him since the very first feature the studio put out, and who were seen as loyal and talented individuals whose expertise led much of Disney's work at the time. They were the Lost Boys to Walt's Pan, though far from refusing to grow up, they went collectively by a name that prematurely aged them.

The Nine Old Men, as Walt referred to the group, were not old at all. Formed to help advise Walt on his various productions in the period after the Second World War, each of the animators was still in their thirties. Having each worked on Disney's films for over a decade, though, the Nine Old Men were more than just experts in their field: they were innovators. Their counsel was deeply valued by Walt, who named them after a bestselling non-fiction book from 1936 that had been written about the ageing justices of the US Supreme Court.

From *Snow White* through to 1986's *The Great Mouse Detective*, there was not a film in the animated canon that wasn't impacted in some way by at least one of the

---

1. Walt's dedication to this railway was remarkable: he had a legal contract made up between himself and his immediate family, protecting his right to build and operate the line, built a curved tunnel into the rock behind his property in order to keep the track from sight, recreated period newspapers at a reduced scale for the sake of authenticity, and even paid for power lines to be moved so that passengers would not see them during the ride.

Nine Old Men. But *Peter Pan* represents an important landmark in their history: the last film that every single member of the group worked on.

* * *

Les Clark joined the Disney studios in 1927. He was fresh out of high school and had been working a summer job at an ice cream shop frequented by the Disney brothers. Clark's lettering on the parlour's menus had caught Walt's eye, and the young artist quickly talked himself into a temporary role as a camera operator.

Clark became the first of the Nine Old Men to secure his place at the studio, working his way up to an ink and paint artist, then an inbetweener, filling out the frames between key drawings by the higher ranking animators. Before long, Clark was animating these scenes himself, working on iconic sequences in the early Silly Symphonies. He wasn't the showiest member of the group by some way, and, generally, his character work was split with others – in *Peter Pan*, he was one of two directing animators to work on Tinker Bell.[2] Clark's dedication to improving his art ensured he was a respected voice within the animation department until his retirement in 1975.

* * *

Marc Davis was one of the group's more ambitious artists. Even Disney himself was known to acknowledge to others that he had under-used the animator's skills, calling him his 'Renaissance Man'. But under-use him Walt did; Davis was so reliable an animator that the studio frequently foisted upon him the characters that were considered the most difficult to draw.

Davis found much of this work dull but nevertheless proved himself the best man for the job time and time again. It wasn't always fun to animate the subtle movements of princesses like Snow White, Cinderella and *Sleeping Beauty*'s Briar Rose, but Davis put extraordinary care into the process, sitting in on voice recordings for characters in order to capture the nuances of the actors' expressions as they spoke. As a result, his reputation extended beyond the animators' studios; Davis was well-loved by the voice artists for being one of the few men in Hollywood who truly appreciated what they brought to each film.

---

2. A brief note on Tinker Bell, as you may have realised this chapter will mostly be about the artists. For all its magic and wonder, *Peter Pan* has dated fairly badly in the seven decades since its release. As well as the racial stereotyping of Native Americans, there's a rich vein of misogyny that runs through the film. Tinker Bell sits at the heart of this – portrayed as a jealous woman who both tricks the Lost Boys into attempted murder and betrays Pan, in each case doing so to remove Wendy from the picture. In Neverland, women are constantly in competition with one another (the mermaids also toy with homicide when Wendy visits), and the men are quick to take advantage of what Smee describes as 'women trouble' whether it furthers their evil plots, or simply boosts their ego.

The last film Davis worked on for Disney was *One Hundred and One Dalmatians* in 1961. His long-standing reputation for being a 'ladies man' (that is, a man who was exceptionally good at drawing ladies) meant he was lumped with the job of designing and animating the straight-laced dog owner Anita Day. As with his work on *Peter Pan*'s Mrs Darling, it was a relatively thankless assignment. But perhaps as a final reprieve, Davis was also given the opportunity to lead on the film's big baddie, Cruella de Vil. After years of pretty young things, Davis revelled in the task; he drew the features of De Vil's face so far in that it took on an almost skull-like quality. The choice was criticised by some of the Nine Old Men as having gone too far – but the ghoulish De Vil became an iconic character and a fantastic last hurrah for a talented animator.

Davis continued working at Disney for another decade or so, focussing his imagination on the nascent Disneyland attraction in California. His work is still visible today on some of the park's most famous rides, from It's a Small World to Pirates of the Caribbean.

* * *

Ollie Johnston was a close friend of Walt's – alongside fellow Old Man Ward Kimball, Johnston had also built a miniature railway in his back garden. Televisions weren't really a thing yet, and the men of the Disney Studio had to entertain themselves somehow, I suppose.

Johnston was rarely seen without his best friend and colleague Frank Thomas, and so it only seems fair that the two of them can sit together here, too. Frank and Ollie, as they were known around the studio (so inseparable that 'Frankenollie' might better capture the pronunciation), were perhaps the most famous of the Old Men. The two had met at Stanford University, where they worked on a student magazine.

Their book, *Disney Animation: The Illusion of Life*, remains one of the most widely revered reference tomes for animators and captures many of the innovations the Old Men developed together. At the heart of the book are the pair's twelve principles of animation that enable artists to create more realistic action within their work.

The two worked side by side on *Peter Pan*, and their artistry – Frank animating Captain Hook and Ollie working on Mr Smee – perfectly embodies the way these twelve principles impact animation. Take the scene in which Hook gently coaxes Tinker Bell to reveal the location of Pan's hideout.[3] The captain is equal parts smooth and deceitful, his animation revealing the insincerity of his words. At the same time, the drunken Smee is a masterclass in physical comedy – his body

3. Tinker Bell, it turns out, is really keen on the details. She walks Hook through the journey on his map – quite literally, her little feet striding across the paper. She gives a starting location, and the amount of paces to be taken, the direction to turn. And then she settles on a specific named location – Hangman's Tree. It's like giving your Uber driver fifteen minutes worth of instructions only to finish with '...and then pull up outside the gates of Buckingham Palace'.

stretches and squashes as he stumbles about the room and gets his finger stuck in the neck of his rum bottle.

Close friends for their entire careers, the pair's final film at Disney was 1981's *The Fox and the Hound*. A young animator on that film contacted Frank and Ollie almost two decades later as he worked on his directorial feature debut – Brad Bird offered the duo a cameo voicing their own caricatures in both *The Iron Giant* and, later, *The Incredibles*.

* * *

Brad Bird's greatest mentor, though, was Milt Kahl. One of five animators to have been given the duty of bringing the animals of *Snow White* to life, Kahl would go on to become a leading animation director at Disney, overseeing much of the character work in *The Sword in the Stone*, *The Jungle Book* and *Robin Hood*.

Milt was given the task of animating the title character for *Peter Pan*, though he was disappointed with the assignment. He'd longed for Captain Hook, a figure that might have better matched his skills.

Curiously, given Pan is so cocky throughout the film, there's no sign of Kahl's signature move. The animator became known for his 'head swaggle' – subtle head movements that were often tied closely to pride. His later work on *The Jungle Book*'s Shere Khan is perhaps the best example of this – Kahl's 'swaggle' bringing him to life.

* * *

Eric Larson was a talented all-rounder, whose work covered every corner of animation during his time at the studio. He'd animated a number of short films for Disney by the time that, alongside Kahl, he took on the forest critters of *Snow White*. He went on to animate scenes featuring Cinderella, Alice, Mowgli and, in this film, Pan, Hook and Wendy.

But Larson's greatest legacy for the studio was in his training programme that, from the early 1970s, brought new recruits up to speed with studio techniques. He became a vital lifeline to the new generation of animators coming up at Disney and, as an animation consultant on *The Great Mouse Detective*, was the last of the Nine Old Men to retire from the organisation.

* * *

Very few of the group made their way to becoming fully-fledged directors for Disney. In many cases, it simply wasn't a priority. John Lounsbery started off about as far as it's possible to be from director. His work as an assistant animator on *Snow White* went uncredited, and though he clearly earned Walt's trust by the time the Nine Old Men were first gathered, he was often given tertiary characters to animate – Jaq the mouse in *Cinderella*, Pongo in *One Hundred and One Dalmatians*. He was eventually given the chance to act as directing animator for the lead character in 1973's *Robin Hood* and, the following year, directed the short film *Winnie the Pooh and Tigger Too*, which would eventually be a part of *The Many Adventures of Winnie the Pooh*. His final film at Disney saw him finally take the reins (alongside two others) for 1977's *The Rescuers*. He passed away during the film's production, aged sixty-five.

* * *

Working alongside his old friend and long-time colleague on that film was Wolfgang Reitherman, known around the Disney studios as 'Woolie'. Of all the Nine Old Men, Reitherman was the most prolific director and perhaps the most central to the studio's work in the wake of Walt's death in 1966.

Reitherman was deeply collaborative and incredibly forthcoming, and would direct a total of seven Disney classics, with *The Jungle Book*, *The Aristocats*, and *Robin Hood* all being produced under his watch.

His methods weren't always popular, though, and Reitherman was responsible for championing much of the recycled animation that plagued the mid-century Disney films. He also had a tendency for nepotism – his three sons each voiced Disney characters. His youngest, Bruce, voiced both Christopher Robin and Mowgli. Prior to this, he'd called upon his older sons, Richard and Robert, to take turns voicing the lead character in *The Sword in the Stone* – they replaced Rickie Sorensen, whose voice had broken during the recording process. As a result, Wart has three very noticeably different voices throughout the film – sometimes changing mid-scene.

* * *

Ward Kimball is perhaps the most interesting of the Nine Old Men – not only was he the artist behind some of *Alice in Wonderland*'s most memorable diversions, but he was also a talented trumpeter and founded the Dixieland jazz band The Firehouse Plus Two. The group comprised a number of animators, including Frank Thomas, and would frequently play Disney events.

Later on in his career, Kimball's work took on a more antagonistic quality. In 1968, while still working at Disney, he released an independent short film of his own making. *Escalation* was an absurdist protest against the Vietnam War. It's both a million miles from his work for Walt, and also closer than you might expect – a significant part of the two-minute film is dedicated to the growth and arousal of Lyndon B. Johnson's nose, which grows in a way that is both deeply phallic *and* a reference to Pinocchio's extending schnozz. Kimball had animated Jiminy Cricket almost thirty years earlier.

He also released two books entitled *Art Afterpieces*, in which he edited famous artworks with incongruous items – turning Jean-François' *Gleaners* into litter-pickers or giving *Madame Hamelin* a truly enormous hamburger to hold. After Kimball's death in 2002, many suggested that similar works by the street artist Banksy were derivative of the animator's ideas.

A hint of this subversion had been seen before when Kimball was the only one of the Nine Old Men to join the animator's strike against Disney. At the time, the studio's pay seemed grossly unfair, with an undefined bonus scheme awarding some artists healthy chunks of money and others nothing at all. A large proportion of the animators took up pickets and, for almost four months in the summer of 1941, Walt's animating staff was cut nearly in half as twenty-four-hour protests ran outside the studio.

It's particularly telling that only one of the Nine Old Men had any involvement in the strike. Walt took the affair intensely personally. He had a deep-seated dislike for union action, having watched his father experience the darker side of it when he was younger. Though the eventual settlement of the strike involved a promise that there would be no prejudice against those involved, Walt stuck closely with those who had remained loyal to him. Kimball was perhaps able to escape his full ire because he had broken ranks as a strikebreaker, and returned to work.

One wonders who else might have been allowed to sit with Walt as one of his Old Men, had they not taken action against him in 1941. Certainly, the strongest case can be made for Art Babbitt, whose rebellion felt particularly unwarranted to Walt. Babbitt was one of the highest-paid animators in Hollywood when he joined the strike as one of its leaders. He wasn't in it for himself, but rather because he believed in the rights of those earning less than him.

Babbitt's pre-strike work was key to the early films of the studio – he animated the Queen in *Snow White*, Geppetto in *Pinocchio* and the stork in *Dumbo*.[4] But once the strike was over, he had lost Walt's respect. The deal the animators struck ensured that Babbitt was given his job back – having been fired alongside sixteen other union members in the lead-up to the industrial action. But Babbitt wasn't given the same opportunities that those among the Nine Old Men were, and he left the studio. His most prominent work after his departure was as lead animator on Richard Williams' cult film *The Thief and the Cobbler*.

* * *

The Nine Old Men weren't always popular among their colleagues at Disney, with a reputation for having unfettered access to, and preference from, Walt himself. It was often suggested that Walt favoured spectacle over substance when it came to pitches, and so quieter members of staff were at a disadvantage when pitted against the charismatic group of trusted advisors.

4. For *Dumbo*, Babbitt also animated the scene in which the clowns decide to hit the boss up for a raise – a small moment of collective action that was assigned to the animator long before his involvement in the industrial action against Walt and the studio.

But it's clear that spectacle was not all Walt favoured. The above are not, after all, Nine Old Animators. They are Nine Old Men, and the absence of anyone else is, at the very least, telling of the gendered workplaces of the era. It's true that Disney paid male and female animators equal wages – at least, they did after the end of the 1941 strike, which was resolved at the request of the US government's National Labor Relations Board. But few and far between are the women of Disney who are recognised at the same level as the men.

There is a world – or at least, there should be – in which Walt Disney included another artist in his group: Mary Blair. Though Blair's work as an animator at Disney was not particularly significant, her art had more of an impact than almost anyone else.

Blair's most prominent work at the company was as a concept artist, creating visions that would define the look of each film long before it reached the screen. She was among the group that travelled to South America with Walt ahead of *Saludos Amigos*, and her influence on the likes of *Cinderella*, *Alice in Wonderland* and, yes, *Peter Pan* is immeasurable.

Mary's artwork was unique, and instantly recognisable as her own – which, on occasion, did cause difficulty for artists looking to translate her vision to the screen. But she was well respected by many of the Nine Old Men – Marc Davis compared her use of colour to that of Matisse. Walt, too, was a huge fan – he relied on her to deliver art that captured the childlike sense of wonder he wanted for his films, and by the time she left the company in the mid-1950s, she had left an indelible mark on the studio's output.

* * *

Peter Pan remains among the most enjoyable of the Silver Age films, with fast-paced storytelling and iconic songs.[5] But at the heart of it all is the animation – a monument to the work of the men and women of Disney who refused to grow up.

5. More songs, even, than fully fit the film. The comic song 'Never Smile at a Crocodile' was written at the very earliest stages of *Peter Pan*'s production, way back in 1939. Only the instrumental version made it to the final film, the rest swallowed up whole like a ringing alarm clock.

Chapter 15

Barks and Recreation

Lady and the Tramp • *1955* • *Clyde Geronimi, Wilfred Jackson, Hamilton Luske*

It is not uncommon for our childhood homes to maintain a remarkable hold over us throughout our lives. I was lucky, in that I lived in the same house from the day I was born until I left for university at eighteen. Even when I returned during the holidays, or for a brief period of transition in the year after I graduated, I was still able to sleep in the bedroom that I had called my own for as long as I could remember. It has been fifteen years since I last stepped foot in that house, but to this day, I will dream myself there, with only the slightest adjustments made to accommodate sleeping logic.

Walt Disney had a few homes during his childhood. He was born in a house that his father had built by hand; a modest building in the Hermosa neighbourhood of Chicago. This home, though no doubt saturated with memories that his parents and his three older brothers could lovingly recall, was barely remembered by Walt. The family moved out when he was just four, and so his prime activities within the house had been, presumably, sleeping, toddling, and more or less quadrupling in size.

Later, the family found themselves in Kansas City, Missouri, but by this point, Walt was almost ten and already taking on responsibilities. He would wake around 4 am each morning to deliver newspapers to a subscriber list his father had purchased. He attended a grammar school and later began to make his first steps in the world of professional cartooning.

And so, for Walt, the most fond memories were attached to the home his family occupied between their time in Chicago and Kansas City: the family farm in the small town of Marceline, Missouri. Walt spent just over four years of his life in Marceline, but the sway that it had over him significantly beats the lingering dream presence that my own childhood home can claim. For Walt, those enduring memories of smalltown America from 1906–1911 would influence not only The Happiest Place on Earth but also, in *Lady and the Tramp*, the *yappiest* place on Earth.[1]

* * *

Whether you are in California, Florida, Paris or Hong Kong, the first area you'll encounter upon entering Disneyland is Main Street, USA. A long stretch of

1. My apologies for this pun, which is both awful and inaccurate. Even within the Disney canon, we must surely accept that One Hundred and One Dalmatians is yappier than this.

buildings that introduces visitors to the park, and presents a dramatic view of the castle, the area simultaneously eases you into the fantasy of Disneyland while raising your anticipation for what lies ahead. One of the key inspirations for the buildings that seem to tower over visitors on each side is the early 1900s architecture Walt remembered from his short time in Marceline.[2]

For Walt, the area was built to directly reflect this period of his life. There are period vehicles that drive around in the quieter morning hours: a horse-drawn trolley, a vintage fire engine. The Main Street Cinema shows early Disney shorts, though when the park initially opened, it played a variety of silent films from the 1910s.

Main Street, USA plays an important part in empowering visitors to get into the spirit of the park. When Disneyland launched in the summer of 1955, the time it evoked was not so distant – Walt wanted the area to serve children and adults alike, and so while younger guests could explore the country's recent history, anybody over the age of forty would begin their Disneyland experience with an overwhelming hit of nostalgia. An equivalent street created today would have to reflect America in the year 1980.[3]

This effort to engage with older visitors to the park was a key part of Walt's vision for Disneyland. He was tired of taking his children to places that served only their needs and left adults bored on the sidelines. Travelling around the world throughout the 1940s, Walt made a point of touring zoos and amusement parks that might inform his plans for an inclusive land of adventure. Critics – even before Disneyland opened – were quick to laugh at the idea of adults enjoying themselves in a children's park. Even today, many people are eager to scorn adult fans of Disney who happily explore the parks regardless of whether or not they have children. But Walt always intended Disneyland to be a place where everyone could feel welcome.

* * *

Less than a month before Disneyland opened its gates to the public, Walt launched another grand project into the world: *Lady and the Tramp*. It was, in some ways, Walt's most personal film yet.

One of Walt's artists, Joe Grant, had been attempting to pitch a film about a dog who finds themselves competing for her owners' attention after the arrival of a new baby. Though the premise was interesting, Walt was never fully convinced. But

---

2. The buildings may *seem* to tower over the park's clientele, but Walt actually employed forced perspective in the design of the structures – making the buildings appear taller than they really are while maintaining the quaint and cosy atmosphere that he desired.
3. I'm not sure which era in American history most heavily influenced my own prominent Disney theme park memory. In the early 2000s, while exploring the Animal Kingdom park, my family were accosted by a free-roaming, talking bin. It promptly took a shine to my young sister, who was so unnerved by it that she fled the scene, hunkering down in the nearby toilets until the bin moved on. I, on the other hand, felt a little sorry for the poor trash can. It had done nothing wrong, and now it was trundling around the food court forlornly calling out my sister's name. Anyway, this is how my family came to have a photo of me hugging a bin at Disney World.

in the mid-1940s, he read a short story in Cosmopolitan magazine called 'Happy Dan, the Whistling Dog' and realised he had found the missing element Grant's canine tale needed. He approached the story's author, Ward Greene, and had him write a new story featuring both Happy Dan and Grant's dog, Lady.

By this point, Grant had left the studio, and so, though it was his dog who had inspired the original story and given the lead character her name, it was Walt who shaped much of the final story we see on screen. Lady's initial presentation as a gift given in a hat box reflects the literal unboxing of a puppy Walt had bought as a present for his wife.[4]

And, like the park that opened a few weeks later, much of *Lady and the Tramp*'s setting is heavily influenced by Marceline. The idyllic town that plays host to the characters is a good deal snowier than its Disneyland partner, but bears many of the same hallmarks, from turn-of-the-century architecture to horse-drawn carriages. There is a sense of security and comfort here. Above all else, there is community – whether it's the friendly relationships one holds with their elderly neighbours, or the generosity of Tony and Joe, the two Italian chefs who act as the ultimate wingman to the local street dog they know as Butch.

The world isn't without its threats, of course – busybody Aunt Sarah is blinded by her love for her cats (whose disruption now ventures beyond the havoc they cause in the house: their racist portrayal means this is one of several animated classics that Disney Plus added a sensitivity warning to upon the launch of their service). There is a dog catcher roaming the streets of the town, too – a curious threat in the otherwise idyllic reflection of Marceline. Perhaps we can see the dog catcher as a reflection of those figures who were already appalled by the idea of a theme park that catered to adults; figures of puffed-up authority determined to decide who should be allowed where. In Tramp's Marceline, as in Disneyland, everyone *should* be welcome, and anyone who suggests otherwise must be the villain of the piece.

I think the real threat within *Lady and the Tramp* is not the faceless municipal worker just doing his job, though. Nor is it the well-meaning but misguided Aunt Sarah. The real threat, the one that triggers the action of the film and upsets Lady's quiet little life with Jim Dear and Darling, is that of change. For Lady, this change isn't wanted – but it pushes her into the world, delivers a new perspective, and offers a spaghetti-scoffing soulmate before allowing her to find her feet in a new, evolved version of the life she had before.

Walt Disney may have held a deep love for his time in Marceline, but he was not tied to it. He was, at his heart, a futurist looking to try new things and improve the world around him. The first thing we see in both *Lady and the Tramp* and Disneyland may be a memory that he was keen to hold onto, but the ultimate message of both is one of embracing change. Main Street, USA is only just the beginning of your time in a Disney park. Tomorrowland is just around the corner.

4. Lily Disney was initially appalled by the hat box – she preferred to choose her own hats. Dogs, apparently, she was less picky about.

Chapter 16

Beautiful Dreamer

Sleeping Beauty • 1959 • Clyde Geronimi

I've always enjoyed the idea of the 'unofficial trilogy' – three films tied closely to one another either in theme or spirit, despite not actually being part of the same franchise. Nicolas Cage's sequence of 90s action films: *The Rock*, *Con Air* and *Face/Off*. Rachel McAdams' three films in which her partner is a time-traveller: *About Time*, *Midnight in Paris* and, of course, *The Time Traveler's Wife*. Park Chan Wook's *Sympathy for Vengeance*, *Oldboy* and *Lady Vengeance* each dealt with such similar themes that even the critics took it upon themselves to refer to the films collectively as his 'Vengeance Trilogy'.

Sleeping Beauty completes the most clear-cut unofficial trilogy within the Disney canon: Walt's Princesses. Coming two decades after *Snow White* and nine years after *Cinderella*, it was the last of the three princess-centred films that Walt would work on in his lifetime.

The fact that he'd already released two films based on fairy tales weighed heavily on Walt's mind throughout production. There were obvious parallels within the plots of each story: the long-suffering princess who would eventually be freed by the true love of a man who just so happened to match up to her hidden royal lineage.

For *Sleeping Beauty*, Walt wanted to find a way to differentiate the film from its predecessors, while still ensuring it stood as an equal to their respective reputations. He honed in on the aesthetic of the piece, spying an opportunity to further push the boundaries of animated cinema and, in doing so, create the film that he believed would be his masterpiece.

Concept art often played a significant role in the creation of a Disney cartoon, and we've seen the reputation that artists like Mary Blair had within the studio as a result of their designs. Walt felt that the animators hadn't yet succeeded in transferring the essential qualities of these artworks – something was always lost along the way.

The solution, Walt decided, was to make a concerted effort to deliver these lush visuals within the cartoon medium. He turned to Eyvind Earle, an experimental background artist who had joined the studio in 1951, and offered him a position that had so far been without precedent at Disney, as the sole artistic director and colour stylist for a feature film.

Earle would have the ultimate say in the design of *Sleeping Beauty*, his decisions impacting everything from the way the characters looked to the artists' ongoing efforts to capture the feel of the film's concept art. Walt wanted the film to look and feel less like a traditional cartoon and more like a moving illustration from a children's fairy tale collection, and Earle would champion this ambitious goal.

Drawing on mediaeval and gothic art, Earle began to form his unique vision for the film, which was to be set in 14th-century France. He pulled ideas from a wide range of sources, including European tapestries, Persian artworks, and illustrated manuscripts such as the Books of Hours. These 15th-century French volumes, commissioned by an uncle of Charles VI, are filled with lush illustrations that accompany prayers for each hour of the day.

However, the vivid nature of Earle's plans created issues for many of the crew working on the picture. The sheer detail and colour that was imbued into many backgrounds meant that, at times, the characters were swallowed up by the scenery around them. The film's supervising director, Clyde Geronimi, found himself at constant odds with Earle and fought tirelessly to bring the characters back to the centre of the animation. Eventually, one year before the film was completed, Earle left to begin work on another project, and Geronimi airbrushed the offending backgrounds to minimise their clash with the characters in the foreground.

Sleeping Beauty's biggest asset, though, remains the stunning and entirely singular visual coherency of the film. As well as his mediaeval influences, Earle's guidance left the film with a distinctly mid-century aesthetic, and the combination of these two contrasting ideas is, at times, breathtaking to look upon. It's just a shame that the story and characters can't keep up.

Given Walt's ambitions to deliver a masterpiece that outdid even *Snow White*, he was relatively hands-off over the course of *Sleeping Beauty*'s production. The process took almost a decade, with the opening of Disneyland falling right in the middle of its creation. Walt was, understandably, distracted. Whether he was modernising the very concept of a theme park, or overseeing the studio's growing live-action branch, he had little time to impart his usual detailed analysis of the project. His focus had been on delivering a film with a unique and groundbreaking visual style – but he failed to recognise that his skill as a producer was imparting life and soul into the characters at the heart of each film. Bob Thomas, Walt's official biographer, suggests that this is why the 'human touch' and humour present in so much of the early Disney canon is sorely lacking in *Sleeping Beauty*.[1]

Sometimes, though, a little otherworldly inhumanity is exactly what a character needs. Enter Maleficent, our smouldering fairy of darkness. The divine evolution of *Snow White*'s evil Queen and, without a doubt, the pettiest of all the Disney villains. The princess Aurora is cursed to die before her sixteenth birthday simply because Maleficent wasn't invited to her christening. This, dear reader, is world-class petty. Most people actively try to get *out* of going to christenings. If Maleficent punishes so small a slight as this with such vigour, one can only imagine how she reacts to other social snubs. Declined to make Maleficent your maid of honour?

1. 'Walt Disney: An American Original' by Bob Thomas, Simon & Schuster, 1976

Your husband's entire family will explode on your ruby wedding anniversary. Briefly forgot Maleficent's name when you bumped into her in Starbucks? Your tongue will turn into a snake the next time you drink a macchiato. Neglected to send Maleficent a postcard from your recent trip to Cardiff? The entire south of Wales has just turned into a lava field, and an octogenarian Shirley Bassey has unexpectedly returned to the charts with a song that consists solely of her singing your internet browsing history.

While the three good fairies spend much of the film fighting over fashion choices, and the title star herself is restricted to just eighteen minutes of screen time, Maleficent's every scene is magisterial, sinister and deeply engrossing.

Meanwhile, the dashing Prince Phillip is precisely as dry as his predecessors – though he is at least given a more active role in Aurora's salvation. With our princess napping through much of the final act, it's down to Phillip to defeat Maleficent. Having struggled to derive much action from the source material, the studio manages to deliver a thrilling conclusion. Phillip gets to dramatically escape from a castle, battle with magical horticulture and, finally, take on Maleficent's horrifying dragon form. *Snow White*'s Prince Charming only had to show up. Cinderella's man didn't even do that, preferring instead to delegate.

It's been six decades since Walt Disney concluded his unofficial trilogy of princess films, which drew up a blueprint for success that the studio has been returning to ever since. Among all of the Disney Princess movies, *Sleeping Beauty* remains the only flop, failing to make back its budget at the domestic box office upon release. Like *Fantasia* before it, though, the film's financial shortcomings are offset by its artistic merits. Walt may not have been at hand to deliver a story or cast of characters as unforgettable as audiences expected, and the soundtrack may offer up only one song of note (with much of the rest of the music drawn directly from Tchaikovsky's 1889 ballet of the same name), but he did achieve the one thing he wanted most: there is no film that quite so emphatically captures the storybook aesthetic as *Sleeping Beauty*.

The Transition Era

Chapter 17

Spot the Difference

One Hundred and One Dalmatians • 1961 •
Clyde Geronimi, Hamilton Luske, Wolfgang Reitherman

I write this with my jaw sitting in the kitchen sink, stunned at the phenomenal success achieved by *One Hundred and One Dalmatians*, an adaptation of the Dodie Smith dognapping novel. Disney needed a hit after *Sleeping Beauty*'s underwhelming performance had left Walt considering the closure of the studio's animation department. And what a hit they had.

I've never quite got the fuss myself. Pongo's erudite narration may be full of charm, and the twilight barking – a messaging chain of pet pooches yelling at each other across the length and breadth of the country – is a fantastically fun idea. But the film is quick to lose momentum, and, besides a bold opening credits sequence and the angular design of its villain, it simply doesn't offer up much of interest to compete against the studio's output on either side of its release.

The artistic style – though innovative – is not particularly appealing. The studio had worked out how to Xerox artist drawings directly onto celluloid. This meant a huge saving for a production that could now cut back on both time and money spent. But it also meant the early, scrappier qualities of the artists' drawings were copied to the screen. And where is the music? Though multiple songs were written for the film, only Roger's sinister tune about his wife's boss gets a full run-through. It's a classic, yes (Marcus Valle's bossa nova take, 'Cruela Cruel' is both a gorgeous cover and a surprising insight into the character's name in Brazil), but it doesn't hold the attention forty minutes down the line when Horace and Jasper are *still* following puppy tracks through the snow.

Not that any of this impacted the film's success. Upon release, *One Hundred and One Dalmatians* became the first animated film to make more than $10 million at the domestic box office. Combined with international takings, and those from four subsequent rereleases over the following thirty years, the movie earned its place as one of the most successful films of all time. Adjusted for inflation, *One Hundred and One Dalmatians* currently ranks just outside of the top ten highest-earning films in the United States and Canada, above *Avengers: Endgame*, *Avatar* and *The Dark Knight*. Of all the animated classics, only *Snow White* beats it.

We shouldn't be surprised, then, that Disney saw it fit for a live-action remake. In 1996 the studio released *101 Dalmatians*, starring Glenn Close as stealer of scenes and puppies alike, Cruella de Vil. The film sticks rather closely to the plot of the original animation but with one curious change: in the remake of the most successful talking animal film of all time, none of the animals can talk.

Despite the new film being a $300 million success in its own right, Disney didn't get carried away with the idea of remaking its old classics for another decade and a half. But when it did return to the remake business, the studio went all in.

In 2010, Disney teamed up with a former animator of theirs, Tim Burton, to release a reimagining of *Alice in Wonderland.* This was a bold choice, given that the first rule of movie remakes – at least since the early 1990s – is *never let Tim Burton near the film*. From *Planet of the Apes* to *Charlie and the Chocolate Factory*, Burton's remakes are universally terrible. His pointedly weird take on *Alice* was atrocious, dropping the gentle absurdity of the 1951 classic in favour of an exhausting action-adventure plotline. Nevertheless, a performance overloaded with forced quirk by a height-of-his-powers Johnny Depp helped the film gross over a billion dollars worldwide. A sequel was guaranteed – as was a flurry of rehashed IPs (including, rather disappointingly, a terrible remake of *Dumbo* directed by – you guessed it – Tim Burton).

The most interesting thing about Disney's run of live-action remakes is rarely the films themselves. Instead, it's how (and if) the studio reimagines their classic stories for modern audiences.

Often the films present Disney with an opportunity to address overt racism present in the original. *Lady and the Tramp*'s Siamese cats are replaced with two new felines who don't present any overt ethnic stereotypes (both are voiced by Black actors, but this doesn't feel problematic in a film with such a diverse cast, in which Lady herself is also voiced by a Black actor). *Peter Pan and Wendy*, which was released directly to Disney Plus in 2023, reframes the role of the Native American Tiger Lily. Where the original film saw her captured and saved by everybody's favourite flying narcissist, David Lowery's adaptation instead allows Wendy's brothers to get kidnapped. Tiger Lily is part of the intrepid rescuing party.

The studio has also been bold with their recasting at times – drawing the ire of petty racists who can't abide the idea that someone else might see themselves reflected in mainstream cinema for once. There was an apoplectic collection of grown adults who fumed at the announcement that *The Little Mermaid*'s Ariel would be played by Black actress Halle Bailey in its live-action remake. 'Why would an underwater creature need that much melanin?' asked irate racists who hitherto had no issue with the science of a half-fish-half-human who could talk to seagulls.

The biggest recasting effort was given to *The Lion King* – easily the studio's most prestigious remake to date.[1] In the original film, Simba's royal parents were voiced by the appropriately stately Black actors James Earl Jones and Madge Sinclair (who had also coupled up to play Eddie Murphy's parents in *Coming to America*). Almost all of the rest of the cast had been white, including Simba himself, who had

1. Though *The Lion King* remake is actually almost entirely animated, it was very much marketed in the same vein as the live-action remakes, so we'll include it here all the same.

been voiced by Jonathan Taylor Thomas and Matthew Broderick. In their remake, Disney injected a great deal of Black talent into the cast. Donald Glover took on the lead role, and Beyoncé voiced his love interest, Nala.

Despite relatively emotionless animation, *The Lion King* remake brought in over half a billion dollars in the US and Canada alone – an incredible feat, even if it can't quite compare to *One Hundred and One Dalmatians*.

Perhaps the most interesting approach Disney has taken to their remakes, though, are the films in which they re-centre the villain as the star of the film. *Maleficent*, an early entry into the trend, retold the story of *Sleeping Beauty* by putting the evil fairy front and centre in the plot. More popular with audiences than it was with critics, the film earned itself a sequel, further expanding a world that otherwise might have been left with a mere 'happily ever after'.

The success of *Maleficent* almost certainly played a role in the revival of another iconic villain for a new live-action adventure. In 2021, Emma Stone took on the title role in an origin story prequel for our gal Cruella de Vil. The film presented a more sympathetic view of de Vil, killing off her mother and really cutting back on the number of animal murder schemes. It is very possibly the best of the live-action reimaginings – precisely because it takes such a left turn from the original film's story.

That said, there is still one take on *One Hundred and One Dalmatians* that I'd like to see: a live-action adaptation of Dodie Smith's sequel to her original book, titled *The Starlight Barking*. On the one hand, it is entirely possible to understand why Disney has yet to take on this particular story: *The Starlight Barking* is the most unhinged sequel one could possibly imagine. In the novel, the dalmatians of the first book awaken one day to find that every other creature on the planet is asleep. Humans, cats, cows – if it isn't a dog, it's locked in an unbreakable slumber. Also: the dogs are telepathic now. Also also: they can fly.

Obviously, the first thought the dogs have is that this global surge in sleepiness must be Cruella's doing, so they go on a mission to murder her. But she's asleep too, and the decision is made for the dogs to leave her be, and fly down to London, where one of the first book's puppies has taken on the role of Prime Minister. It only gets stranger from here: the dogs are contacted by Sirius, a literal star, who informs them that he has frozen the world so that the dogs might escape the inevitable nuclear war that human existence will eventually bring about. The dogs all consider his offer, before ultimately deciding that humans are pretty good fun, and obliteration by nuclear holocaust will be worth it for all the belly rubs and games of fetch they'll get in the meantime. I'm paraphrasing a little, of course. Still, if audiences are going to continue to be subjected to live-action versions of the classics, the least Disney can do is throw in something wild like *The Starlight Barking* to keep things interesting for a while.

Chapter 18

The King's Hand

The Sword in the Stone • *1963* • *Wolfgang Reitherman*

How apt that the last film completed under Walt Disney's watch is about a land in disarray, and the power vacuum left behind by the death of the 'good king'. The question that hangs over *The Sword in the Stone* is one of succession, and like those at the Disney company in the years following Walt's death, everybody in mediaeval England seems content to just do without a clear leader until someone magically turns up to give the place some meaning.

Let's not get ahead of ourselves with who will fill that role for Disney – we're only just about to begin the studio's long period of disarray. For England, though, it is the young Wart who will eventually take the reins of the nation, his rightful place upon the throne decided by that one scene in the dying moments of the film, where he finds a sword in a rock and pulls it out.

It's a drab and underwhelming conclusion to the film, in much the same way that *The Sword in the Stone* is a drab and underwhelming conclusion to the Walt years at Disney. There's an aimlessness to the plot, which takes T. H. White's 1938 novel of the same name and delivers an episodic and relatively shallow adaptation.

Theoretically, the film is about the education of a future king, bestowed by a great wizard. In practice, though, *The Sword in the Stone* spends most of its energy on turning Wart into an animal and trying to kill him.

First, Merlin transforms the boy into a fish and watches on impotently as a pike tries to eat him.

Next, Merlin transforms Wart into a squirrel, and then sings a song where the implicit message seems to be: 'You, a 12-year-old boy in the form of a small mammal, should probably just have sex with that lady squirrel'. He also watches on impotently as a wolf tries to eat Wart.

Finally, Merlin transforms Wart into a bird and completely ignores him while a hawk attempts to, you guessed it, eat the poor lad. Thankfully, the wizard does decide to step in when Wart crash lands in the cottage of Mad Madam Mim, the witch. Who also attempts to eat the young monarch-to-be. The magical battle that follows is the highlight of the film and almost distracts the audience from the fact that the entire movie seems determined to swallow its hero whole.

Compared to the films that had come before it – and particularly those of Disney's Golden Age, *The Sword in the Stone* is scrappy and deeply unfocused. It may be the last film that Walt completed prior to his death, but it lacks his insightful touch, which had made classics of so many movies before.

Of all Disney's films, none had quite so much of Walt's attention as *Snow White.* It had been his greatest labour of love, and thousands of hours of his time were spent ensuring that it lived up to his exacting vision.

Though he was able to step back a little for the films that followed, Walt still remained heavily involved in both the development and production process for many years. His notes frequently had a significant impact on the plot and characters. If Walt felt development wasn't heading in the right direction, he would shut down the film entirely until an idea somewhere down the line inspired its revival. So many of the films released during Walt's lifetime had production periods that spanned a decade or more as Walt tried to ensure every piece of the puzzle was in the right place.

But as the studio grew, so did Walt's ambitions. And before long there were other projects pulling his attention from the animation department. In the early 1940s, Walt was distracted by battles at home (the animator's strike) and overseas (a literal World War). A few years later, he was focused on his burgeoning live-action films, and then on the development of Disneyland in California.

By the end of his life, Walt had found another fixation that was taking up most of his time: his 'Florida Project', which would incorporate a new theme park complex and an experimental 'community of tomorrow'. And so, as story artist Bill Peet hammered out the plot of *The Sword in the Stone*, Walt was in the Sunshine State building a very different sort of Magic Kingdom.

Without his guidance, *The Sword and the Stone* evolved into a project that would foreshadow the haphazard and often lazy filmmaking of the decade and a half that followed. Wolfgang Reitherman, of Walt's Nine Old Men, reused old animation to the point of distraction – one scene in Merlin's cottage at the beginning of the film features the same shot of an agog Wart twice in close succession.

Even the sound of the film couldn't escape Reitherman's cost-cutting techniques. Rick Sorensen's voice was breaking during the process of recording his lines as Wart, and rather than start again from scratch, Reitherman simply had two of his sons take turns to complete the dialogue. The result is jarring – in some scenes, the actor audibly changes from line to line. What's more, anytime Wart trips or falls (which is a lot – the boy is in the midst of puberty and can't even maintain a consistent voice, let alone control his growing limbs), he makes the exact same noise – a sort of 'Woah-whip-wow!' that occurs at least *five times* over the course of the film.

Ultimately, *The Sword in the Stone* floundered at the box office – Disney's most underwhelming performance in over a decade. Walt clearly recognised the need for improvement and took a little more interest in the production of the studio's next film, *The Jungle Book.*

But this solution was just a sticking plaster that did not deal with the wound beneath. When Walt died in 1966, before *The Jungle Book* was completed, the studio fell right back into the bad habits we see on display here. The throne was empty, and there was no magic sword to help the company find a successor to the king.

Chapter 19

Marvelling at the Cinematic Universe

The Jungle Book • *1967* • *Wolfgang Reitherman*

You'd be hard pressed to convince my wife of this, so often do I return from the shop with everything but the one item I had been meaning to buy, but I've got a pretty good memory. My problem is that it only has two basic functions: remembering the sort of film trivia that everybody else could find on IMdB anyway, and recalling with unnerving accuracy photographic details about my early years. I could, if pressed, draw an accurate floor plan of the nursery I attended when I was two years old. I would be able to give you a tour of a holiday cottage I stayed in only once when I was four, or effortlessly guide you around the Dorset town of Wimborne Minster despite not having visited in almost thirty years.[1] I can also picture, with startling clarity, the day I made my first-ever trip to the cinema.

In my memory, I am standing between my father and my uncle on a pavement in Colchester, waving goodbye to my mother, aunt, and younger sister. In a moment, I will turn around and be led by hand into the foyer. My father will buy a Coca-Cola for himself and – I think – a carton of apple juice for me. This isn't part of the actual memory; I just consumed so much apple juice as a child that my family may well have been better off simply buying a small orchard to cut out the middleman. As a drink for my first cinema trip, it feels like a safe assumption. Finally, my father, my uncle and I would walk into the cinema, and I would see my first ever movie on the big screen: *The Jungle Book*.

With the possible exception of 2011's *Winnie the Pooh*, I'm not sure there is a more perfect film in the Disney canon for a child to see during their first cinema experience. *The Jungle Book* is a near-perfect film, of course, but it's also particularly accessible to younger audiences; a fun and colourful adventure that is relatively light on peril. Yes, the villain is a hulking tiger whose only goal is to devour the film's child hero – but Shere Khan sets about on his mission with so much elegance one suspects most of his victims are consumed by his charm long before his digestive system gets a look-in.

At the other end of the charisma scale is the man-cub Mowgli, who sulks his way through the forest, leaving much of the film's emotional heft to its supporting

1. This is, of course, assuming that Wimborne has not changed in any way whatsoever since the mid-1990s. Given the vibes the place gave off at the time, I honestly suspect that might be the case.

cast and, in particular, the odd couple pairing of Baloo and Bagheera. Story artist Bill Peet reversed the personalities of these two characters in his early treatment for the film. In Kipling's stories, Baloo has a more serious quality, acting as a mentor to Mowgli, while Bagheera is distinctly more laid-back. These positions put the duo at odds, and one of the most effective and moving scenes in the film is an understated sequence after the pair have saved Mowgli from King Louie's crumbling temple. In a duologue of careful debate and negotiation, Bagheera sensitively convinces Baloo that Mowgli will never be safe in the jungle. In this moment their relationship subtly shifts, their rivalry making way for the arm-in-arm retreat into the sunset that will act as the film's finale.

Not that young audiences will notice this in the moment of discussion. They will, instead, still be reeling from the high-energy rescue sequence at the temple, and the irresistible rhythm of King Louie's tune 'I Wan'na Be Like You' – one of five original songs written for the film by Robert and Richard Sherman.

These musical numbers are another reason the film works so well for inaugural cinemagoers – there is little downtime between them, and almost every song is among the finest that Disney ever recorded. Even the gentle 'Trust in Me', the sibilant song of the unscrupulous Kaa, is mesmeric. Its melody was originally written some years earlier for *Mary Poppins*.

The musical centrepiece of the film is, of course, 'The Bare Necessities' – the only song here not to have been written by Robert and Richard Sherman. Instead, it's a lingering remnant from Peet's early draft of the film, which (despite the upbeat mood of its one surviving tune) was much darker in tone. Terry Gilkyson had been the songwriter for this initial version of *The Jungle Book*, and so claims the credit for the film's best song (alongside legendary songwriter Van Dyke Parks, who arranged it for the final soundtrack).

The film was the last of the animated canon that Walt had an active role in producing – he was diagnosed with cancer in November 1966 and passed away from related causes just a few weeks later.

Walt's death had a smaller impact on the making of *The Jungle Book* than you might expect. He had been engaged in the production process, but even after *The Sword in the Stone*, he was far less involved than in the earliest days of the studio. It's understood that some of the jazzier elements of the soundtrack only made their way in after his passing, but for the most part, the film is a loyal representation of everything that Walt wanted from his films. That is to say, it is a reimagining of a classic story that plays fast and loose with its source material. *The Jungle Book* is more interested in being fun (and funny) than offering up a perfect narrative – perhaps why Mowgli is more upset about leaving the jungle than he is about leaving the family of wolves that raised him, and being tricked into doing so without even saying goodbye.

One area in which Walt's death did have some impact was the box office – the film was a huge success, driven in no small part by the sentiment that the public as a whole felt towards the late Walt Disney. There had been fears for the studio in the months leading up to *The Jungle Book*'s release – would it even be able to continue on without Walt at the helm? The emphatic response to the film presented a clear answer – and also ensured that a generation of 1960s kids would remember *The Jungle Book* as their first time in a cinema.

There is something magical about the cinema when you are a child. It is, of course, an *occasion* – a treat for many, and a moment to savour. It is an experience simply to step into the room itself, with its towering screen, and its sprawling seating. For some children it will be the largest indoor space they have yet seen. Every sense comes into play, building anticipation. The smell of popcorn, the sheer volume of the adverts, the way your feet dangle from the edge of the seat. The luckiest of us hold on to this sense of wonder for the rest of our lives. The biggest screens still loom over us, even as adults. That buzz of excitement runs through me even now whenever the lights dim, and the British Board of Film Classification certificate fills the screen – the last teetering moment before you are allowed to freefall into another world.

And so it is perhaps a little strange that, despite remembering the moments before my first-ever trip to the cinema, I recall nothing of the screening itself. Maybe I was lost in the moment, so excited that my brain forgot to record the memory – it's a common occurrence, often seen in popstar's mega-fans after a much-anticipated gig. Or perhaps I've simply let the memories meld in with all the other viewings of *The Jungle Book*. The film was put out on VHS shortly after the 1993 rerelease that served as my introduction, and it was my favourite of the few Disney videos we had at home at the time. I suspect I have watched the film more than almost any other over the course of my lifetime. But here's the true joy of *The Jungle Book*: it is so sweet, so vibrant, and so timeless that I doubt I will ever get bored of it.

In 2022, a few months before I signed the deal to write this book, Disney sent *The Jungle Book* back to cinemas for the first time in almost thirty years as part of its centennial celebrations. One Saturday morning, I took myself down to the nearest cinema and sat back to enjoy the film that, for me at least, started it all. Just ahead of me, there sat a father with his child, a young boy who could barely see over the seat in front of him. They had shuffled in just as the film was about to start, and I remember the boy's father leaning over to him in the last moment before George Bruns's perfect overture pulled us into the forests of central India.

"If you enjoy this," he said, "we can come back next weekend too."

The Bronze Age

Chapter 20

Cat's Got His Tongue

The Aristocats • *1970* • *Wolfgang Reitherman*

Easily one of the most underrated films in the Disney canon, *The Aristocats* came out in the midst of the studio's transition after Walt's death. It offered audiences hope for the immediate future, effortlessly capturing the spirit of the Silver Age. Though the film is the first wholly original story in the studio's history (and would remain the only one until *The Lion King*, almost a quarter of a century later), it feels deeply familiar.

The story of kidnapped animals making their way back home recalls *One Hundred and One Dalmatians*, while the combination of upper-crust house pet and happy-go-lucky stray is taken straight from *Lady and the Tramp*, which also shares its penchant for racially stereotyped Asian cats.

But the key factor in the instant nostalgia that *The Aristocats* provides is surely its stellar cast, which features a wealth of actors who, between them, had already appeared in over half of the studio's animated films.

Of these, the film's most enjoyable performance must surely go to Phil Harris, who voices the immensely charming ginger tom cat, Thomas O'Malley. Introduced with an equally delightful song, O'Malley is among the most likeable rogues in all of cinema. The repartee between his character and Eva Gabor's elegant yet sharp-minded Duchess is the making of the film: a call back to the charismatic romances of screwball comedies in the 1930s and 40s. Though things might not go exactly as he plans – it's pretty clear O'Malley just wanted to hook up with Duchess – the tom cat's heart is set firmly in the right place, and throughout the film, he goes out of his way to save the lost family (and in particular Marie, who perhaps should learn to stay on the ground, having fallen off of both a milk truck and a fifty-foot tall railway bridge over a fast-moving river).[1]

1. The three kittens – whose provenance we probably shouldn't overthink, given how eagerly Duchess is engaging with O'Malley, despite the fact her children can't be more than three months old – are each named after famous French figures. Toulouse, who is shown to have pretty credible artistic skills for a housecat, is named after the painter Henri de Toulouse-Lautrec. Berlioz, who honestly plays the piano better than I could ever hope, despite being so young he genuinely might not even know how to use a litter box yet, is named after the composer Hector Berlioz. Marie, on the other hand, is named after Marie Antoinette – presumably because after all the trouble she puts them through, the rest of the characters are seriously considering having her beheaded.

Harris was something of the studio's golden boy at the time – a favoured actor who appears here in the second in a row of three Disney classics. In the other two, he is more ursine than feline, playing Baloo in *The Jungle Book* and Little John in *Robin Hood.* All three roles are, admittedly, very similar. Disney needed a confident, rebellious anti-hero working against the established system. Phil Harris was their man.

There are plenty of other repeat offenders, too. The voice of Bill Thompson, who turns up here in the relatively minor role of the marinated Uncle Waldo, is barely recognisable from earlier roles as *Alice in Wonderland*'s White Rabbit, or *Peter Pan*'s Smee.

Thurl Ravenscroft has perhaps the most extensive Disney-centric CV of all, though he almost exclusively filled small roles or took on singing duties across the twelve animated classics he appeared in throughout his career. His credits include Monstro, the whale in *Pinocchio*, the alligator in the zoo in *Lady and the Tramp* and one of Colonel Hathi's elephant brigade in *The Jungle Book.* He appears here as the Russian cat, Billy Bass.[2]

Ravenscroft's most famous contributions to pop culture actually came from beyond the world of Disney – his distinct baritone is behind both the song 'You're a Mean One, Mr. Grinch' from the 1966 Seussian Christmas classic *and* the distinctive 'They're grreeeaattt!' catchphrase of Frosties' Tony the Tiger.

The Aristocats also serves as a Disney debut for Pat Buttram, who had already been acting for some twenty-five years when he turned up here as Napoleon, one of the film's two comic relief dogs. Having appeared in over a dozen westerns across the forties and fifties, Buttram had struggled to adapt to the changing cinema landscape after the genre faded from audience favour. Voice acting provided something of a career revival, and he would go on to play prominent roles in *Robin Hood* and *The Fox and the Hound*, as well as appearing in *The Rescuers*, *Who Framed Roger Rabbit* and, for his final role, *A Goofy Movie.*

But the real runaway hero of Disney voice acting is Sterling Holloway, whose seven appearances in the canon may not match up to Ravenscroft in number, but certainly do in impact.

Holloway's voice is so distinct, so recognisable, that it's hard to believe we've let him get away with defining the sound of so many of Disney's iconic characters. Among the roles that benefited from his warm, nasal rasp (and believe me, I know how unpleasant sounding that description is) are *Alice in Wonderland*'s Cheshire Cat, *The Jungle Book*'s Kaa and, most famously of all, the title character in *Winnie the Pooh.* Though these prime roles didn't start turning up until the early 1950s, Holloway had long been a go-to for Walt, who at one point considered him for the voice of Sleepy in *Snow White.* His earliest work for the studio ended up being

2. That's 'bass' as in 'double bass', the instrument his character plays. Ravenscroft's character is no relation to the turn-of-the-millennium singing rubber fish phenomenon that was Big Mouth Billy Bass.

in *Dumbo*, where he has the first speaking role in the film. Next time you watch it, look out for Mr. Stork. Holloway turns up in *The Aristocats* as the well-meaning but repeatedly ineffectual mouse, Roquefort.

Repeat performers have continued to appear in Disney films in the years since *The Aristocats*. Gabor herself would return for *The Rescuers* and *The Rescuers Down Under*. But three men in particular stand out as the latter-day successors to the likes of Ravenscroft and Holloway.

One of the earliest roles Jim Cummings took on was as a replacement for Holloway after the latter's retirement. Since 1988 he has been Disney's go-to actor for voicing Winnie the Pooh. By 2000, he had taken over the role of Tigger, too, replacing the original actor Paul Winchell (who also turns up here as Shun Gon, the Chinese alley cat whose racial stereotyping single-handedly earns this film a place on the list of Disney Plus titles not accessible to under sevens).

Cummings is one of the last great voice actors in a time when most big roles are taken by Chris Pratt or, if he isn't available, some other Hollywood A-lister. His knack for impersonation has meant that as well as originating roles like Ed the hyena in *The Lion King*, he has also revived a huge amount of classic Disney figures, either in film or television. During the production of *The Lion King*, he also stepped in to save one of the film's musical numbers. While recording 'Be Prepared', Jeremy Irons developed a vocal problem that meant he was unable to deliver the song's dramatic climax. Listening to the track now, you wouldn't have a clue that the final third is actually being sung by Cummings. To date, the actor has appeared in twelve classics, equalling Ravenscroft's record.

In the 1990s, another actor made a credible run of appearances across the canon. David Ogden Stiers was already a hugely respected actor best known for his role as Major Charles Emerson Winchester III in over 130 episodes of the smash-hit television programme *M*A*S*H*. In 1991, he took on the role of Cogsworth in *Beauty and the Beast*, perfectly echoing Winchester's snooty outer shell. He would go on to appear in *The Hunchback of Notre Dame* and *Atlantis: The Lost Empire*, as well as playing the villainous Governor Ratcliffe in *Pocahontas* and the wannabe-villainous Dr. Jumba in *Lilo & Stitch*.

We are currently in the midst of the greatest run of all, though. Since 2012, Alan Tudyk has appeared, without fail, in every single Walt Disney Animation Studios film. Like Stiers, Tudyk was already recognisable to audiences for a range of roles, most notably as the lovable Wat in *A Knight's Tale*, the lovable Wash in the television series *Firefly* and its film sequel *Serenity*, and as the lovable Tucker in hugely underrated horror comedy *Tucker and Dale vs. Evil*. What can I say? If you want a friendly face, you bring in Alan Tudyk.

His remarkable run of films features some pretty significant roles, including King Candy in *Wreck-It Ralph*, Alistair Krei in *Big Hero 6* and talking goat Valentino in the recent *Wish*. But one gets the sense that he's very actively going for the record: he has appeared in several films playing non-speaking animal roles. If you were wondering who voices Tuk Tuk, the giant armadillo/woodlouse in *Raya and the*

Last Dragon, or Heihei, the (figuratively) headless (literal) chicken in *Moana*, it's your boy, the Juilliard-educated actor, Alan Tudyk.

At the time of writing this book, Tudyk has already matched the twelve classics that Ravenscroft and Cummings have to their name. But by the time you read this, he'll have broken the record, reviving the role of Heihei for *Moana 2*. Next up will be *Zootopia 2*, and given that Tudyk already turned up in the original as a criminal weasel, I'd bet good money he'll have reached fourteen (consecutive!) Disney films by the end of 2025.

The Aristocats makes the most of a voice cast that features so many of Disney's most loyal stars – but as they each returned time and again to take on different roles for the studio, it's perhaps proof that the film's irresistible show-stopping song was wrong after all. Not *everybody* wants to be a cat. Sometimes they want to be a jovial yellow bear, or a stuffy old clock, or – if it helps them become the most prolific voice actor in the animated canon – a gigantic, rideable woodlouse.

Chapter 21

Hot in Nottingham

Robin Hood • *1973* • *David Hand, Wolfgang Reitherman*

There is no film in the Disney canon more hot under the collar than *Robin Hood.* The film is absolutely ripe with desire. There's an undeniable crackle of sexual frisson between the petulant Prince John and his loyal but perpetually frustrated advisor Sir Hiss. Little John flirts with just about every character in the movie – from the aforementioned Prince to the titular outlaw that he enjoys domestic bliss with in the forest. Lady Cluck plays her own sordid games, encouraging Maid Marian to act out an imaginary love affair with a local child roleplaying as her old boyfriend. Even Friar Tuck has *something* going on, physically bouncing the Sheriff out of his church before being thrust into bondage and led away by a chain connected to a collar.

And at the heart of it all, we have Robin and Marian themselves – a strangely chaste couple who are wholly hung up on one another, despite having no idea whatsoever about the natural order of things. The pair agree on how many children they'll have (a dozen at least) before even sharing a kiss.

Perhaps we can forgive them for moving so fast – both Robin and Marian are hot property on the singles market and might be snatched up at any minute. Ask any ten people about their first crush, and you can confidently expect at least a couple of mentions for the absolute foxes at the heart of this underrated Disney classic.

We discover our sexuality in much the same way that we discover language. Though others may try to teach us, the majority of our education comes simply from existing in the world, seeing it in action and learning how to understand it on our own terms.

Unlike language, much of the sexuality we see expressed in the world is still discussed through whispers and allusions, and so this education is eked out over a great many years. We might be able to hold a basic conversation when we are just a few years old, but most of us are unable to express (or even understand) our sexual desires until much later.

The early examples of sexuality we see in the world are all the more important for this. They ease us into a complex new way of comprehending our own existence, and the actions of those around us. They have the power to teach us that love, and its kissing cousin sensuality, are inherently good things and that their definitions can be fluid, varying from person to person with equal validity. Some groups seek to deny our children this early education, and the results are always telling. Those exposed to a new language in later life tend to lack the fluency of those who picked it up naturally along the way. They express themselves awkwardly and are more prone to mistakes.

Besides the relationships shared between parents and family members in our earliest years, the films and television we watch as children offer up some of our first experiences of sexuality. These moments of exposure are tame and broadly conform to heteronormative world views, but they are important nonetheless, attempting to build a positive foundation upon which the framework of sexuality can be, ahem, erected.

In contrast to those who would not educate on sexuality at all, there are many who oppose these early impressions for much healthier reasons. As we grow older, we realise that animated films (and we often pin this specifically to Disney, with its princess stories and global reach) have given us unhealthy expectations of love. Many of the great Disney romances are built around terrible compromises – almost always on the part of the woman, who may give up her voice for a man she's never spoken to, or find love with the beast who holds her captive. But these opinions are almost always expressed by people who are retroactively shocked at the stories they grew up watching. They are themselves proof that the foundations do not dictate every aspect of what is built upon them; formative years filled with Disney's love stories can still produce adults capable of a thoughtful and well-rounded understanding of healthy sexual expression.

The representations of sexuality we first see in films and television as children are an important part of our development, but I don't believe for a second that any child bases their entire worldview on the romantic lives of anthropomorphic foxes, or fairy tale princesses. I think we are always looking for a chance to connect with real-world experiences – even as children. Animation just offers us a safe, chaste means by which to do so.

I've been asking my friends about their childhood Disney crushes recently. None of the answers really surprised me. Princess Jasmine was mentioned a few times, as was her boy Aladdin and my own personal first love, Meg from *Hercules*.

A few people hesitantly offered furrier options: Adult Simba was a popular choice (always with his age very purposefully specified), as was Beast (this time always with the proviso that he was only fanciable in his cursed form) and, of course, Robin Hood.

I don't find any of these particularly strange. Each of these characters has a commanding presence, and each of them is generally pretty fun (even when the Evil Queen in *Snow White* got a nomination, it was backed up with an explanation that included her shape-shifting abilities. That, and her perfect cheekbones). And there's another key element that each of the choices shares: an irresistible voice.

Robin Hood is filled with great voice acting, from Peter Ustinov's comedy turn as Prince John to Phil Harris' now-familiar warmth, put into good use as Little John (who looks, sounds and acts like a more put-together version of Harris' *Jungle Book* character, Baloo). Marian, another popular Disney crush, is voiced with easy elegance by Monica Evans. But it is Robin himself who, despite being one of the most straightforward figures in a film filled with eccentric characters, steals the show. Surely this is down to veteran British actor Brian Bedford, a man who gifts the fox with a smoky voice that is so assured, so full of charm, that Robin even moves the dial on my own personal Kinsey scale by a notch or two.[1]

Adult Simba's voice – provided by Matthew Broderick – was mentioned as a factor in his nominations. And surely it should be noted that Beast's voice post-transformation was a world away from his animalistic gruffness.

As children, these first crushes play formative roles in our initial sexual development. There is something reassuring about the fact that so many of our romantic infatuations in animated films seem to be connected to the voice. We may be attracted to a witch's high cheekbones or that specific look Nala gives Simba as they lay in the grass together – you know the one – but ultimately, the thing that sticks with us is the one element of the entire film that has been transferred directly over from reality. We are drawn not to the world of the film, but to the lingering traces of the world that we are only just starting to discover.

1. Robin is also, I think, serenely comfortable with his own sexuality. There is not an ounce of toxic masculinity in his little orange body. He happily daydreams of his love, and discusses it with his best friend. He *loves* dressing up, and has no qualms about donning women's clothing. One of the frequent claims made about *Robin Hood* is that the film inspired significant areas of the furry community – a community that often enjoys dressing up in elaborate animal costumes. It's fitting, then, that Robin gets so much joy from dressing up in a wide variety of human outfits. Anyway, this footnote – and this footnote alone – is why my internet browsing history now includes a visit to the website 'Wikifur'.

Chapter 22

Oh Bother, Where Art Thou?

The Many Adventures of Winnie the Pooh • *1977* •
John Lounsbery, Wolfgang Reitherman

First things first: Gopher isn't in the book. It's my duty as an Englishman – possibly the only such duty I will ever fulfil – to point this out. Though, to his credit, Gopher says as much himself on a number of occasions – a little joke about not being in the phone book that plays to his anachronistic presence in this anthology film, which compiles three featurettes released between 1966 and 1974 and adds a melancholic little epilogue to wrap up everything neatly.

He may not belong in the Hundred Acre Wood, but Gopher has become an important part of Winnie the Pooh lore, representing one of the ways Disney attempted to draw American audiences into the distinctly English world of the stories.

Walt first encountered AA Milne's books through his daughter, who would read them in their family home. He began seeking film rights in the wake of *Snow White*'s release but didn't obtain them until 1961. It was only as he began developing the film that he realised how unfamiliar the stories were with American audiences. Walt shifted his plan a little: he would still release a Winnie the Pooh feature, but not before he had taken the time to present the characters to the public.

1966's featurette, *Winnie the Pooh and the Honey Tree*, marked the first of these introductions. The twenty-six-minute short drew from the first two chapters of Milne's *Winnie-the-Pooh*. Gopher's role was to inject a little American humour into proceedings – and he certainly does that, in part, by cribbing his entire personality from the beaver in *Lady and the Tramp*. Still, the plan worked: American audiences loved the short and all of the characters – including the brash Gopher.

British crowds were less impressed with the little interloper, though – not least because the studio had not even bothered to include one of the book's most beloved characters, Piglet.[1] As it happened, Gopher was originally intended to replace Piglet

1. It always strikes me that poor Christopher Robin has rather a bad deal in his friendship with Pooh. After all, if you ask anyone who Christopher Robin's best friend is, they will answer 'Pooh Bear', or something to that effect. But if you ask the same person who Pooh's best friend is, they will surely answer 'Piglet'. No wonder the real Christopher Robin hated his role in the books so much: he was written as the child who had an unrequited friendship with his own teddy bear.

in the films – a terrible decision that was reversed for the second featurette, 1968's *Winnie the Pooh and the Blustery Day*.

The nature of releasing featurettes over the course of almost a decade meant that the young actors playing both Christopher Robin and joey Roo had to be replaced as they outgrew their roles. There is a little inconsistency between performances and even the quality of production across the three shorts that combine to make the finished film, though it's less noticeable than in *The Sword in the Stone*, at least.

One area that remains reliable across the featurettes is the music, which was written wholly by Walt's favourite songwriting team, the Sherman Brothers. Whether you know it or not, you have been singing songs by the Sherman Brothers your whole life.

The two siblings, Robert and Richard, were born in the 1920s. They were the sons of Tin Pan Alley songwriter Al Sherman,[2] and the pair first started writing together in response to a challenge their father had set them. Before long, the Shermans had their first taste of success when 'Tall Paul', a song they had written for Annette Funicello, reached the top ten. It was the first time a female singer had done so well with a rock and roll track. Funicello was one of the original Mouseketeers on *The Mickey Mouse Club* TV show, and Walt paid attention to the hit. He beckoned the Sherman Brothers to the studio, and the boys were hired as staff writers.

Their early work at Disney was largely featured in live-action films that have long since been forgotten, but Walt saw the pair's potential and encouraged them to work on songs for a feature-length adaptation of *Mary Poppins* – despite not yet having obtained the rights from the infamously crotchety author PL Travers.

The impact of Robert and Richard on *Mary Poppins* cannot be understated – it was their advice that saw the action shift from the 1930s to the spring of 1910. Their songs are integral to the story, and saw the Shermans' profiles skyrocket after the film's release. 'Chim Chim Cher-ee' won an Academy Award for Best Song, and their score took home a second Oscar to boot. If you've ever sung 'Supercalifragilisticexpialidocious' or 'Feed the Birds' to yourself, you've sung a Sherman Brothers song.

The boys would continue to work as Walt's go-to songwriters until his death in 1966, and their work is heard not only in films of the era but also in the Disney theme parks. Their most notorious song is so catchy that just muttering its name will lodge it in your head for weeks. So I'll whisper the title in a footnote and hope we get away with it.[3]

Though the pair returned to Disney for occasional films after Walt's passing, things were never the same. It didn't help, either, that the brothers had a difficult relationship throughout their shared career. In 2009, their respective sons Gregory

---

2. Al Sherman had a decent amount of success himself, mostly across the 1920s to 1940s. One of his biggest hits was written for Walt's early rival Max Fleischer, and featured in a Betty Boop short. Alas, almost all of Sherman's songs have faded from the public consciousness today, with one exception: 'Livin' in the Sunlight, Lovin' in the Moonlight', which found notoriety in 1968 when the eccentric Tiny Tim released a particularly deranged cover.
3. 'It's A Small World (After All)'

and Jeffrey came together to direct 'The Boys', a documentary that told both the story of their fathers' remarkable legacies and of the rift between them that meant the two sides of the family barely spoke for many decades, even while the brothers sat together at a piano to write their unforgettable songs. The saddest part of all: there was no major incident at the heart of their estrangement. They were simply two brothers who had very little in common besides their work.

Nevertheless, the two continued to collaborate until the death of Robert, the eldest of the brothers, in 2012. By this point, they had amassed a back catalogue of classics that had been heard around the world. As well as non-Disney films like *Chitty Chitty Bang Bang* and *Charlotte's Web*, the Shermans had delivered iconic soundtracks for *The Aristocats*, *Bedknobs and Broomsticks*, *The Sword in the Stone* and *The Jungle Book*.[4] And, of course, *The Many Adventures of Winnie the Pooh*.

Though this film is by its very nature an episodic affair, it's the Sherman Brothers' charming songs that hold it together. They capture the very essence of the books – no mean feat given that when first given the gig, neither brother could get their head around the source material's appeal. In their struggle, they reached out to the British set and costume designer, Tony Walton, who was in the studio prepping *Mary Poppins*. Walton reacted exactly as I might have, and spoke so enthusiastically about the books that the Shermans finally understood the task at hand.

The final songs reflect the lightweight nature of those Pooh sings to himself in Milne's books – they float on the breeze, drifting out like half-formed thoughts, or they capture the simple innocence of childlike play. 'The Wonderful Thing About Tiggers' is among their most memorable songs, and the sweet to-and-fro of 'Little Black Rain Cloud' is perfectly understated. In 'Heffalumps and Woozles', another element of the film that diverges a little from the books, they deliver a pachyderm nightmare that is deeply indebted to (and only marginally less disturbing than) *Dumbo*'s 'Pink Elephants on Parade'.

Piglet turns up, eventually, during the second Pooh featurette within the film. The facts all point to this being a response to the livid British response to his absence in the first short. But there's a case to be made for an alternative reason: Disney simply realised that American audiences didn't need to be drawn into the film by a fellow countryman gopher when the Sherman Brother's magical songs were doing all the heavy lifting already.

4. For *The Jungle Book*, they wrote every song *except* 'The Bare Necessities'. Surviving brother Richard would also rewrite the lyrics to 'I Wan'na Be Like You' for the 2016 live action remake of the film, in which King Louie is a prehistoric gigantopithecus, which Richard gamely rhymes with 'magnificus'.

Chapter 23

Hide and Squeak

The Rescuers • *1977* • *John Lounsbery, Wolfgang Reitherman, Art Stevens*

Upon its release in the summer of 1977, *The Rescuers* was received as the best Disney film in over a decade. This is surprising for a number of reasons, very few of which we need to bother with because, above all else, it simply isn't a good film.

You might be instinctively inclined to disagree with me here; I have upset people in the past by claiming that *The Rescuers* is a fundamentally unenjoyable watch. Give it another go, and I think you'll understand.

There is no dirtier-looking film in the Disney canon. Despite the vivid colours of the movie's poster, the entire thing appears to have been animated under a thick layer of grime, as though the animators were forced to use New York subway platforms for desks. It is an unrelentingly bleak-looking movie, in which our intrepid heroes, Bernard and Bianca, appear to have their priorities entirely wrong. They shouldn't be looking for the missing orphan Penny, but rather the sun itself, which is taken hostage somewhere after the opening scene and not spotted again until the film's sequel, a full thirteen years later.

The plot here is tiresomely straightforward: Penny, the aforementioned runaway orphan, has gone missing. Technically, she's missing twice over. First, she ran away, and then she was kidnapped for the most boutique child labour camp in cinema history – a cushty little enslavement deal in which Penny is the only member, regularly thrust down one specific hole in the midst of Louisiana's swampland. Her kidnappers are a classic Disney pairing: the foul and controlling Madame Medusa, and her bumbling short king Mr Snoops.[1]

Who will come to Penny's rescue? Why, the International Rescue Aid Society – rodentia's answer to *Thunderbirds*' International Rescue. Except where the Tracy family sent space-age rocket ships to save the needy, the Rescue Aid Society sends a Hungarian diplomat and a superstitious janitor. Both of whom are mice.

---

1. Mr Snoops, it should be said, is a fantastic villain name. 5% sinister, 95% comedy impotence. A man with evil intentions, but only the slightest ability to follow through. Snoops' design was based on the journalist John Culhane, who had been working on a piece about the studio's animators during the pre-production of *The Rescuers*. Culhane was thrilled about the caricature, though surprised. He was clearly well loved at Disney, though – his likeness turns up again in *Fantasia 2000*'s 'Rhapsody in Blue' section.

Actually, let's pull back a bit here. The International Rescue Aid Society is easily the most shambolic international organisation in the history of cinema. We join them at the very beginning of *The Rescuers*, watching a selection of distinctly international-looking mice gather at the headquarters of the United Nations. They've each travelled secretly in the luggage of their human counterparts. The Austrian mouse wears a little Tyrolean hat. The Scottish mouse, a tiny kilt. A couple of Asian mice each have a Fu Manchu moustache, but at least these caricatures are used to show a functioning international community of well-meaning ambassadors. The purpose of the emergency meeting, for which at least five dozen delegates have travelled from across the globe, is to respond to a message in a bottle from the kidnapped Penny.

Not that the Society would know that. When the bottle is brought in, it remains closed. Nobody has opened it, let alone read the message inside! Yes, it clearly says 'HELP' on the paper within the bottle, but that could have been anything. How embarrassed would the portly chairmouse be if the message was unfurled to read 'HELP WANTED: JOIN YOUR LOCAL CO-OP TODAY', or 'HELP US OVERTHROW DEMOCRACY NOW – FASCISM NEEDS YOU'.

Anyway, the good news for the Rescue Aid Society is that it turns out a small girl has been kidnapped. Bad news for the girl, sure, but no egg on the face of whoever was in charge of sending out the invites.

I want you to bear in mind the size of this society once again, if only for a moment. Not the average size – that's about three inches, though you'd be right to identify this as an issue in the prickly world of missing person recovery. But rather, let's remember for the moment that at least sixty mice have travelled from – as far as overt cartoon racial profiling can tell – every corner of the globe. And they have travelled solely to attend a meeting regarding one specific mystery call for help. There are literally two items on the agenda: second, an emergency response to a call for help that has already been sitting unread in a bottle for at least a week, and also, before any of that, singing a little song.

Anyway, sixty mice have come to this meeting for these two purposes. So tell me why the two who end up taking on the case are an Eva Gabor-esque socialite, voiced (for extra authenticity) by Eva Gabor, and the janitor. Don't worry, actually, I know the answer: everybody else is only there for the song. And fair. It's not Disney's finest musical number, but it's pretty easy to sing.

Fortunately for Bernard and Bianca, the clues are incredibly easy to follow, and before long the pair are helping young Penny find a rare diamond, escape Madame Medusa, and get the best of her two pet alligators.

So, a simple plot and grotty visuals that are among the very worst of Disney's post-war run. There's little to get out of this film, which relies mostly on nostalgia to get audiences across the finish line.

One home video release did offer another incentive to watch the film, though you'd need to be a little creep with split-second pause button precision to make the most of it. In 1999, Disney recalled almost 3.5 million copies of the film's second VHS release after it was discovered that two frames of Bernard and Bianca's haphazard flight through New York featured an image of a topless woman.

It emerged that an employee at Disney had – for reasons unknown – spliced the non-consecutive frames into the film during its initial post-production in 1977. The prior video release had used a different print, and so the explicit images escaped the audience's attention for over two decades.

It wasn't the first time that Disney had attracted ire for adult imagery in their films – though it was the first time the accusations were technically correct. In 1994, some viewers commented that a scene in *The Lion King* featured the word 'SEX' written out in the sky by a puff of dust. It's a stretch even viewing in slow motion – *not that I have* – and some have cited Disney animator Tom Sito as saying that the message actually reads 'SFX', a calling card left by the film's special effects team.

The *Lion King* rumour was given a public airing by the conservative Christian group American Life League in 1995, which highlighted it among a number of concerns about subliminal messaging in Disney cartoons. They also suggested that the priest in the final act of *The Little Mermaid* is hiding something of an arousal beneath his liturgical vestments. Watch the film for just a moment longer, and you'll see that all he's hiding is a terrifically knobbly knee.

Disney isn't beyond hiding little easter eggs in their films – it's just that they generally aren't as interesting as erect men of the cloth. Instead, much like the *Rescuers* themselves, these surprises are usually mice hiding in plain sight.

Hidden Mickeys are secret glimpses of the iconic Mickey Mouse silhouette that are often tucked away in the backgrounds of Disney's films. The most hardcore of fans – more hardcore even than a thirty-something man who writes an entire book about Disney movies – have been taking note of these Hidden Mickeys for years, sharing their findings online. Sometimes these discoveries feel entirely subjective – the image of two circles atop a larger circle can be easier to find if you're willing to grossly skew the positioning of each shape, and easier still if you include any scene where there are a lot of bubbles, or puffs of smoke or dust (clearly people are willing to spot just about *anything* in dust).

Others feel more purposeful, though – Mickey's distinctive silhouettes appearing in the spots on various dalmatians, among a pile of fruit in *Lilo and Stitch*, or as a patch on Aladdin's clothing for a split second after Jafar reveals him to be a pauper.

There is, in fact, a Hidden Mickey tucked away in *The Rescuers*, though you'll be forgiven for missing it – firstly, it isn't his famous silhouette, but rather a low-res image of the iconic Mickey Mouse clock face, in which his hands point to the time. Secondly, the image appears in the one scene of the film where you'll be too distracted to notice a tiny Mickey Mouse. It hangs on the back wall of the Rescue Aid Society's chambers, and you'll be preoccupied with trying to comprehend every single decision the organisation ever made.

Chapter 24

Hounded Out and Hunted Down

The Fox and the Hound • 1981 • Ted Berman, Richard Rich, Art Stevens

There's a strange melancholia that runs through *The Fox and the Hound.* Centred on the doomed relationship between the titular characters, Tod and Copper, it's clear that there is no real happy ending in sight from the very first scene, which wastes no time killing off the fox's mother.

Even the youngest audience members quickly realise that while Tod and Copper plan to be best friends forever, their destinies are intertwined very differently. This is a film about the hunter and the hunted. Inevitably, it makes for one of the most moving and downright depressing films within the Disney canon. It could have been worse – the novel that the film is based on more or less kills off every character going. For a while, even this adaptation considered an onscreen death for one of the characters.

Midway through the film, Tod and Copper find themselves engaged in a thrilling chase that will cement the new dynamic between them. Copper is joined by Chief, an experienced hunting dog voiced by Disney regular Pat Buttram. It is Chief who briefly seems to have the upper hand in the chase, driving the adolescent fox onto a bridge and looking like the inevitable victor. And then the steam train comes.

Barrelling down the tracks, the train surprises both fox and dog alike. Tod is terrified, but quick to react. Chief is too slow. We see him tumble from the bridge, crashing into the cliffside as he falls into the river below. It's enough to kill an old hunting dog – and, indeed, that was the original plan. Watching the film today it's still clear that the incident was intended to be the end of Chief. He lies prostrate among the rocks, his head slumping lifelessly when prodded by Copper. And then his eyes open just slightly. Just enough to let us know that he has escaped death.

The decision to spare Chief's life was a matter of deep contention between Disney's old guard, including Wolfgang Reitherman, Frank Thomas and Ollie Johnston, and the young and upcoming artists the studio was training to replace them. The Nine Old Men were mostly retired now, and *The Fox and the Hound* marked the first feature for a new wave of animators keen to make an impression at the studio that had first inspired them.

There was plenty of respect between the fresh-faced artists and the legendary animators who had helped Walt build the studio into the American titan it had become. But this transitional period was rife with clashes as Disney's management –

including Walt's son-in-law Ron Miller, who had just been made CEO – disagreed with the new generation of animators over what Disney should stand for. Was it good old-fashioned family values, or the development and delivery of bold and exciting new ideas?

Before long, a number of *The Fox and the Hound*'s younger contributors would find themselves pushed out of Disney. Some left of their own accord – in 1979, the influential animator Don Bluth left the studio mid-way through the production of the film, taking with him almost a dozen of the studio's animators. The mass departure hit *The Fox and the Hound* hard and would prove a thorn in Disney's side for years to come, as Bluth's own feature films – many of which were produced by Steven Spielberg – became critical and commercial successes in their own right. Though films like *An American Tail*, *The Land Before Time*, and *All Dogs Go To Heaven* haven't necessarily broken into the consciousness of the generations that have followed, they remain distinctly-styled semi-classics that more than matched up against the faltering Disney releases of the mid-1980s.

Other animators were forced out of Disney, though. Given marching orders for failing to maintain the status quo in a studio that desperately needed to adopt change in order to secure a future for itself.

Brad Bird was one of these artists, a recent graduate of the California Institute of the Arts, which was better known as CalArts among the myriad young animators who had studied there and were now breaking into the industry en masse.

Like many of the new artists joining Disney, Bird had been a huge fan of the studio growing up. He had formed a friendship of sorts with Mitt Kahl, one of the Nine Old Men, and as a teenager had been invited to visit the lot whenever he was in town. This first-person experience of seeing the studio in action had left Bird with strong ideas about where Disney stood, and what it represented. He believed the studio needed to take more creative risks in order to live up to the principles Walt had founded it with. Management disagreed, and after just two years, he was fired. He had worked on only two features: *The Fox and the Hound* and *The Black Cauldron*.

Bird had plenty of ideas of his own, though, and quickly went about looking for homes for his various projects. One of his concepts, *Family Dog*, eventually led to a poorly-rated adult-oriented cartoon series. It flopped terribly, but his talent was noticed, and production company Klasky Csupo hired him to act as an executive consultant on a brand new animated sitcom that they were working on: *The Simpsons*.

Bird's work on *The Simpsons* had a significant impact on the early years of the show – he designed the character Sideshow Bob and helped shape the visual approach that differentiated the programme from anything else on television. His profile boosted, he was afforded the opportunity to direct his first feature animation, and in 1999 released *The Iron Giant* – still arguably the greatest traditionally animated film America has produced beyond the walls of the Disney lot.

In 2008, Bird was beckoned back to Disney, directing the live-action sci-fi feature *Tomorrowland*, a box-office disappointment. But by this point, he'd more than made his point to his former employers, who had already distributed two Academy

Award-winning films that he had made for Pixar: *The Incredibles* and *Ratatouille*. Among the very best of Pixar's output to date, these two films demonstrated for Disney the rich rewards that were on offer for animators willing to take risks.

Fittingly, Bird's opportunity to work with Pixar came about as a direct result of his friendship with a CalArts classmate who had also been fired from Disney in the 1980s. John Lasseter joined the studio in 1979, hired straight after graduation thanks to his student film, *Lady and the Lamp*. It was a short, traditionally animated cartoon that offered the first glimpse at an idea Lasseter would return to throughout his professional career: what if an inanimate object came to life?

Like Bird, Lasseter felt Disney had lost its way a little – but he was keen to work on projects that could revive the studio's fortune. Like Walt before him, Lasseter was passionate about making the most of new technologies – he became enamoured with the potential he saw in computer-generated graphics. He wanted to incorporate computer-animated backgrounds with traditionally animated characters and pitched consistently for projects that would allow experimentation in this area. Ron Miller couldn't see how CGI would offer any benefit from a cost perspective, and in 1984 Lasseter was fired from Disney – by animation administrator Ed Hansen, the same man who had let Bird go a couple of years earlier.

Lasseter soon found work at the computer graphics department of Lucasfilm, the production company of *Star Wars* creator George Lucas. He became close friends with the group's Vice President, Ed Catmull. Here, Lasseter began to realise how even he had been underestimating the possibilities CGI offered the filmmaking industry. He worked on short films in which every aspect was computer-generated – even the characters, which he had previously thought would be too complex a prospect. When Lucas had to sell the department to fund his divorce proceedings, Apple co-founder Steve Jobs came aboard, and the team reformed as Pixar.

In 1995, Lasseter shot to global fame as the director of the first full-length computer-animated feature, Pixar's *Toy Story*. He went on to direct the studio's next two features as well, acting as executive producer on the rest of their output. Disney, who had realised all too late how prescient Lasseter had been regarding CGI, came on board as a distributor for Pixar's early films. In 2006, Disney bought Pixar for over $7 billion. Over two decades after firing Lasseter for his relentless championing of CGI, the studio made him the Chief Creative Officer of their three animation studios. The eleven films in this book that were released during his tenure represented a new renaissance for a studio that had once again been faltering.

Brad Bird had wanted Disney to take more storytelling risks – he was among the young animators pushing for Chief's death in *The Fox and the Hound*. John Lasseter was fired for wanting the studio to take more technical risks. And then there was a third animator, who was fired for taking stylistic risks.

It's hard to imagine now how the director Tim Burton ever could have slotted into the family-friendly animated style of Disney's canon. Burton's artwork has always been deeply distinctive, and a world away from the studio's tried-and-tested formula of cute animals and sweet children. And yet, for a short while, the future hero of Hot Topic goths was a concept artist and animator, sharing studio space with Lasseter and the other animators. It was a baffling mix. James B. Stewart's corporate exposé *DisneyWar* relishes in anecdotes of Burton, fresh from dental surgery, returning to the Disney offices to loom over his colleague's desks, blood dripping from his mouth onto their workspaces.

For *The Fox and the Hound*, Burton was tasked with animating Vixey – a bright-eyed love interest for Tod the fox. The artist reportedly had to 'work up' to drawing a scene in which Vixey is shown in close quarters, smiling kindly at the audience. Burton – whose artwork tended towards the ghoulish, couldn't simply leap into such a sweet vision.

Though his style was at odds with their clean-cut image, Disney tried their best to work with Burton's obvious talent. He directed a stop-motion short about a young boy who dreams of being horror icon Vincent Price, and a curious live-action version of *Hansel and Gretal* that screened on the Disney Channel once on Halloween night, and then never again. His next project, a thirty-minute featurette about reviving the corpse of your dead dog, proved too much for Disney, and he was finally let go.

Though Burton's unique style was deemed unsuitable for Disney, it was increasingly in demand elsewhere. He was quickly picked up to direct *Pee-wee's Big Adventure*, a film that took Paul Reubens' cult character Pee-wee Herman into the mainstream. He directed Michael Keaton in the dark comedy *Beetlejuice* and, later, in *Batman* and *Batman Returns*. By the mid-nineties, he was one of the most recognisable directors on the planet. His unique visual style, which had once been too dark for Disney, was at the heart of his success. In 1993, less than a decade after the studio fired him, Burton was brought back into the fold for *The Nightmare Before Christmas*. The director was too busy with other projects to take the reins but produced the film, which was based on an original story he had conceived. Another former *Fox and the Hounds* crew member, Henry Selick, directed. Even now, the film was deemed too dark for a straight Disney release, and so it was produced under subsidiary studio Touchstone Pictures.

Disney beckoned Burton back again in 2010, offering him the chance to direct a live-action reimagining of *Alice in Wonderland* that they had been developing. He would also deliver a new take on *Dumbo* in 2019. But the real victory, surely, was the project he helmed for Disney in between these two films: a feature-length stop-motion remake of *Frankenweenie*, the dog-reviving story that had got him fired two decades earlier by the exact same studio.

In most versions of the story, that would act as a neat little bow to wrap up a redemption narrative – but that was never really Tim Burton's style. Speaking at the Lumiere Film Festival in 2022, the director admitted that he couldn't see himself working with Disney again in the future. His reasoning was an interesting echo of the views his classmates held during the production of *The Fox and the Hound*. Disney is playing things too safe, he believes, with an overreliance on existing IPs. With Burton, Bird and Lasseter all working on projects elsewhere now, it looks like an opportune time for a new generation of disruptive animators to offer their vision for the studio's future.

Chapter 25

Toil and Trouble

The Black Cauldron • 1985 • Ted Berman, Richard Rich

All art is a miracle; the culmination of millions of years of evolution, and the entirety of all human civilisation up until the singular moment in time in which an artwork was created. There is, in a sense, as much wonder in the first finger painting of a toddler as there is in all of the Sistine Chapel. That the human mind so consistently creates something out of nothing and is capable of capturing the imagination in visual, aural or physical form is perhaps the most incomprehensibly magical thing we see in all life on planet Earth.

That said, *The Black Cauldron* really is a steaming pile of pig excrement.

If, somehow, you've yet to work out that this book is not a credible academic document (in which case, congratulations on picking it up in a bookshop and happening to turn to this precise page on your first go), let my unrelenting hatred for this film erase your last doubts.

I'm not alone in my aversion to *The Black Cauldron* – it was such a flop upon release that Disney's new management almost shut down the animation department forever. Picture that for a moment: The Walt Disney Company, whose very existence was founded on animated films, both short and feature-length, almost gave up on the artform entirely because after a string of disappointing releases, *The Black Cauldron* looked like the last of the dirty bathwater swirling inevitably around the drain.

The film is a relatively loose adaptation of the first two novels of Lloyd Alexander's *The Chronicles of Prydain* series. The high fantasy story stands in stark comparison to the studio's previous releases, though animators working on the project believed that it had the potential to match up to the artistry and wonder of *Sleeping Beauty*. It's a nice idea, but one that was doomed from the start.

Like so many fairy tales, the story of *Sleeping Beauty* is essentially a very simple one. One can't say the same for a series of books with deep lore drawing on ancient Welsh mythology. From the start, the team of young animators working on *The Black Cauldron* found themselves attempting to create a coherent story from a wealth of material. This isn't necessarily an impossible task – the studio approached Ralph Bakshi to work on the project after the relative success of his 1978 adaptation of *The Lord of the Rings*, which packed the first two volumes of that series into a two-and-a-quarter-hour film.

Brevity was not the only issue *The Black Cauldron* faced. Though the studio often made significant changes to the dark original endings of fairy tales like

Snow White, *Cinderella* and *Sleeping Beauty*, little effort was made to lighten the content of Alexander's stories. And so, when appointed CEO of The Walt Disney Company in 1984, Michael Eisner was appalled to find that their next animated film featured undead corpses and, in one since-deleted scene, a man developing grotesque boils and lacerations before rotting away on screen. Eisner's right-hand man Jeffrey Katzenberg was no stranger to such imagery – he had been president of production at Paramount when *Temple of Doom*, the most gruesome Indiana Jones film, was being made. But Disney was a family company, and its audiences would look very different. A few months before *The Black Cauldron*'s release date in the winter of 1984, a disastrous test screening saw one family after another walking out of the final act of the film, their children unable to handle the horrors onscreen.

Katzenberg ordered a significant re-edit despite directors Ted Berman and Richard Rich protesting that it simply wasn't possible. Animated films are meticulously planned to save costs on the expensive animation processes, and editing happens during storyboarding to minimise needless work later. Katzenberg wouldn't listen and ultimately removed around twelve minutes from the film.

Without seeing the uncut version that was already complete when Katzenberg joined the studio, it's impossible to say whether the film would have benefitted from being left as it was. I'm personally inclined towards *more* cuts. The comic relief character Gurgi, who appears to be a cross between Smeagol and Elmo, but is somehow a thousand times more grating, could stand to be removed entirely. I am not a man of violence, but if I were ever to come across Gurgi in real life, I would be inclined to punt him into the film's death-bringing cauldron with all the force of Katzenberg shoe-horning his way into an editor's suite.

One thing is certain, though: had the film been released unedited, it would have plausibly received an R rating in American cinemas, indicating it was unsuitable for children. As it was, the release was delayed until the summer of 1985. Even with the cuts, it earned the studio its first-ever PG rating for an animated classic.[1]

The Black Cauldron was a significant commercial flop, scraping back less than half of its budget in domestic markets. Neither Berman nor Rich would make another feature-length film with Disney. A tremendous amount of work had gone into the film, and more work still had been piled on top in a desperate attempt to salvage something positive.

Sometimes this is how it goes. All art is a miracle, but that isn't because all art is necessarily *good*. Art is a miracle because it represents humanity's innate need to create. Its desire to add something to the world, to try something new and see what happens. Art is a miracle because even when it fails, it is still art. You've still made something. And there's still something to take away. *The Black Cauldron* did fail

1. Even without the cuts, had it simply been held back until the summer of 1985 the full version of *The Black Cauldron* would likely have received a PG-13 rating. In a sense, even this chance to escape the dreaded R rating could have been partly attributed to Katzenberg. PG-13 only came into effect in 1985, in part as a response to the darkness abound in the aforementioned *Indiana Jones and the Temple of Doom*.

– rather spectacularly. But it taught some valuable lessons to all of those involved, from the young animators cutting their teeth on the project to Katzenberg, who was adapting his successful work in the film industry to the animated market. *The Black Cauldron* almost killed Disney's animation department. But it also showed them that they needed to rethink everything if they were to survive.

Chapter 26

Big Cheese

The Great Mouse Detective • 1986 • Ron Clements, Burny Mattinson, Dave Michener, John Musker

Ask someone when the Disney Renaissance began and – assuming they don't look at you in utter bewilderment, unsure how to explain to a grown adult that Goofy and Machiavelli didn't run in the same circles – most people will name *The Little Mermaid*. It's a fair shout. Critically acclaimed and commercially successful, it marked the first time since Walt's death that the studio seemed truly comfortable in its own shoes.

But creative shifts like these rarely happen unprompted, particularly when the process is as collaborative an endeavour as the production of an animated film. Rather, it is possible to trace the incremental changes to attitudes, methodology, and culture and understand how they influence a work. We look backwards, reversing the butterfly effect, analysing the path of the tornado to such a depth that we can pick out the individual wingbeats that kicked the storm into motion.

All of which is to say: *The Little Mermaid* might have been the turning point for Disney animation, but *The Great Mouse Detective* represents one of the more decisive flutters of the butterfly's wings.

The 1970s were a period of tremendous turmoil within the Walt Disney Company, which had lost the leadership of both Walt (in 1966) and Roy (in 1971). Everybody knew how instrumental the brothers had been in guiding the business as it grew from a small outfit animating short films into one of Hollywood's largest studios, but few had anticipated just how ill-equipped their successors were to fill the void.

Everything the studio did felt tied to the recent past – the 1950s sensibilities of the nuclear family. Swathes of wholesome, toothless live-action films with inexplicably dull names: *No Deposit, No Return* and *The Biscuit Eater*, *The North Avenue Irregulars* and *The Barefoot Executive*.[1] Desperate to cling on to the last remnants of Walt's creativity, the studio repeatedly returned to the final film he'd worked on – *The Love Bug* – releasing three further sequels starring Herbie, the sentient Volkswagen Beetle.

1. The comedian and cartoonist Sam Schafer points out that *The Barefoot Executive* does benefit from one fantastic element: a mealy-mouthed theme song that sounds deeply onanistic if one isn't paying enough attention to the chorus. I fully recommend digging it up online.

Very few of these films made an impact at the box office – the studio's new president, Card Walker, didn't believe that marketing offered value to the organisation. In his book *DisneyWar*, James B. Stewart highlights *Tron* as being particularly underserved by Walker's policies. It was released just weeks after Steven Spielberg's *ET the Extra-Terrestrial*, and sank without a trace. The film had cost almost twice as much to make as *ET* and would be mostly forgotten for decades to come, loved only by the earliest gamers and two French guys pretending to be robots.

Disney Animation was fumbling its legacy, too. Wolfgang Reitherman's cost-cutting techniques had led to a marked decline in the quality of the animation and though the studio managed to release a few wonderful films in the years after Walt's death, contemporary critics were mostly underwhelmed. Box office returns reflected an image of a studio resting a little too heavily on its laurels. Though *The Rescuers* was considered a success upon its release, drawing in healthy US box office takings, Disney was unable to replicate its popularity with any consistency.

By 1984, things were looking exceptionally bleak. Share prices were less than half of what they had been at the studio's peak, and the studio was still reeling from Don Bluth's mutiny, which had taken 17% of its animators. Taking advantage of the situation, billionaire financier Saul Steinberg attempted a hostile takeover. Disney managed to hold on – but took on significant new debts to do so.

Serious changes were clearly needed, and with the current CEO (and Walt's son-in-law) Ron Miller dilly-dallying about making them, the company's shareholders – led by Roy Disney's son Roy E. Disney – forced their hand. Miller was ousted.

Brought in to replace the business's senior leadership were two men: Michael Eisner and Frank Wells. Eisner, the new CEO, had seen enormous success as president at Paramount Pictures. His strong head for business was matched by an incisive creative instinct. He had been involved in the greenlighting of major hits, including the first *Indiana Jones* film and *Beverly Hills Cop*. He also had a built-in right-hand man – a former colleague from Paramount, Jeffrey Katzenberg.

The new president, Frank Wells, had spent much of his career at Warner Bros. Though Eisner was initially hesitant about how their partnership would work, they soon fell into a dynamic that in many ways echoed the one Walt and his brother had shared: Eisner the creative who pushed the company forward, and Wells the facilitator who took on the brunt of the difficult jobs to ensure ambitions were met.

Still, neither had any real experience in animation, which put the struggling division under immense pressure. Conversations were had about dropping the department entirely – an incredible move for a company built on a foundation of cartoons. Roy E. Disney was more aware of this than anyone – he had been instrumental in bringing Eisner and Wells in and had considered their strengths and weaknesses. As part of the transition, the new leadership came to Roy and asked where he saw himself within the business. He acknowledged that he could offer animation the experience they lacked, and asked to head up the division. It was the least Eisner could do. Had Roy not stepped up to the plate, this book may very well have ended with the previous chapter, which would have been the direct opposite of 'happily ever after': 'and so Disney shut down, sadly, with a pig keeper'.

Though little could be done to salvage *The Black Cauldron*, production on its follow-up, *Basil of Baker Street*, was still in the earlier stages of development. Eisner and Katzenberg took a keen interest in the project – their first chance to impact Disney's struggling animation department. An early review of the story reel led to significant rewrites. At the same time, Eisner demonstrated a willingness to shake up the genteel corporate culture at Disney, cutting both the budget and project timeline in half.

It's hard to say exactly what impact these changes had on the finished film, but few Disney fans would argue that it isn't a significant improvement on *The Black Cauldron*. Plotting is tighter, characters are more likeable, and there are flashes of experimentation within the work. The finale, which takes place among the cogs of Big Ben,[2] represents the first uses of CGI in a Disney film – though in this early incarnation, an element of traditional animation clings on. The gears of the clock were rendered as computer graphics and then printed directly onto cels that the animators could add colour and characters to.

Though Eisner's input was a net positive for the film, one decision deeply rankled the crew working on the project. Believing that *Basil of Baker Street* sounded 'too English' for domestic marketing purposes, he renamed the film *The Great Mouse Detective*.

Many in the studio felt that this new title was too simplistic – a lowest common denominator name for people devoid of imagination. One animator wrote a notorious interoffice memo, masquerading as a studio executive. It claimed that the rest of Disney's animated films to date would also be renamed. Among these new titles were 'Seven Little Men Help a Girl', 'The Wooden Boy Who Became Real' and 'Puppies Taken Away'.[3]

The Great Mouse Detective was a modest success upon release – roughly double the box office take of *The Black Cauldron*, but at a third of the cost. There were still plenty of elements that felt out of place within the wider Disney canon, though. The curious darkness of Bronze Age Disney regularly seeps into the film – in particular during an extended nightclub sequence, during which:

- An overtly sexualised female mouse sings a song titled 'Let Me Be Good To You' to a titillated male crowd.
- Basil's sidekick Dr Dawson has his drink spiked.
- A brawl breaks out, during which shots are fired, and one character strangles another.

2. Yes, I know Big Ben is the bell. Just like I know that you're a pedant and everybody around you finds it very tedious.
3. My favourite part of the memo is that of the 18 films listed, just one is permitted to keep its original title: *Aristocats*. Given that since the film's release, most children learn about 'Aristocats' before they learn about the concept of 'aristocrats', it is perhaps the only movie that actually might have benefitted from a new name.

Still, the scene also introduces one of the best couples' fancy dress costumes in the Disney oeuvre – Basil's moustachioed sailor disguise, and Dawson's pot-bellied, eye-patched counterpart.

While we're at it: Dawson's storied past poses a question that haunts me to this day: what does mouse war look like? In the film's opening scene, Dawson explains that his arrival in London follows lengthy service in Afghanistan. Are we to infer that there are international mouse wars? That, like her human counterpart, Queen Moustoria[4] is waging a war thousands of miles away in the Middle East? And to what end? The Second Anglo-Afghan War stemmed mostly from international tension with Russia – are global mouse relations so fraught as to warrant a war of their own? Or are the British mice acting in collaboration with the human armies – chewing vital lines of communication, perhaps? Maybe the war shares the cynical motivating factors of modern conflicts – but how much oil can the mice really need for their tiny lamps? What is the mouse equivalent of oil? Actually, we all know this. But is Afghanistan's cheese of choice, kishmish paneer, really worth the toll that war takes upon a rodent nation?

Perhaps, bearing all this in mind, the villainous Rattigan is simply trying to bring the conflict to a peaceful conclusion. Probably not, though. He is, after all, a prototypical over-the-top villain. He has a pet cat who he feeds his henchmen too whenever they fail him. He has an elaborate scheme to replace the monarch with a janky clockwork robot. He's voiced by Vincent Price, which is an absolutely inspired piece of casting. And, best of all, he sets up an incredibly overwrought Rube Goldberg machine to kill his greatest foe – complete with a jaunty farewell song that appears to have been written, recorded and committed to vinyl solely for the occasion of murdering the mouse detective.

Compared to the films being released just a few years later, *The Great Mouse Detective* remains rough around the edges. But it has an undeniable charm – and marks the beginning of Eisner and Katzenberg's great intervention. The result is twofold: the best Disney film in a decade, and the first tentative steps along the path towards the studio's remarkable resurgence.

4. I'm going to put the laziness of this name down to the entire story team being too busy rewriting old film titles for a silly memo.

Chapter 27

Cool Cats and Hotdogs

Oliver & Company • 1988 • George Scribner

After entering the filmmaking process once production had already started on *The Black Cauldron* and *The Great Mouse Detective*, Jeffrey Katzenberg was ready to make a splash with the first Disney animation greenlit under his leadership.

As a film executive, Katzenberg had been attempting to adapt Charles Dickens's classic novel *Oliver Twist* for some time. When story artist Pete Young pitched an animated version with dogs, Katzenberg was quick to approve the idea and send it into development.

Over the course of 1986 and well into 1987, the story took on a variety of forms, some grossly diverging from the source novel. Roy E. Disney wanted the down-and-out Fagin to attempt a live animal heist from New York Zoo, with Dodger and his gang seeking to steal a panda. Later, Oliver's origins were given a twist more apt for the city of Gotham – an opening was planned in which his parents were killed by Sykes' dobermans, Roscoe and DeSoto. Much of his motivation for joining Fagin's doggy syndicate would have been the opportunity for vengeance.

Eventually, the film settled into a simpler, lighter story that made the most of its New York setting. From the opening scene, audiences are treated to perhaps the most beautifully realised vision of the city yet seen in an animated film. We see the buzz of the streets by day and the melancholic blues of the same block on a rainy night. CGI is used to capture the grandeur of the Brooklyn Bridge and other landmarks, but at the same time, the Twin Towers of the World Trade Center stand proudly in the background of the opening sequence, expressively drawn by hand.

Over a decade later, in 2001, Disney considered removing images of the recently felled towers from their films. It was a strange time for America, and the grief around the 9/11 terrorist attacks was so great that many studios edited new films to remove shots – *Spider-Man*, *Zoolander*, *Stuart Little 2* and *Men in Black 2* all came out the following year having made changes. Disney's 1998 blockbuster *Armageddon* was edited so that television broadcasts would exclude a scene in which the towers were struck by meteors, and the entire finale of *Lilo & Stitch*, that other great ampersand animated classic, had to be rewritten; the film initially featured a hijacked airliner careening through a busy metropolis and crashing off of high-rise buildings. Ultimately, though, the World Trade Centre remains front and centre in the very opening shot of *Oliver & Company*. The film had already seen a hugely successful release on VHS just a few years earlier, and the effort warranted to remove the towers seemed silly when so many families had the footage in their homes already.

Another two decades down the line, and it's a huge relief. *Oliver & Company* is a child-friendly portrayal of rough-and-ready 1980s New York. It finds beauty in the duality of grit and hope that the city represents. The Twin Towers were part of that landscape, and their presence in those opening moments reflects the sheer scope of the film's location.

Disney leaned in on the contemporary urban setting of the film, pitching it as a cool new take of the genre. One of the taglines the studio used to draw audiences in was 'The first Disney movie with attitude', which is almost embarrassingly try-hard by modern standards.

In fairness, though, the studio's attempts to actually deliver a zeitgeisty animated feature that would draw in young, hip 1980s audiences were also pretty damn try-hard. Chart-topping artists like Huey Lewis and, um, one of The Pointer Sisters were brought in to sing big, bold pop songs. Katzenberg even went a step further, personally reaching out to encourage pop star Billy Joel to voice Dodger, arguably the real star of the film.

Now, if there's one thing you should know about me here, it's this: I *love* Billy Joel. Where other kids were raised on their dad's Pink Floyd or Fleetwood Mac albums, I was raised by my mother's all-encompassing appreciation of the Piano Man. And so I speak to you on this matter with as much authority as any millennial might reasonably be able to offer the subject: Billy Joel is fundamentally not cool.

Billy Joel is one of the best songwriters to come out of the United States. He's the fourth best-selling solo artist in the country's history and has – by my count – at least five no-skip albums. But he's also the man who named his most famous song 'Piano Man' and then played its iconic melody on a harmonica.

More remarkable still – Billy Joel had never acted for film or television before *Oliver & Company*. His only appearances since have been cameos as himself on sitcoms like *Mad About You* and *Kevin Can Wait*. Of the fifty-six acting credits on Billy Joel's IMDb page, fifty-one of them are in his own music videos. And, as someone who has watched most of those videos, I can tell you that in a live-action scenario, Joel has all the charisma of a New York City manhole cover.

And yet, for his one starring role, he smashes it out of the park. It turns out that when you don't have to watch him attempting to work out what his face should do, Billy Joel is a pretty solid actor.[1] As Dodger, he is charming, smooth and lovable – even when he's caught out in a lie, or stealing a string of hotdogs from a lonely orphaned street cat.

The effect is lost somewhat if you watch footage of him recording his lines. In true rock star fashion, Joel wore sunglasses indoors throughout the process. But that's what you need to do, I suppose, to deliver Disney's first movie with *attitude*.

1. Joel auditioned for the role over the phone, so this might explain how he got the part.

Joel is also gifted with the film's best song, 'Why Should I Worry?', which is – and I will give Disney this – the coolest song in an animated classic since *The Aristocats*'s 'Thomas O'Malley'. Dodger brings New York to a standstill as he struts through construction sites and traffic, coaxing every dog in a five-block radius to join his carefree howling.[2]

Released on the 60th anniversary of Disney's first real success, *Steamboat Willie*, the film found itself up against the newest work to emerge from former Disney animator Don Bluth. On opening week, *Oliver & Company* floundered in fourth place, while *The Land Before Time* took the top spot. Still, *Oliver* won audiences over through word of mouth, and by the end of their respective runs, Disney proved to be the top dog for domestic takes.

Despite being among the less recognisable titles in the canon today, *Oliver & Company* was the strongest Disney film in over fifteen years at the time of release. It holds up, too – remarkable given that its idea of 'cool' is so dated that Bette Midler plays another of the characters, a vindictive prize poodle who delivers an enjoyable and knowing show-tune about how exceptional she is. Come to think of it, there's a surprising amount of songs in this film that comprise solely of a dog boasting about how great they are.

At last, there was a glimmer of hope for Disney. Their new leadership had an eye for a good movie and was just starting to realise how to translate this talent into animated films. Katzenberg turned his attention to another film greenlit during the same meeting that had brought him *Oliver & Company*: a new take on the classic fairytale formula that Disney had found success in so many times before.

2. A number of other Disney dogs cameo in the sequence, including Pongo from *One Hundred and One Dalmatians* and three of the supporting cast from *Lady and the Tramp*.

The Disney Renaissance

Chapter 28

Renaissance Men

The Little Mermaid • *1989* • *Ron Clements, John Musker*

The success of *Oliver & Company* was more than just a welcome relief for the relatively new leadership at Disney: it was a mandate of sorts. The film had proven that there was still an appetite for all-singing, all-dancing animated movies, and Katzenberg took steps to up the ante for the studio's next release. He'd already committed to a new release schedule of one animated film a year – a huge increase from the past decade or so, where new features often came out at intervals of three to four years. Now he needed to make sure these new releases could warrant such investment.

The Little Mermaid had been greenlit on the same day as *Oliver & Company*, despite initial concerns from Katzenberg that the film would only appeal to girls. Clements and Musker, who had been behind *The Great Mouse Detective*, were put in charge of taking the classic Hans Christian Anderson tale and bringing it to the big screen. But they were not the only creative force shaping the film.

In the mid-1980s, Katzenberg had reached out to an upcoming talent from the New York theatre scene. Howard Ashman had made a name for himself as both the lyricist and director of *Little Shop of Horrors*, an off-Broadway adaptation of a schlocky low-budget B-movie from 1960. Ashman, and his musical partner Alan Menken, had revived the film as a camp doo-wop masterpiece filled with knowing lyrics and social satire. Katzenberg saw an opportunity and suggested to Ashman that his talents were a perfect fit for Disney.

Ashman's first work for the studio had been as a lyricist on the opening number of *Oliver & Company* – the Huey Lewis song 'Once Upon a Time in New York City'. It's a soaring, emotional number to begin the film on, but a mildly curious entity on a soundtrack that never settles on any particular theme (which is no surprise, given that the five songs written for the movie were each written by entirely different teams). *The Little Mermaid* would be different: Ashman brought his old partner Menken onboard, and the two would be responsible for all the music in the film: Menken also provided the score.

Ashman and Menken would prove to be vital to Disney's success – not just with regards to the film, but in building the foundations upon which the studio's remarkable revitalisation would be built. The two worked closely with Clements and Musker to reshape the story of *The Little Mermaid* so that its songs would more closely follow the structure of a Broadway musical. Each number would land at a crucial plot juncture, pushing the story forward. In 'Part of Your World' Ashman and Menken delivered one of the greatest 'I Want' songs of all time.[1] In fact, let's be honest: 'Part of Your World' has a very strong claim to being the best song in the entire Disney canon.

And yet, Ariel's show-stopping moment almost didn't make it into the film. During an early test screening, young audience members seemed to lose focus during the scene, and Katzenberg wanted to drop it from the film altogether. The directors fought for its inclusion; they reasoned that animation for the sequence wasn't yet finished and that it might fare better once colourised. A few months later, a different audience saw a more complete version, and the reaction was strong enough to warrant a place in the final film. Even so, 'Part of Your World' continued to be oddly under-valued: it wasn't nominated for the Academy Awards the following year, while both 'Kiss the Girl' and 'Under the Sea' were. The latter won, with Menken also taking home a statuette for Best Score.

Both of the nominated songs are undeniably great tunes, too, of course. That's the wonder of Ashman and Menken at their best – every song they touch is ten times as good as the best track in any other film's soundtrack. Even a throwaway song here – 'Les Poissons' – is a sheer joy, filled with inspired lyrics (Ashman rhymes 'poissons' with the most intensely French laugh in cinematic history: 'hee hee hee, *hon hon hon*'). It's performed by the absolutely unhinged chef Louis, who spends most of his time hanging out in the kitchen singing about how much he loves chopping up fish and then, when confronted with a live crab, essentially devolves into Wile E. Coyote – a deeply ineffective killing machine who seems capable of destroying only himself. The song's melody is very familiar, too – Menken would upgrade it a few years later to serve another French house servant, Lumiere, for *Beauty and the Beast*'s 'Be Our Guest'.

Ashman's input stretched beyond the music, too – he played a significant role in highlighting the drag artist Divine as an influence on the design of sea witch Ursula. Later, it was Ashman who first suggested *Aladdin* as a future project for the studio.

For a brief moment in time, it looked like Ashman and Menken would be at the heart of Disney's new approach to animated cinema. *The Little Mermaid* was a phenomenal success, and the two were hard at work on *Beauty and the Beast* and *Aladdin*, the films that would cement the beginning of what would become the Renaissance era. Their influence was already greater than any musician who had previously worked at Disney. The Sherman Brothers had been songwriting geniuses, but Ashman and Menken were shaping the very films themselves.

Behind the scenes, though, Ashman was enduring a private hell. It was the peak of the Aids crisis in America, and Ashman, a gay man living in New York, was at the heart of the devastation. Like many in the city, he had already lost loved ones

1. An 'I Want' song is a staple of musical theatre – the big number in which a protagonist longingly sets out their heart's desire. Think 'Over the Rainbow' from *The Wizard of Oz*, or even 'My Shot' from *Hamilton*. Ashman and Menken had already turned the idea on its head with the gorgeous 'Somewhere That's Green' from *Little Shop of Horrors*.

to the still deeply misunderstood disease. He had reconciled with a past boyfriend who had been diagnosed HIV positive and offered much-needed solidarity in their last months. In January 1988, while deep into the production of *The Little Mermaid*, Ashman himself was diagnosed.

It was a devastating blow at a time when the disease was more or less understood to be a death sentence. Ashman was also aware of the stigma around the illness as well as the resulting moral panic around homosexuality that had been seen across America. He was hesitant to tell anyone at the family-oriented Disney company, but shortly after the release of *The Little Mermaid*, Ashman opened up to Katzenberg.

We'll cover Katzenberg a lot over the coming chapters, and we've already seen a little already of his ruthless managerial approach and his occasionally questionable creative decisions. But here is something that Katzenberg will always have to his credit: he was phenomenally kind to Howard Ashman throughout his illness. He had the team for *Beauty and the Beast* relocate across the country so that work could accommodate Ashman's needs and enabled a dying man to continue living out his dream for as long as possible. Later, Katzenberg would arrange for fundraisers to support Aids charities and, when *Beauty and the Beast* was adapted to stage, ensured that Ashman's partner, Bill Lauch, was involved in the process.

In March 1991, Ashman passed away. He was just forty years old.

It had been less than five years since Ashman had first come to Disney to write a single song on a relatively minor release. And yet, in that time, he had become perhaps the most influential figure for the studio since Walt himself. He completed the lyrics for only two films – *The Little Mermaid* and *Beauty and the Beast*, as well as a handful of songs for *Aladdin*, a project that wouldn't have existed without his initial input. But more than that, he helped restructure the studio's very approach to animated musicals. From *The Lion King* to *Frozen*, all of Disney's most successful musical films since Ashman's passing owe a debt to his vision for the medium.

And, of course, they also owe a debt to Ashman's musical partner, Alan Menken. Together, the pair began a journey that Menken has continued on ever since. Ashman's influence on Disney was seismic, and no small part of this has been due to the ongoing presence of Menken at the studio. In the wake of his close friend's passing, Menken collaborated with lyricist Tim Rice to ensure that *Aladdin* could be completed. He would go on to compose the score and songs for three more Renaissance-era classics, as well as writing music for *Home on the Range*, the second *Wreck-It Ralph* film and, in 2018, *Howard* – a documentary about the life and impact of the other half of Disney's greatest ever creative pairing.

Chapter 29

Sloppy Seconds

The Rescuers Down Under • 1990 • Hendel Butoy, Mike Gabriel

The Dark Knight, *The Empire Strikes Back*, *Terminator 2* and *The Rescuers Down Under*: all sequels that surpass the original, and perhaps none of these more so than the latter. Disney may have chosen one of the lesser classics for their first-ever follow-up within the animated canon, but *Rescuers Down Under* undoubtedly benefits from this decision. Though the first film had done unexpectedly well at the box office, it didn't have quite the same emotional baggage as the greats. It would be a brave soul who would choose to make a sequel to a film that had a gilded shrine in the hearts of millions. What sort of fool would want to make a sequel to *The Little Mermaid*, *The Jungle Book* or – god forbid – *Bambi*?

Except, of course, this was exactly what Disney doubled down on doing for an exhausting decade and a bit, starting in the mid-nineties. It's hard to know exactly where to place the straight-to-video sequels with regard to the Disney canon. They *aren't* the canon, that's for sure. But they are intricately connected with it, and occupy a strange place, with many of the films being released to universal disdain even as the studio enjoyed its most creative run in fifty years.

It would be easy to think that the success of *The Rescuers Down Under*, an official animated classic, led the studio to explore other follow-ups. But the film was actually the only true flop within the Disney Renaissance, making less than $50 million at the global box office. Rather fittingly, the real source of the straight-to-video sequels lay on the small screen.

Disney had been making television shows ever since Walt began funding the creation of Disneyland with a series of the same name. In 1983, the company launched the Disney Channel, a premium cable network that existed mostly to let school children know exactly how wealthy their parents were. Early shows for the network included a terrifying live-action Winnie the Pooh show,[1] the truly iconic *DuckTales*, and *Chip 'n Dale: Rescue Rangers*, a show that offered eye-opening adventure for kids (the female mechanic mouse Gadget also providing sexual awakenings to boys and girls alike), and represented voice-over torture to adults, thanks to the lead characters' gratingly high-pitched voices.

1. *Welcome to Pooh Corner*'s most iconic episode was a forty-minute special in which the characters teach audience members about stranger danger. There are multiple songs about not being tricked by grown-ups, including one particularly jaw-dropping number about what to do when an adult attempts to touch your private places.

The beginning of the nineties saw a new branch of animated shows, though: the movie spin-off. The first of these was a well-liked prequel series featuring *The Little Mermaid*'s Ariel. And then, in 1994, the Disney Channel launched *Aladdin*, a follow-up to the film of the same name.

The first few episodes of the *Aladdin* TV show were intended to run as a multi-part story that would introduce the wider series. The team behind the show – and in particular producer Tad Stones – were looking for ways to boost their budget and pitched this initial story as a straight-to-video sequel, hoping the extra revenue from sales would feed back (at least in part) to their productions. They were turned down initially, but after Disney released the original film on VHS and it did phenomenally well, the sequel was given the green light. *The Return of Jafar* was released in May 1994 (almost four months after the premiere of the animated series it was intended to launch) and sold over 15 million copies on VHS. It grossed $300 million, sixty times its budget. The straight-to-video sequel era was born.

The big difference between the films of this period and the canon sequels, (*Rescuers Down Under*, *Fantasia 2000*, *Winnie the Pooh*, *Ralph Breaks the Internet*, *Frozen II* and *Moana 2*) was the animating studio. The straight-to-video films were created by Disney MovieToons, the studio that was also behind the *DuckTales* film, and *A Goofy Movie*. Though it operated on a fraction of the budget that Walt Disney Animation Studios (then Walt Disney Feature Animation) enjoyed, MovieToons initially did its best with what it had. For *Return of Jafar*, all the principal cast members from the first film returned, bar Robin Williams. The actor returned for the third film in the franchise, *Aladdin and the King of Thieves*, which brought in another $100 million in video sales.

But the good intentions were quickly hampered by Disney's eagerness to push out more sequels. In 1998, MovieToons released three films over the course of just eight months. *The Lion King II: Simba's Pride*, which echoed the first film's *Hamlet* inspiration with a plot that broadly resembled *Romeo and Juliet*, was a relative success (that also made use of Lebo M's magnificent 'He Lives in You', a song originally written for a 1995 album inspired by his work on *The Lion King*). But the other films showed the cracks already appearing in this new corner of the business. *Pocahontas II: Journey to a New World* managed the impressive feat of being judged both bland *and* crass by audiences and critics alike, and *Belle's Magical World* was little more than a compilation of three episodes of an unreleased *Beauty and the Beast* TV series, with a runtime of a little over an hour. Even so, this hodge podge of ideas sold more than a million copies, and Michael Eisner felt more than justified in continuing the project.

The new millennium brought sequels to *The Little Mermaid* (Ariel's daughter wants to go back to the sea!), *Peter Pan* (Wendy's daughter wants to go back to Neverland!) and *The Jungle Book* (Mowgli wants to go back to the… you get the idea). Despite the early successes, none of these films were particularly liked by critics or audiences – though the videos continued to sell. Disney was beginning to discover that brand recognition was more important than actual quality, and it began to feel like MovieToons was happy to cut back on the latter if it made things easier. The studio released more films that compiled episodes from unfinished TV series, including terrible sequels for both *Cinderella* and *Atlantis: The Lost Empire*.

There was a brief glimmer of enjoyment to be had in 2004, when the now rechristened Disneytoon Studios released a much anticipated third *Lion King* film, confusingly titled *The Lion King 1 1/2*. In a way, this movie may be the most highbrow piece of art that Disney has ever released. Once again riffing on the original's *Hamlet* connection, *The Lion King 1 1/2* takes audiences on a journey through the plot of the first film, as seen through the eyes of Timon and Pumbaa. It is, in short, Disney's take on the Tom Stoppard play *Rosencrantz and Guildenstern Are Dead*.

Disneytoon stumbled onwards, becoming increasingly weighed down by its reputation for soiling the good name of classic animated films. Eventually, in 2008, good taste stepped in. Recent films like *Bambi II*, *The Fox and the Hound 2* and a *Little Mermaid* prequel that was essentially underwater *Footloose* had continued to draw in sales – but a change of personnel at the top meant that Pixar's John Lasseter was in charge of Disney's animation departments. A proposed sequel to *The Aristocats* was dumped, and Disneytoon spent its last few years focussed solely on a popular series of Tinker Bell films, and spin-offs of Lasseter's pet project, *Cars*.

We're free now of the Disney sequels – despite the fact that most people who complained about the films never actually had to watch them. In fact, with time, the whole run of movies feels pretty uninvasive. Yes, the films are now available on Disney's streaming service. But at the time, you'd have to actively choose to buy a VHS or DVD and take it home to watch. Now we are in the midst of a far more pervasive trend, as Disney's newest trick for exploiting the back catalogue brings us live-action remake after live-action remake. These films are in our cinemas, promoted by marketing campaigns with millions of dollars behind them, before ultimately being available to any child with the technical nous to navigate a streaming service menu (which is to say: any child above the age of three).

It makes you long for the novelty of *The Rescuers Down Under*, which marked the first time Disney's writing teams had recognised the value of their existing intellectual property. The film is often forgotten within the context of the Disney Renaissance, being sandwiched between two cinematic phenomena. But I reckon it's overdue for a re-evaluation.

The film's use of Disney's new CAPS technology, which had been developed with a promising young company called Pixar, allowed the entire film to be compiled digitally. The process of filmmaking was cut down by several months, but the real benefit came in the look of the film itself. With special effects, animation, colouring and CGI elements all combined in a more organic manner, the look of the film was a world away from the scrappy cartoons Disney had been putting out for most of the 1970s and 80s.

The Rescuers Down Under looks stunning. From an opening scene that rockets the audience across a field of rich purple wildflowers to the fantastic looming behemoth

1. Pioneering animator Quirino Cristiani bears a passing resemblance to Walt Disney.

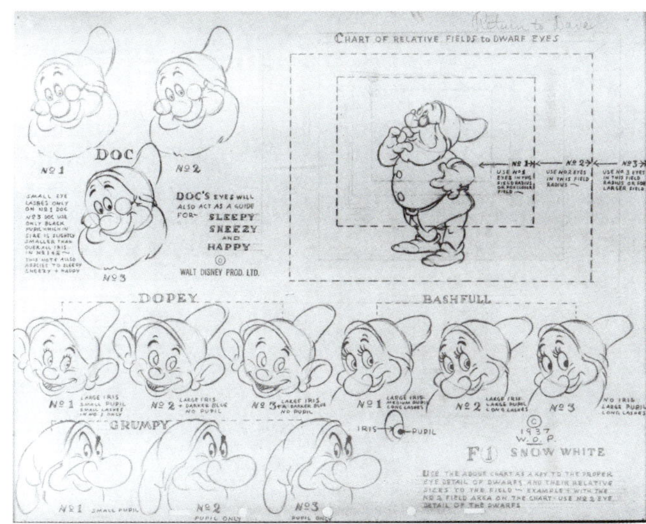

2. An in-depth guide to drawing the dwarfs' eyes ensured consistency among animators on Snow White and the Seven Dwarfs.

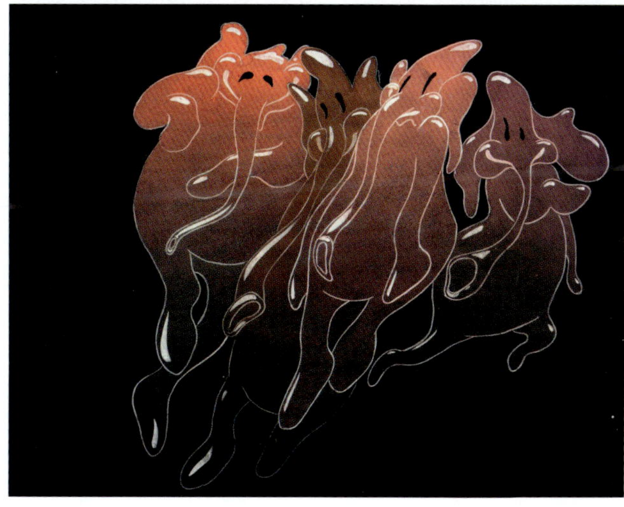

3. Sinister bubble pachyderms from Dumbo's 'Pink Elephants on Parade' sequence.

4. One of the many illustrations drawn by animators on the 'Good Neighbor' trip to South America that informed *Saludos Amigos* and *The Three Caballeros*.

5. Mary Blair was a key figure in the studio in the 1950s, creating concept art that informed the look of films like *Cinderella*.

6. The contrast between light and dark in Blair's *Alice in Wonderland* concept art is easy to see within the final film.

7. Blair's artwork wasn't always easy to translate into animation.

8. Live-action footage offered guidance for complex animated scenes.

9. Disney's childhood home in Marceline informed the architecture of *Lady and the Tramp*.

10. The ornate backgrounds from *Sleeping Beauty* presented new challenges for Disney's animators.

11. Glenn Close brought Cruella De Vil to life in 1996's live-action *101 Dalmatians*.

12. Sterling Holloway was one of Disney's most prolific voice actors, playing characters including Winnie the Pooh, the Cheshire Cat and *The Jungle Book*'s Kaa.

13. Two absolute foxes, each behind the sexual awakening of millions.

14. And another fox, from a pivotal scene in *The Fox and the Hound* that Tim Burton had to work himself up to animate.

15. An early piece of concept art for *The Black Cauldron*, displaying the signature style of animator Tim Burton.

16. This grotesque glimpse of suffering was cut from *The Black Cauldron* after test audiences walked out of early screenings.

17. You can tell Billy Joel's character, Dodger, is cool because he wears sunglasses.

18. The big question here is how Flounder - a fish - managed to move this stone statue of Prince Eric into Ariel's cavern of trinkets. I think it just happened to sink right in that spot, and Flounder claimed credit for a complete coincidence.

19. New animation techniques almost made it possible to ignore how absolutely massive that ruddy eagle is in *The Rescuers Down Under*.

20. What are Gaston's real motivations in *Beauty and the Beast*?

21. Robin Williams changed the voiceover game with his role as Genie in *Aladdin*.

22. Early concept art for *The Lion King* shows a young Simba casually shattering a generation's hearts into a million pieces.

23. The Shakespearean drama of *The Lion King*'s final act comes to life in this concept art.

24. Wishful thinking: Pocahontas watches the English leave peacefully in *Pocahontas*.

25. A moment of lustful anguish for Frollo during the 'Hellfire' sequence in *The Hunchback of Notre Dame*.

26. Foreshadowing, as Mulan uses a firework to foil Shan Yu's plans (by killing a couple of thousand people).

27. A serene moment in *Fantasia 2000*.

28. The one that got away: *The Wild* was briefly considered an animated classic in Europe.

29. Gorgeous watercolour backgrounds gave Disney's masterpiece *Lilo & Stitch* a unique feel within the canon.

30. *The Princess and the Frog*'s Tiana, the first Black Disney Princess.

31. The complexities of animating Rapunzel's hair sent production costs skyrocketing in *Tangled*.

32. An illustration of Poohsticks Bridge that closely replicates the one found in the depths of the Ashdown Forest in Sussex.

33. Bowser and Dr. Eggman are among the many video game characters who make a cameo in *Wreck-It Ralph*.

34. Drew Struzan's artwork for *DuckTales: The Movie* echoes the iconic look of Indiana Jones.

35. Elsa's song 'Let It Go' is among the most iconic scenes in the modern Disney canon.

36. Disney brought together their princesses (and Anna and Elsa) in *Ralph Breaks the Internet*. But where's Princess Leia?

37. A perfect family portrait courtesy of the Madrigals.

38. And a less perfect one courtesy of the author's family.

39. The emotions of Star from *Wish* draw inspiration from those of Mickey Mouse in his early shorts.

that is poacher McLeach's ominous truck, the studio was able to deliver complex animation that still looks fantastic three and a half decades down the line.

The film's new characters add charm too – besides, perhaps, the one-note kangaroo rat, Jake. George C Scott delivers an understated masterclass as McLeach, while John Candy plays John Candy exceptionally well, albeit in the guise of Wilbur. Why play a character when you *are* a character? The original Rescuers return, too – Eva Gabor in her final film role, and Bob Newhart as Bernard, a mouse who has his heart set on marrying somebody he still refers to as 'Miss'. There is one missed opportunity: the directors were initially keen on having Cody, the young boy at the centre of the film, be an Aboriginal Australian – a choice that would have represented a real landmark for Indigenous inclusion in mainstream Hollywood. Unfortunately, the idea was quickly shut down by Katzenberg, who preferred what he perceived to be a more audience-friendly little blonde boy.

Perhaps the only lingering problem with the whole thing is how quickly it wraps up. After all, the most interesting part of the film surely comes after the end credits roll. How does the boy explain where he's been for the past three months? His mother may believe him, but we've seen that the media has been on the case too, and lord knows that the Australian press in the 1980s struggled to believe tragic stories. After all, if nobody in the country was convinced by 'a dingo ate my baby', poor Cody is really going to struggle to sell 'I free soloed a two-hundred-foot cliff, rescued an eagle the size of a family car, was captured by a poacher, and ultimately saved by three talking mice before riding the eagle to safety'.

Actually, I can see why he took the story to Disney. Put it on a VHS, and those guys can sell *anything*.

Chapter 30

Something There

Beauty and the Beast • *1991* • *Gary Trousdale, Kirk Wise*

Howard Ashman was reluctant to work on *Beauty and the Beast*. It was, he thought, a distraction from his pet project, *Aladdin*. His health had begun to deteriorate more quickly, and sensing how little time he had left and how difficult work would soon become, the film was not a priority.

But the input of Ashman and Menken was sorely needed. The project had been underway for two years already when, in 1989, Jeffrey Katzenberg decided big changes were needed. British director Richard Purdum left the project, and two first-timers were installed in his place. Kirk Wise and Gary Trousdale had each started as animators on Disney's middling 1980s releases, before uniting within the story department and working on *The Rescuers Down Under*. Now they had been given their first directorial role – and just two years to deliver it.

Beauty and the Beast is the story of individuals facing up to frightening challenges, overcoming hidden pain, and finding greatness through coming together. Which is all a bit saccharine, but hey, it's Disney.

In fact, today, *Beauty and the Beast* is almost the most emblematic of all Disney features. It has the princess, the castle, the love story and, of course, the songs. But the film as a whole is also composed with an elegance and stateliness that is equal to any of Walt's passion projects. It is the princess story refined, polished, and ever so slightly upgraded for contemporary audiences.

The Disney musical, outdated and neglected for too long, had been given a vital adrenaline shot with *The Little Mermaid*, and the Broadway-esque structure that the film's songwriters had brought to that film's proceedings is back again in full force. Ashman would have been forgiven for delivering a few half-hearted tunes while he longed to get back to writing for *Aladdin*, but there is not a single dud in the *Beauty and the Beast* soundtrack.

The opening number, 'Belle', is perhaps the best screen showcase for the pair's talents as Broadway songwriters. The fast-moving ensemble piece is crammed with jokes and introduces two of the film's main characters. We quickly learn that Belle is seen as an outcast in town – her vociferous reading habits seem to be her worst crime.[1] Gaston, meanwhile, is established as a universally loved macho man, fawned

1. I have no idea how the kindly bookseller survives in a town where the residents harbour deep suspicions towards anyone who reads, and the sole bookworm doesn't seem to understand the difference between a bookshop and a library.

over in equal measure by a trio of buxom bimbettes (Disney's term, not mine) and his best friend/hype man LeFou. The song would be the obvious stand-out of any other film or musical, but in *Beauty and the Beast*, it finds itself amid stiff competition. Gaston's big number is perhaps the funniest of all Disney songs, skewering the arrogance and bravado of toxic masculinity, and offering glimpses at the character's vulnerability. 'Be Our Guest' is magnificent, too, an all-out show tune fit to end the first act of any Broadway musical.[2] The song had originally been written to be sung to Belle's father, Maurice, when he first arrived at the castle – the production team had recorded and even begun animating the scene when the switch was made.

My favourite story behind a *Beauty and the Beast* song belongs to the title track itself, though. The song underscores the change in the relationship between the two leads, who dance together in the castle's stunning ballroom – the most impressive early use of CGI in a Disney feature, and still an astonishing piece of art over three decades later. Angela Lansbury, the voice of Mrs Potts, didn't believe she was up to the challenge of singing the song. Though she encouraged Ashman and Menken to find someone else to record the vocals, the pair eventually convinced her to record just a single take, in case they were unable to find anyone. That lone recording, approached with breathtaking tenderness, is the version we hear in the film today.

The final movie owes as much to Jean Cocteau's 1946 adaptation as it does to the 18th-century tellings that form its core plot; it's a fitting influence, seeing as the film's release is believed to have played a large part in Walt shelving his own early plans for a retelling. As in Cocteau's film, the castle is filled with enchanted furnishings. Here, they are more fully realised characters, filling out the cast sheet and offering charm and comic relief in the gloomy chateau. The intimate bickering of Lumière and Cogsworth provides plenty of joy. Even Chip, a teacup whose presence lends itself to more questions than answers,[3] transcends the usual precocious child role within the film. The character was originally intended to have only a single line, but actor Bradley Pierce was so impressive that the role was significantly expanded.

Beauty and the Beast was an instant hit, echoing the success of *The Little Mermaid* two years previously. Like many of the Renaissance era films, it has become increasingly popular in the decades since. Its critics cite the apparent glamorisation of Stockholm Syndrome, but this remains a rare film within the Disney canon in

2. The song is actually the penultimate number of the first act in the film's theatrical adaptation, which opened at the Palace Theatre in New York in 1994.
3. Over the course of the film we establish that the curse will end – for better or worse – on the Beast's twenty-first birthday. Lumière tells us that the palace staff have been rusting for ten years. The obvious takeaway here is that the young prince was cursed because he turned away a stranger from his door when he was just eleven years old – a harsh sentence when 'stranger danger' is still very much a part of your school curriculum. But the secondary response must surely be: where the heck did Chip come from, given he is clearly no more than six years old? It gives a whole new meaning to 'bone china'.

which the male lead is saved by the woman, instead of the other way around.[4] Belle doesn't so much soften up to the Beast as the Beast softens up to her.

The story's focus on outcasts has made it prime material for fans to project their own deeper meanings onto. Perhaps unsurprisingly, given the film's preoccupation with what it is to live in persecution, there have been dozens of queer readings of the narrative over the years. In a 2005 essay for *Pop Culture Review*, H. Peter Steeves argues that all three of the film's main characters are meant to be read as homosexual. On a fundamental level, the Beast is cursed because he turns away a woman, and Steeves poses that his animalistic form is a representation of the way the homophobic townsfolk would see him if they were to find out. I'm not convinced by that myself, though Steeves is far from the only person to posit such an idea. Neither am I persuaded by his case for Belle's queerness. Yes, we know she is considered 'different', 'odd' and 'peculiar' by the townsfolk, but the author's argument only works if Beast is gay himself – and thus an 'opportunity' for Belle to essentially shack up in a celibate relationship with someone in exchange for the world's biggest library. Admittedly not the worst offer in the world, but not one I'm willing to accept here.

Where Steeves does make an interesting case, though, is with the third of the film's leads: Gaston. Early designs of the character by the gay animator Andreas Deja presented Gaston as closer to the traditional Disney villain – often queer-coded, presenting characteristics associated with the LGBTQ+ community without ever actually being revealed to belong to it.[5] It was Katzenberg who encouraged the hyper-masculinity of the final character. Steeves asks if we might see this as over-compensation on Gaston's part, born from internalised homophobia, as well as a fear of how the village will respond to him should he be found out (which, again, fair: they see a woman who could read and perform a whole song and dance about it).

And so Gaston chases Belle – the one woman in town that he knows despises him. The one woman in town who will never accept his advances. In pursuing someone who will only ever deny him, Gaston engineers a situation in which he

4. Also, take a moment right now to familiarise yourself with the actual origins of the term 'Stockholm syndrome'. Spoiler alert: it was less about the hostages sympathising with their captors than it was that the hostages were treated with such little regard by the police that they ended up carrying out negotiations themselves. The police criminologist, Nils Bejerot, frequently agitated the bank robbers, putting the hostages in further danger, and then had to come up with a term to describe their animosity towards him upon their emergence, rather than accept that he'd been part of the problem. Anyway, what I'm saying is that *Beauty and the Beast* is *absolutely* a film about Stockholm Syndrome, in that after a couple of weeks in the castle with a single captor whose main character flaws are a short temper and a tendency to moult, the situation probably would look preferable to returning to a village where you're frequently sexually harassed and are considered a crackpot just because you're a bit of a hardback queen.
5. Take your pick: the sharp-tongued theatricality of male villains like Hades, Scar and Jafar, the androgynous glamour of Maleficent, or our gal Ursula and her drag queen origins. Disney often seems to be happy to display queer traits as long as it's in a villain who will end up either dead or disgraced.

never has to face up to his true self. Suddenly our villain becomes a tragic figure, though still very much complicit in his actions, fighting against his own truth until the last rather than attempting to find peace, even when Beast presents him with an opportunity to leave peacefully after their fight.

Another popular understanding of the film is borne from the experiences of its lyricist. In the documentary *Howard*, producer Thomas Schumacher says that the film is intrinsically influenced by Ashman's experience with HIV and Aids. Given the heightened fear and lack of understanding around the illness in the late 80s and early 90s, it's easy to imagine the songwriter connecting with Beast. The character locks himself away, (correctly) assuming that others will see him as a monster, and not as a human being in pain. As Ashman wrote the songs for the film, the production crew frequently travelled to and fro across the country to collaborate with him. None of them knew that they were accommodating a man who was too unwell to travel. The songs were written by a man who was afraid to reveal himself. Even if his illness was not a direct influence on the film, which Ashman also executive produced, it was certainly on his mind.

Queer readings of Disney films have become increasingly popular in recent years, in no small part due to the increased visibility and representation of LGBTQ+ issues in the public sphere. There are trans men and women who see themselves reflected in Ariel's physical transformation and Mulan's struggles to meet societal expectations, and a very vocal online clamouring for *Frozen*'s Elsa to find love with another woman in the forthcoming *Frozen III*.[6] Disney has made strides towards more inclusive storytelling over the last two decades, but these efforts have been mostly limited to representing the experiences and cultures of different nationalities. When it comes to the matter of sharing the stories of queer communities (a group of people estimated to be larger in number than any one nation on the planet), it has been less forthcoming. The first gay couple shown in an animated classic didn't come until 2016's *Zootopia* – even then, it was a pair of cohabiting antelopes who could just as easily be read as housemates, and whose primary characteristic is that they're always arguing with one another. Eventually, in *Strange World*, Disney's 61st film in the canon, we are given a character whose queerness is clear-cut. As we'll see later, it wasn't exactly a happy ending.

Perhaps most galling of all is that even Disney attempted to have a go at offering up a queer reading of *Beauty and the Beast*. Ahead of the release of his garish 2017 live-action remake, director Bill Condon teased an 'exclusively gay moment' within the film. It was clearly a matter of some pride to Condon, a gay man whose previous films include *Gods and Monsters* and *Kinsey*, which both explore themes around the discovery and repression of sexuality. The term 'exclusively gay moment' is a strange one – anticipative audiences might have been left wondering what it might

6. Elsa's own experience echoes that of the Beast: she is called a 'monster' for displaying behaviours that her people do not understand, and responds by shutting herself away from society in a remote castle.

mean for a moment to be 'exclusively gay'. Maybe the couple would sign some sort of declaration afterwards?

As it turned out, Condon's meaning of an 'exclusively gay moment' was a moment that entirely excluded any obvious gay activity whatsoever. During the finale of the film, Gaston's former henchman, LeFou, is seen dancing with a woman. The woman then swaps out – as part of the dance itself – with a man. For less than three seconds, the men are on screen, dancing. Neither shows any real emotion towards the other. LeFou doesn't react in horror to the physical touch of another man – I suppose we can give Disney that? Just three seconds of two men in brief, romance-free contact with one another. And then the camera cuts away, and back to Belle and the transformed Prince (who also have absolutely no chemistry with one another, but I suspect that isn't intended).

Disney came under fire for such a muted attempt at queer inclusion. It doesn't help that they chose the laziest reading possible to pick the obsequious LeFou for their 'exclusively gay moment', either. Nor was it ideal that LeFou's name translates literally to 'the fool', and has been used in France both to mean 'madman' and as a slur against gay people. But it was the entire lack of inherent gayness in that gay moment that hurt the most. If you need to gauge how entirely non-existent the moment was, consider this: Russia and Malaysia decided not to ban the film, despite having plenty of form in that area.[7] One cinema in Alabama decided not to screen the film, but, honestly, if your movie isn't upsetting at least one person in Alabama, are you even making art?

People will always attach meaning to the films they love. Sometimes it's wishful thinking, and sometimes – as trans fans of *The Matrix* films were thrilled to find out – they were right all along. But it's a shame that for so many Disney fans, queer readings remain the only way to see their lived experiences in the films they love.

7. Russian law prohibits content that affirms "nontraditional" sexual relations or relationships, while the Film Censorship Board of Malaysia banned the Pixar film *Lightyear* on initial release due to a brief same-sex kiss. The film is now available to stream on Disney Plus, but has an 18+ rating. Kuwait, meanwhile, *did* decide to ban the film, but they'll ban *anything*. Kuwait banned Pixar's *Turning Red* because it featured *puberty*.

Chapter 31

When You Wish Upon a Corporate Entity

Aladdin • *1992* • *Ron Clements, John Musker*

The Little Mermaid may have kicked off the Disney Renaissance, and *Beauty and the Beast* may have been proof that the film's success wasn't a fluke, but it was *Aladdin* that truly cemented the understanding that Disney was back in the business of churning out hits. In fact, it wouldn't be entirely unfair to say that Disney was *finally* in the business of churning out hits. After all, the studio had never really hit a consistent run of box office smashes before, preferring instead to release occasional masterpieces and then slowly stumble towards the oblivion of bankruptcy before deciding once again to risk the financial viability of the entire company on a ludicrously ambitious passion project.

The seismic success of *The Little Mermaid* had knocked Disney out of this rhythm though, and *Aladdin* marked the third critical and commercial smash in just four years. It is perhaps the most poorly dated of the Renaissance era's biggest hits – though its often clichéd take on Arabian life had its detractors from the start. A lyric from the original release that claimed the 'barbaric' locals would 'cut off your ear if they don't like your face' was quickly dropped from future editions. Agrabah's locals are often grotesque caricatures, while Aladdin and Jasmine are given gentle features that are broadly Westernised (the design of the titular street rat was initially based on Michael J. Fox, before studio bosses decided that he should be modelled on someone more muscular, opting for Tom Cruise as inspiration instead).

But gripes like these aside, *Aladdin* remains a fast-paced and hugely enjoyable movie that takes the Disney fairytale business plan and broadens its horizons, making way for future adaptations like *Hercules* and *Mulan*. Howard Ashman's last songs are supplemented perfectly with new music from Tim Rice, who stepped in after the former's death. Alan Menken's score is suitably grandiose, reflecting the scale of the David Lean epics that heavily inspired Clements and Musker.

Aladdin himself is charming and roguish, Jasmine savvy and just slightly more feminist than Disney had yet managed. Jafar and Iago balance each other out perfectly, one calculated and reserved, the other brash and abrasive (in early drafts, these characteristics were reversed, with Iago being the more sophisticated of the two). Even Jasmine's father, the portly man-child sultan, is an absolute joy. Yes, he isn't great at listening to his daughter's needs, like so many Disney dads before (and after) him – but it's only because he's too busy playing with toys, or magical home furnishings.

Of course, the real star of the show doesn't get top billing – or even turn up on screen until over half an hour into the film. But the effect of Genie's arrival is immediate, the film's fun factor instantly turned up to eleven.

The key to this phenomenal key change is not the fact that Robin Williams is the Genie. It's that the Genie *is* Robin Williams, and was always intended to be. Clements and Musker wrote the character specifically with Williams in mind, attempting to capture some of his madcap energy and harness it through the playfulness of animation.

When it came to actually pitching the role to Williams, the directors dreamt up a clever ploy: they took a recording of one of the actor's old stand-up bits and had the Genie's supervising animator create a rough sequence of the lines being delivered by the character. The reel had the desired effect – Williams watched the Genie riffing on schizophrenia, a second head appearing on the character's shoulder in order to have a conversation with himself. He couldn't stop laughing.

Williams was onboard – and was willing to take on the role for union scale pay, taking his usual fee of around $8 million down to just $75 thousand. It was a gesture of goodwill towards the studio, who had backed him when his Hollywood career seemed dead in the water. During his early success in *Happy Days* spin-off *Mork & Mindy*, Williams had taken on the title role in a live-action adaptation of *Popeye*. The film had performed terribly, hindered both by the inexplicable decision to let the idiosyncratic auteur Robert Altman take the helm, and by Williams' own performance. Keen to present an authentic representation of the classic cartoon character, the actor's line delivery was mostly inaudible and had to be dubbed later. It is very obvious when watching the film, though only one of many, many issues.

Under the new leadership of Michael Eisner, Disney launched Touchstone Films in the 1980s – a new studio to put out less family-oriented material. Eisner also believed in making high-concept films with low budgets, which often meant paying lower fees to out-of-favour actors. A screenplay that Williams had been championing, about a military DJ making waves while on assignment overseas, seemed a perfect fit for this ideology. In 1987, Touchstone released *Good Morning, Vietnam*. Williams was a natural fit for the role, and the huge success of the film opened up new opportunities in Hollywood. Two years later, Williams returned to Touchstone for another film about an unorthodox mind in a regimented world. *Dead Poets Society* was set in an elite boarding school. It follows many of the same beats as *Good Morning, Vietnam* but is tinged with more sadness. Both films earned the actor an Oscar nomination.

And so, Williams was more than happy to take a role in *Aladdin* as a way of saying thank you while also becoming a part of American animated film history. He did have a couple of provisos, though. Williams didn't want his voice to be used to sell merchandise to children, and he didn't want the Genie to become the sole focus when advertising the movie, demanding that Disney only use the character for 25% of the film's marketing.

Looking back at these stipulations with modern eyes, it's incredible to imagine an actor ever credibly making them to a major film studio like Disney. It's more incredible still to imagine Disney actually accepting Williams' conditions – but that's exactly what they did, and the actor signed on to the film, recording his lines and improvising so many more that the movie was deemed ineligible for a screenplay nod at the Academy Awards.

But Disney is in the business of wishes and (more so than even the Genie himself) understands that delivery is all about interpretation. Robin Williams had not wished on a monkey's paw, but Mickey's four-fingered handshake could be just as tricksy. Before long, adverts were all over television sets around the world. Genie was selling everything, from Burger King kids' meals to children's toys. Williams was furious, though Disney hadn't broken their contract. They'd simply found a way around his requests, overdubbing the character so it wasn't Williams whose voice was selling things – but it *was* the Genie's.

The studio was even sneakier with the other proviso. They had agreed with Williams that the Genie would only be used in 25% of the film's marketing. The actor had intended for that to mean that only one in four posters would feature the character – the stunning teaser, featuring only the lamp, was a great example of this vision in action. But Disney quickly realised that the agreement's wording left plenty of room for interpretation. Soon Genie was featured on posters and in adverts everywhere – but with careful precision by Disney to ensure that he never took up more than 25% of the frame.

Williams was furious, and in a move uncharacteristic of a leading Hollywood actor, was not afraid to show it. He appeared in the press and on television, complaining about how Disney had betrayed his trust and claiming he would never appear in a Disney film again.

Disney had a double-edged approach to his complaints. They released a public response that implied Williams was belligerent because the film had done well and he was retroactively unhappy with the financial deal he had agreed to. At the same time, the studio sent a painting by Picasso to him in an attempt to make amends. Williams, having avowed that he was well and truly done with his blue period, was unimpressed.

The direct-to-video sequel *The Return of Jafar* was produced with all of the original film's voice actors returning – with the exception of Williams, who was replaced by Dan Castellaneta, the voice of Homer Simpson.

Eventually, the Genie and the Mouse made up: Jeffrey Katzenberg, who had been at the heart of Disney's dealings with Williams, left the studio. His replacement, Joe Roth, publicly apologised to the actor, admitting that the studio had exploited him and promising to make amends. Roth admitted, too, that Disney should have been more active in shutting down suggestions that the feud had only been based on the actor's desire for more money.

It was enough for Williams, who returned for the third entry in the series, *Aladdin and the King of Thieves*. For four years, fans wished the studio would bring back the unmistakable celebrity voice that had made the first film such a success. At last, that wish was granted. But we all know just how wishes work by now: in the wake of the Robin Williams affair, studios across Hollywood realised that even when their faces aren't on screen, audiences love that unmistakable celebrity voice. Animated films have never been the same since.

Chapter 32

Shakespeare on the Savannah

The Lion King • *1994* • *Roger Allers, Rob Minkoff*

The sun shimmers on the horizon, the start of something wholly new. In the first light of dawn, a rhinoceros breaks from grazing, and hartebeests raise their heads to the east. A flock of marabou storks take to the air, passing through the mists of Victoria Falls. Guineafowl scatter in the path of a gargantuan elephant, and leafcutter ants march on the branches above a dazzle of zebras.

Despite the cases that can, have and will be made for why millennials have connected with Disney's films more than any group before them, perhaps the simplest argument is this: for a brief moment in time, just as their generation grew old enough to enjoy feature-length films, Disney had the most remarkable run of movies in cinema history.

For all the musical vibrancy of *The Little Mermaid* and *Aladdin* and the theatrical scope of *Beauty and the Beast*, there was nothing in the Renaissance era that could stand toe-to-toe with the sheer *ambition* that *The Lion King* offered, or the wide-eyed wonder that it delivered to audiences upon release.

The film's first trailer, released in November 1993, seemed to understand exactly what the film had in store for fans. Some marketing campaigns launch with fast-paced action sequences and broad introductions to characters. Others lean in on the gags. For *The Lion King*, Disney simply released the entire opening sequence, from the shimmering sun to the triumphant presentation of Simba at Pride Rock. It was a decision that spoke of the confidence the studio had in the quality of the film's artistry and music, and its awe-inspiring scope. And yet, until the studio was fairly deep into the production process, very few people at Disney realised just how special *The Lion King* was.

The project had first been touted in the late 1980s when a pitch was made for a story set in Africa, in which the main characters would be animals. Jeffrey Katzenberg took an early interest in the premise, and more than any other film he would work on during his time at Disney, *The Lion King* would become a passion project that he would not let go of. Katzenberg's ideas shaped the film drastically, helping to create the foundations of its plot, and making decisions throughout the production process that were integral to the film we know today.

In the earliest days of development, *King of the Kalahari* already bore familiar traits: a young lion prince, separated from his pride; a fight to take his rightful place as king;

and baboon as a mentor.[1] During this time the idea was to deliver a film that looked and felt like an animated nature documentary; a trip the production team made to Kenya in 1991 instilled a sense of awe at the majesty of the African landscapes.

The sprawling scope of the scenery paired well with Katzenberg's ambitions for the film, in which the animals' experiences would act as a metaphor for some of the most important lessons of human life. From the initial conversations in the 1980s, Katzenberg made it clear that the film would, in its way, echo his own life. In particular, he was inspired by a period in 1972 when he was a member of the team behind John Lindsay's presidential campaign. Amid the murky deals of politicking, Katzenberg's youthful naivete had been extinguished – he was ultimately pulled before a grand jury investigating cash dealings between the candidate and a campaign donor with corporate interests.

But there were many other influences on the film, too. Perhaps the most famous of these is Shakespeare's *Hamlet*, in which a young man must kill his uncle to avenge the death of his father, a king who has a habit of appearing to him in ghostly form.[2] But the film also echoes elements of parts one and two of another Shakespearean play, *Henry IV*. Here, a prince shirks his responsibilities while a rebellion is at hand. What is 'hakuna matata' if not a handy stand-in for Falstaff's plea to the young Henry to 'banish all the world'?

These particular influences were heavily encouraged by Katzenberg, riffing on an idea by Eisner to model the story after *King Lear*. As the production team evolved the film to more closely reflect *Hamlet*, they also threw in biblical touches that echo the stories of Moses and Joseph, important figures separated from their destinies but finding their way back. This, of course, is a motif that is found in ancient mythologies across the world.

I'd be remiss to mention the animated tales that must have had some sort of influence on the film. *Bambi* shares several of the same beats as *The Lion King*. In a later chapter we'll also explore the venn diagram that unites Simba and a young anime lion named Kimba.

Perhaps a hint of another great story made its way into the film, too – the Epic of Sunjata, a story passed down through the oral tradition of West Africa's Malinke people that has its basis in real historical figures. Sunjata is the son of a king, exiled after his father's death. In his banishment, Sunjata grows strong and eventually is encouraged to return home in order to fulfil his destiny and become the first ruler of the Mali Empire. Sunjata has often been referred to as the 'Lion of Mali'.

* * *

1. In one draft, a tribe of baboons were the primary antagonists, led by a character named Scar. The final film is obviously very different, and baboons don't appear to feature at all. Rafiki is, of course, not a baboon, but rather a mandrill. But you already knew that, didn't you? This whole footnote exists because you already know that, and I need to cover my back so I'm not swamped with emails from amateur monkey specialists.
2. Simba was also meant to die in a version of *The Lion King* that made it as far as storyboarding, with Scar cribbing a line directly from Hamlet's Horatio: "Good night, sweet prince."

If we accept that the above influences were no more than loose inspirations for the film, then *The Lion King* was only the second Disney feature that told a single story that was not based on a pre-existing property.[3] For many at the studio, this marked the film out as a wildly ambitious gamble – and this was reflected in the approach the animation team took to the production process. 1995's *Pocahontas* was being developed in unison with *The Lion King*, and even Katzenberg – the film's greatest champion – expected the former to take the, ahem, lion's share of the accolades. This led to the studio's most senior and experienced artists flocking to that project, leaving *The Lion King* with Disney's less tried and tested animators (as well as a few who were particularly keen on the challenge of bringing animal characters to life).

Watch *The Lion King* now, though, and you'd have no idea that the film was created by first-time character supervisors and staff at Disney's less prestigious Florida animation studio (which occupied space in the backlot of the Disney-MGM Studios theme park and had previously been used for only minor supplementary animation work on the classics). *The Lion King* is a breathtakingly beautiful film, that frequently takes bold and experimental risks with its artwork – something that would no doubt have been difficult were the animators under the heightened pressure that a tent-pole release usually comes with.

Some of the most striking visual moments come during the film's musical numbers – in particular, the technicolour fantasy of 'I Just Can't Wait to Be King' and Scar's underrated villain song, 'Be Prepared', which sees hyenas goose-stepping across the screen in shots directly modelled on *Triumph of the Will*, the Nazi propaganda film directed by Leni Riefenstahl.[4]

Elton John was not the first choice to compose the music for the film's songs – initially, the film's lyricist, Tim Rice, had approached ABBA – despite the band not having existed for over a decade. Rice had collaborated with Benny Andersson and Björn Ulvaeus for the 1980s musical *Chess* and was disappointed to find that the pair were already occupied with another musical during the production of the film. And so he turned to John and collaborated on what would become the all-time biggest selling soundtrack to an animated film.

Even so, Rice and John had to repeatedly fight for their music. Katzenberg was their biggest antagonist, rejecting the original melody for 'Circle of Life' and unceremoniously dumping 'Can You Feel the Love Tonight' ahead of a screening attended by John. The latter decision went down terribly, and Katzenberg was the recipient of a furious phone call from John, who saw the song as his opportunity

3. The first was *The Aristocats*, almost a quarter of a century earlier.
4. Curiously, this is not Riefenstahl's most direct connection with Disney. In 1938, she travelled to the US to present screenings of her documentary *Olympia*. During the first week of her trip, the Nazis carried out a coordinated wave of violence against German Jews – *Kristallnacht* – and an outraged Hollywood shut Riefenstahl out for the remainder of her time in the States. One notable exception, however, was Walt Disney, who gave Riefenstahl a tour of his studio, showing her work-in-progress from his forthcoming film, *Fantasia*.

for a radio hit from the soundtrack. The track made the final cut, shifted so that it was better placed within the film. The song was a top twenty hit on both sides of the Atlantic and won Elton John his first Academy Award.[5]

It was Hans Zimmer, composer of the film's score, that came to the rescue for 'Circle of Life', delivering an arrangement for the opening sequence that incorporated a dramatic opening sung in Zulu by his friend and collaborator Lebo M.[6] Zimmer's score represents the pinnacle of his composing career, in my book.[7] Like John, Zimmer's first Oscar was earned for his work here, and there are some gorgeous highlights across the film – be it the thrill of 'Remember Who You Are' or the mounting dread of 'Stampede'.[8] For me, though, the highlight is the understated piece that plays as Simba finds the body of his father in the aftermath of that stampede. For all the great losses of animated cinema, in *Bambi*, *Up*, *Inside Out* or *The Iron Giant*, none is as well conceived, nor earns its emotional impact, as much as the death of Mufasa.

* * *

There is only one figure, then, who remains adrift in this tale. Jeffrey Katzenberg left Disney in 1994, frustrated at not being promoted to president in the wake of the death of Frank Wells that April. The events of that summer clouded what should have been a celebratory moment for Katzenberg. Instead, he lost his opportunity at a senior leadership role he believed had been promised to him, and left Disney under a cloud. Don't feel too sorry for Katzenberg – he sued the company for money owed and came away with an estimated $250 million dollar settlement. Though Katzenberg originally saw *The Lion King* as an echo of his experience in 1970s politics, he might now have an argument that it predicted his public banishment from Disney twenty years later amid the film's release.

Of course, though Katzenberg himself was too embroiled in corporate infighting to appreciate it, the film defied all expectations upon release. It quickly eclipsed *Aladdin*'s $500 million box office takings to become the highest-grossing animated film of all time (and second highest overall, after the previous year's *Jurassic Park*). To this day, it still sits very comfortably in the top twenty most successful animated

---

5. Honestly, though, the man was more or less guaranteed an Oscar at the 1995 awards – his competition in the Best Original Song category was a track from the Danny DeVito/Arnold Schwarzenegger comedy *Junior*, a weak Randy Newman effort from the long-forgotten film *The Paper*, and… two more songs from *The Lion King*.
6. Disney also dubbed the film into Zulu for release in South Africa. Incredibly, to this day this is the only time the studio has dubbed a film into any African language besides Arabic.
7. And this very much *is* my book – check the cover.
8. That wildebeest stampede represented one of the most impressive uses of CGI to date at the time of release, with hundreds of animals replicated from just a few base models and given paths by the computer that would ensure the creatures moved seamlessly around both the scenery and each other. The sequence took a team of five over two years to complete. It runs to less than three minutes of screen time.

films, the only entry in the top fifty to have been released before 2000. Sitting at the very top of the pile now? The 2019 version of *The Lion King*.

This is, after all, a tale of succession. Of the rightful heir finding the throne. The new film may not be perfect – instilling photo-realistic animals with emotion proved a step too far for the animators. But if the rightful king can't sit on the throne any longer, it seems only fitting that the title should go to its direct heir.[9]

9. In late 2024, Pixar's *Inside Out 2* took the title from the *Lion King* remake. Since then, the title has been snatched again, this time by Chinese CGI mythology-fest *Ne Zha 2*. But I wrote this chapter before all that happened, and I felt this was a really neat ending for it, so let's just pretend none of that happened, yeah?

Chapter 33

And They All Lived…

Pocahontas • *1995* • *Mike Gabriel, Eric Goldberg*

There were very fine people on both sides. That's the takeaway from Disney's *Pocahontas,* which attempts to tell the story of a Native American peacekeeper but delivers a watered-down morality tale that ends with the English getting back on their ships and heading home having learnt the errors of their ways. Good news for the locals, at least. I wonder what became of them.

The film arrived with tremendous fanfare in 1995, Disney riding high after the back-to-back successes of *Beauty and the Beast, Aladdin* and *The Lion King.* It wasn't just the critics and audiences who expected *Pocahontas* to be another record-breaking success, with many of the studio's animators opting to work on the film instead of wasting their time on the 'experimental' lion film.

Pocahontas's premiere was among the largest ever held. Four screens were raised in New York's Central Park, and as many as 100,000 fans piled in to see the story of an American icon unfold. The result was by no means a poor film – the animation is frequently gorgeous, the animal companions charming, and the song 'Colors of the Wind' stands comfortably alongside the other great numbers of the Renaissance era. But with expectations so high, a backlash was inevitable.

For *Pocahontas,* it came in two forms. Some critics decreed the film to be the worst thing a children's movie can be: a bit boring. And it's true that the songs are underwhelming once you put aside 'Colors of the Wind' and the chorus of 'Just Around the Riverbend'. Mel Gibson's John Smith is curiously devoid of personality, and the villainous Governor Ratcliffe is unlikeable, yes, but also uninteresting. You want to be able to root for a villain – at least a little bit. But after the toxic masculinity of Gaston and the complex and grubby power-grabbing of *The Lion King*'s Scar, Ratcliffe's character seems rather shallow. He likes gold and is racist. We know people like this. We do not enjoy people like this.

The other complaint was made by a range of voices, from audiences to critics and even those working on the film: 'This isn't how the story goes'.

Disney has a long history of changing the endings of their films in order to make them more palatable to young audiences. It began, as so much of Disney's history does, with *Snow White.* In the Brothers Grimm's earlier telling, the Evil Queen does not die falling from a cliff. Instead, she is captured during Snow White's wedding to the prince and made to wear slippers made of red-hot iron and then to dance until she dies. It's an odd choice for the entertainment portion of the reception but, honestly, more interesting than some weddings I've been to.

Disney has ignored similarly dark endings in other fairy tales, too. In *Cinderella*, the Brothers Grimm once again turned the karma up to eleven, this time directing their wrath at the step-sisters, who are blinded by doves during the climactic nuptials.[1]

Hans Christian Andersen's original version of *The Little Mermaid* ends not with a battle at sea and true love conquering all, but with the title character having to decide whether or not to kill the prince while he sleeps. Unable to bring herself to do it, she dissipates into sea foam and spends the next 300 years or so floating around in purgatory somewhere above the North Sea.

Disney's non-fairy tale adaptations have famously strayed from the source material, too. Both Victor Hugo and the studio's animated *Hunchback of Notre Dame* deny Quasimodo a happy ending with his crush, Esmeralda. But Hugo goes a step further, hanging the poor woman. Quasimodo is understandably distraught and disappears without a trace. Years later, his skeleton is found draped over that of Esmeralda. As unhappy alternate endings go, this is at least morbidly romantic – though Hugo soon puts an end to that. As the men who found the two intertwined corpses attempt to pull them apart, Quasimodo's crumbles into dust.

These are all relatively well-known changes made by Disney, though. One of the less familiar endings is found in *The Fox and the Hound's* source material, originally published under the same name by Daniel P. Mannix in 1967. The novel offers a stark contrast to the film, having been written primarily for adult audiences. Accordingly, the plot is darker throughout and offers a stark representation of civilisation encroaching upon wild spaces. Also, it's absolutely miserable. Copper the dog and Tod the fox are never friends – in fact, Copper is trained to essentially act solely as a Tod-killing machine, ignoring all other foxes as long as Tod lives. If the film were to be made today, true to the original plot, Copper would be played by Liam Neeson, and Tod would spend the entire runtime quaking in his den.

The climactic chase from the film adaptation is even more gruelling in the novel – it ends with Tod collapsing and dying from literal exhaustion, pushed to the very limit by his canine rival. Copper almost dies too, but survives and makes a full recovery, only to be – and this will hurt, so look away now if you're of a sensitive disposition – taken outside and shot when his owner needs to move into a nursing home.

All of these changes are understandable, given the nature of Disney's audiences. However, they also differ from *Pocahontas* in one very significant matter: Pocahontas

1. By this point, one has to wonder just what was going on at weddings in Hanover in the early 1800s. They were either absolutely terrifying affairs, in which unpopular family members were ritually humiliated, or simply so boring that the Grimms were driven into their own imagination in a desperate attempt to stay awake. Either way, it may explain why only one of the brothers ever got married. If the choice was bachelorhood or being permanently disabled by a famously peaceful species of bird, I'd probably opt for the slightly less humiliating choice of singledom too.

was a real person. The story that Disney was drawing from for its thirty-third animated classic was something that had actually happened. More importantly still, it was a singular moment in a complex and deeply troubling period of American history that doesn't really warrant a retelling focused on balancing the vices and virtues of the participants. It was not a matter of white settlers who were a little greedy versus an indigenous people who weren't eager enough to share. It was a situation in which one party believed they had an inherent superiority over a native population. At the end of *Pocahontas*, the English make peace with the Native Americans and head home. In real life, the events that are very loosely portrayed in this film were far more complex.

It's hard to know exactly how inaccurate *Pocahontas* is, but we know the scale starts at 'very' and moves quickly up to 'entirely'. Part of the problem is that even our historical documents regarding the real-life Matoaka (Pocahontas was a nickname) are skewed by European eyes – and, in particular, those of John Smith.

We know that Pocahontas did not have any sort of romantic relationship with Smith – this was wholly a creation of Disney's writers. The two met – but the exact circumstances are uncertain because they were reported solely by Smith, who changed his story across the years to suit his needs at the time.

When Smith and Pocahontas first met, she was not a young adult, as the film suggests. Instead, she may have been as young as ten, and probably no older than thirteen. Smith's claim that she saved him from execution only emerged later, when Pocahontas had travelled to England, and Smith was eager for her to meet the Queen.

By then, she had married another Englishman, John Rolfe, and had converted to Christianity. Both of these events happened while she was held prisoner by the English in Virginia, a hostage during the First Anglo-Powhatan War. Indigenous oral tradition claims that she was sexually assaulted during this time.

On the one hand, it's easy to see why Disney decided to change the story so much to present an iconic figure of American history to families in a palatable way. But then, the question surely must be: should we make this story more palatable in the first place? Should Pocahontas be viewed as an icon or as a peacemaker, when so little about her can be known for sure, and when the facts that we can pin down frequently place her as yet another victim of a white supremacist worldview, and of the genocide that it empowered?

These aren't really questions that Disney should seek to answer. Hell, they aren't really questions that *this* book is equipped to answer. But one thing is clear enough: the horrific and exploitative history of European settlers in Native American lands should not first be encountered by children through an animated film featuring a greedy raccoon and a pampered pug.

Fairy tales are folk tales, and they evolve through time with the tellings we pass down to the next generation. In the earliest versions of *Sleeping Beauty*, the princess is raped as she sleeps; she gives birth to children before she wakes. By the time the Brothers Grimm came to tell the story, this awful plotline had turned into a simple kiss that breaks her slumber, a change that makes it into Disney's adaptation.

But this is neither a fairy tale nor a folk tale. It is the story of a young woman caught up in a conflict fuelled by European greed and racism. It is the story of a young woman who died in a strange land and was buried in an unmarked grave an ocean away from her home. A woman who was perhaps just 21 years old, and who was brought to England as the embodiment of a 'civilised savage'. It is a story that needs to be told, but that needs to be told in good faith. Because the story of Pocahontas is a variation on that of literally millions of Native Americans who died as a result of Western colonisation. It is their story to tell, and no matter how beautiful the animation, no matter how breathtaking the songs, Disney forgot this when they released *Pocahontas*, a story of two star-crossed lovers who could bring peace to a world that, in reality, would never see it again.

Chapter 34

French Horn

The Hunchback of Notre Dame • 1996 •
Gary Trousdale, Kirk Wise

Hollywood finances can be hard to get your head around. Unless you're earning what I'm going to politely call 'tyrant cash' – the sort of money that buys houses without neighbours, vehicles without wheels, and influence without accountability – it can be hard to understand exactly how impressive a film's box office take is.

Beauty and the Beast made $330 million dollars globally during its initial release, but how can we gauge what that meant for Disney? Well, we can look at the directors' next film for the studio: *The Hunchback of Notre Dame*. Because here's how much goodwill the studio had for the men behind their biggest hit since *Snow White*: they let Gary Trousdale and Kirk Wise put out one of the darkest and most ambitious family films in cinema history.

That's a bold statement, I know – but I'm willing to bring receipts. Because *Hunchback* opens with attempted infanticide and only builds from there. It's pre-revolutionary Paris, and the city's streets are governed by the Minister of Justice, Judge Claude Frollo. And, like all authority figures, Frollo is an absolutely bang-up fella – real good egg. Lovely guy. Invite him round for a barbecue next Friday, because our Frollo? He's the bee's knees.

Just kidding. Of course, Frollo is among the most vile and monstrous of all Disney villains. From his very introduction, we see him having to be talked out of dropping a baby down a well. This is not how we make a good first impression, Frollo. This is not how it's done. If I'm in a job interview and they ask me how my weekend was, I'm not answering with 'It was alright. I almost dropped a baby down a well, but a priest turned up and said I probably shouldn't.' I'm not answering that, even if that is *exactly* what I got up to that weekend.[1]

And it's worth noting, too, that Frollo isn't convinced not to drop the baby down the well because it's the right thing to do. He's convinced because he's already killed an innocent woman that evening, and the priest points out that there are only so many murders you can do each day before God starts questioning whether you're going to be a liability when you get to Heaven.

1. I should add here, I *very* rarely find myself in this position. I mean, really, how often do you see a well these days?

Anyway, from here on in, Frollo's crimes continue to rack up. He essentially spends the entire film advocating for genocide while bullying and berating Quasimodo, the disabled man that the baby grew up to be.[2]

In Victor Hugo's classic novel, upon which the film is fairly loosely based, Frollo is actually an Archdeacon. Trousdale and Wise changed this, a decision reflected through many of the film adaptations that came before Disney's. Among the reasons for this change was a concern that making such an evil character a representative of the church would upset religious groups. But good news, iconoclasts: they still managed to upset a *lot* of religious groups with this film.

Because here's the thing: whether he is officially sanctioned by the church or not, Disney's version of Claude Frollo is still a deeply religious man who frequently cites his faith as the motive for his horrendous actions.

This darkness comes to a head with Frollo's big musical number, 'Hellfire'.[3] The song is paired both in the film and on the soundtrack with Quasimodo's 'Heaven's Light', and the two stand beside each other in stark contrast. 'Heaven's Light' sees the film's hero finding hope in the kindness that Esmeralda has shown him – to Quasimodo, she is a beacon of goodness in a world of cruelty. In 'Hellfire', though, Frollo sees the same woman as the direct opposite – a temptress sent from the depths of hell itself to draw men into sin. Naturally, Frollo's response to this is a sinister lust that burns with hypocrisy, as he denies responsibility for his desire and instead blames it solely on the object of his obsession.

'Hellfire' stands as one of the most complex, daring and effective songs in the Disney canon. Over the course of three minutes, Frollo evolves from a devout and dreadful persecutor of the innocent to an explicitly compromised sinner whose religion does not save him from his flaws but rather fuels them. He is proud of his perceived virtue and looks down on the world around him with disgust. His lust for Esmeralda can be quelled, he says, but only by taking sole ownership of her. In his greed, he sets out his mission for the film's final half: to take Esmeralda or see her burn.

And while it's fair to say that other religious figures in the film stand in firm opposition to Frollo's hateful use of scripture – the cathedral's archdeacon is a constant barrier to his darkest urges, and Notre Dame itself is championed as a sanctuary for any who need it – it's easy to see why groups like The Southern Baptist Convention were able to ramp up campaigns against Disney, claiming that the studio was disparaging Christian values. Their frustrations spread far beyond the film, too – they felt particularly threatened by Ellen DeGeneres simultaneously

2. I'm sorry I didn't mention earlier that the baby was also disabled. I thought the fact it was a baby would be enough reason not to drop it down the well. But yeah, old Frollo finds a way to make it even worse.

3. The fact that this film is also a musical does capture some of the difficulty the studio had balancing the themes of their film with traditional Disney filmmaking. There are stark tonal shifts throughout, from a Goofy holler in the midst of a tense battle, to more or less every single appearance by Hugo, Jason Alexander's stone grotesque, who spends the film playing pigeons at poker and sexually harassing a goat.

being lesbian and having a TV show, and the fact that there were annual Gay Days at Disney World in Florida[4].

From Frollo's racism towards the Roma community to his misogynistic view of women, *Hunchback* pulled no punches. It offered a significant challenge for not only Trousdale and Wise but also for the studio itself. How far was too far? Where should the line be drawn? 'Hellfire' sat at the heart of many of these conversations – animator Floyd Norman tells of an early performance making Disney executives nervous, with the production team being encouraged not to make the film – which, we should bear in mind, was set in a cathedral – too religious.[5] It's a slightly confusing ask, given that even the film's production notes compare Quasimodo to an angel.[6]

The song was also a point of contention with the Motion Picture Association of America (MPAA), who asked the studio to make two changes to the sequence in order to retain a G rating. Accordingly, Disney drowned out the use of the word 'sin' in the lyrics and adapted the animation of the fiery apparition of Esmeralda to make it clearer that she was wearing clothes.

The film came out in the summer of 1996, having managed to score the precious G rating, and was promptly criticised by delicate parents and members of the media for being too scary for young children – even one of the film's stars, Jason Alexander, claimed he wouldn't be taking his 4-year-old son to see it.

But ask children of the 90s which films scared them when they were growing up, and *Hunchback* rarely gets mentioned. Perhaps the nuance of 'Hellfire' escaped them – perhaps it was quickly forgotten, sandwiched between a scene where Quasimodo's grotesque friends[7] draw pictures while he sings, and an action-filled sequence in which Phoebus, the captain of Frollo's guard, finally turns against him. But equally, perhaps children are just happy to enjoy a thrilling film where everything ends well for all but the villain, who gets a comeuppance rich with dramatic irony: shortly after reciting what sounds like a Bible quote about sinners being plunged into a pit of fire, Frollo is plun… well, you know dramatic irony works.[8]

---

4. These days aren't even run by Disney – they're just unofficial events in which a lot of members of the LGBTQ+ community choose to descend on the parks and enjoy them collectively. But Disney hasn't taken to banning people from the parks on the basis of sexuality, and this is upsetting to the sorts of people who watched Frollo not drop a baby down a well and thought 'hey, maybe we should all be giving this guy a break'.
5. Norman, Floyd, *Animated Life: A Lifetime of tips, tricks, techniques and stories from a Disney Legend* (Taylor & Francis, 2013)
6. *The Secret of the Hunchback*, a direct-to-video cash grab released the same year as Disney's film leans even further into this idea, with a twist ending that revealed Quasimodo's hunch to have been hiding angel wings all along. It is fundamentally terrible, but might go down better with the Southern Baptist crowd.
7. I'm not being rude – that's what they are. Gargoyles have spouts that allow them to carry rainwater away from the building.
8. Interestingly, the scripture Frollo cites appears nowhere in the Bible. You can choose to take this as you like: a final burst of ignorant religion from a hypocrite whose faith is not built around actual teachings, or a savvy move to avoid upsetting Christian audience members.

For all its darkness, *Hunchback* remains an incredibly enjoyable film. Visually, it's among the finest films the studio has released. It echoes the darkest moments of *Fantasia* and builds upon the grandest moments of spectacle from *Beauty and the Beast* and *The Lion King*. Sweeping shots around Paris – and in particular, about the stunning facade of the titular cathedral, which was intricately realised using both hand-drawn and CGI animation, capture the audience's imagination. The scope of the crowd scenes led to the team developing new CGI software, and, as a result, the film feels bigger than any Disney classic that had come before it. 'Hellfire' aside, the songs may not match up to those from the earlier Renaissance films – but their grandeur more than met the brief that composers Alan Menken and Stephen Schwartz were given: to create a soundtrack that recalled pop opera musicals like *Phantom of the Opera* and *Les Miserables*. Fittingly, *Hunchback* debuted as a stage musical in Berlin in 1999. Though the production's book was originally written in English, it was translated into German – the original version did not reach the United States until 2014. For my money, the original cast recording of 'Hellfire' from the Berlin production – retitled 'Das Feuer der Hölle' in German, is the most breathtaking version of all.

It takes some gall to approach a Gallic classic like Victor Hugo's novel and adapt it into a children's film. But in giving Trousdale and Wise the benefit of the doubt Disney enabled them to deliver something that, if not necessarily in the spirit of the source material, still delivers a dark and surprisingly nuanced story. Watching *Hunchback* in a contemporary context, the complexity of the film's narrative is clearer than ever. Though many see a morality tale about acceptance, both of oneself and others, it's also a story about the sort of men who preach traditional values as a way to cover for – and empower – their own hypocrisy, misogyny, and hate.

Chapter 35

Drawing on the Classics

Hercules • *1997* • *Ron Clements, John Musker*

From a classical point of view, *Hercules* is a hot mess. Disney stuffed a bunch of animators into a giant wooden horse, rolled it into the world of Greek mythology, and unleashed absolute mayhem. Even the film's name is wrong; Hercules is the Roman name given to a man better known to the Greeks as Heracles.

The film had intended to premiere in the heart of Athens, near the ancient ruins of The Pnyx, but such were the liberties taken with the plot that the idea was shut down by the Greek government. We'll have to guess which change was most offensive to critics and audiences in Greece. Maybe it was the name change or the idea that Hades was a villain, when he often seemed to be among the more benevolent of the Greek gods. Perhaps it was the fact that Megara was not Heracles' one great love, but rather the first of four wives.[1]

In fact, Hercules' backstory in the film rings truer to that of another mythological figure: Oedipus. In Ron Clements and John Musker's film, two farmers find Hercules at the foot of a mountain and take him in. It seems they had been struggling to have a child of their own – Hercules is a miracle that will finally enable them to have a son. This is more or less exactly how the myth of Oedipus begins. Heracles, by comparison, resulted from an affair between Zeus and the mortal woman Alcmene. Where Hera serves as his mother in the film, in the original myth, she was the humiliated goddess of marriage – more or less the worst person one could cheat on. Hera had a habit of attempting to kill the children from her partner Zeus's numerous affairs – Heracles was so-called in a vain gambit by his parents to mollify Hera and put an end to her attempts to kill him.[2]

We've already seen how Disney plays fast and loose with established stories, though, so it should be of no surprise that the frequently promiscuous adventures

1. And many more sexual partners to boot. In fact, as a reward for killing the Lion of Cithaeron, Heracles was offered the chance to bed all *fifty* of the king's daughters in one night. Proving to have not only superhuman strength but superhuman stamina too, he happily agreed – impregnating every last one of them. Being Ancient Greece, Heracles also had a number of male lovers. A hero beloved by all, then.
2. In a fun twist, Heracles' strength is attributed to Hera accidentally breastfeeding him with godly milk on one occasion. The baby bit too hard, causing Hera to pull away and spray her milk across the heavens. And that, my friends, is how the Milky Way came to be – at least according to some very imaginative Ancient Greeks.

of the Greek gods morphed into something more family-friendly under Disney's watchful eye. Besides, there were other classics that informed the film's production, and *Hercules* is much more successful in paying tribute to them.

* * *

Meet John Doe is now something of a forgotten entry in the filmography of Frank Capra – the legendary director behind iconic James Stewart films *It's a Wonderful Life* and *Mr. Smith Goes to Washington*. Give it a watch, though, and you'll find something familiar in the cynical and yet irrepressible Ann Mitchell, played by Barbara Stanwyck.

Stanwyck's role in *Meet John Doe* was the chief inspiration behind the creation of Meg, a female lead who stands out among her Disney contemporaries. There is a determined independence to Meg, who has been burned by men before, and has nothing to show for it but a steely demeanour and a near-literal deal with the devil. It's precisely this protective will that defines 'I Won't Say (I'm In Love)', which replaced a romantic ballad that was considered out of character for the emotionally closed-off Meg. A happy rewrite: the song remains one of the most enjoyable and underrated in all of Disney's animated classics. It is – and I've checked, this is the technical term – an absolute banger.

It's strange now to think that Susan Egan had to fight for the role of Meg. She delivers her lines so dryly you fear a fire might break out in the projection room. But at the time of production, Egan was already known to Disney for playing one of the company's most iconic princesses. She originated the role of Belle in the Broadway adaptation of *Beauty and the Beast*, winning a Tony Award in the process. Alan Menken, who had worked alongside Egan for that production, was the co-writer of the music for *Hercules* and initially didn't even want to offer an audition to the actress.

It's a good thing Menken relented – Egan's work, as well as that of James Woods as Hades, make the film. Until Woods accepted the role, Hades had been imagined as a very different character – a slow, methodical god who bore more than a little resemblance to Jack Nicholson. Nicholson had, in fact, been the first choice for the role – recommended by *One Flew Over the Cuckoo's Nest* castmate and voice of Philoctetes, Danny DeVito. Negotiations had been quick with Nicholson, but not for a good reason: Disney was prepared to offer $500,000 for the role. Nicholson wanted thirty times that amount and a fifty-percent cut of all merch proceeds for the character.

When Woods auditioned for the role, his quick, wry delivery surprised the directors. He felt like an obvious choice that had hitherto been missed. Now Hades and Meg would be able to sling quips back and forth, like the characters in the 1940s classics that had already informed the script.

* * *

The final piece of the puzzle was the design, which stands apart from anything Disney had ever released before. John Musker had been a fan of the British artist Gerald Scarfe since the late 1960s when the artist had modelled a grotesque caricature of The Beatles for the cover of Time Magazine. Scarfe had been hugely successful in Britain for decades, creating political cartoons, and iconic imagery for Pink Floyd. Noting a similarity between the artist's work and the imagery found on Greek vases, the directors brought Scarfe in as a production designer for the film.

Though Scarfe was not an obvious fit for Disney animation, he became the leading artistic influence on *Hercules*. Contracted to produce only a dozen drawings to inform the animators, he ended up delivering more than 700 over the course of the production.

Translating these ideas to screen was not always easy. The experienced animator Andreas Deja, who was thrilled to take the lead on the film's hero after making his name on villains Gaston, Jafar and Scar in recent years,[3] understood that Hercules would need to be drawn with both weight and subtlety in order to work on screen. Scarfe understood his limitations as a character designer, giving Deja permission to make the changes necessary to deliver this nuance.

The sharp points and swirling curves of Scarfe's work often needed to be softened for *Hercules*. Still, in balancing out his more outlandish flourishes, the animators delivered a unique film within the Disney canon. It often feels as though *Hercules* is left behind a little when considering the back-to-back hits of the Renaissance era. With the exception of *The Rescuers Down Under*, itself a sequel, it's the only film from the period not to have received a straight-to-video feature length follow-up. But that's for the best. Almost three decades later, *Hercules* remains a testament to the benefits of bringing diverse influences together to create something that feels wholly new.

3. Though it wasn't Deja's idea, the writers threw him a fun little in-joke to play with: while posing for a portrait, Hercules is shown wearing the pelt of a lion bearing an uncanny resemblance to Scar.

Chapter 36

Exit, Propelled by a Firework

Mulan • *1998* • *Tony Bancroft, Barry Cook*

Animation exaggerates, but it can also have the effect of minimising the more horrific elements of a story. Take a central scene in *Mulan*, in which our intrepid undercover heroine and her friends find themselves under attack by an entire army of invaders. With steadfast determination, Mulan runs into action, prepares a rocket launcher and successfully triggers an avalanche. It's a thrilling sequence, from the digitally rendered masses of Shan Yu's troops to the dramatic cliff-edge finale. It is also a scene in which a Disney Princess is single-handedly responsible for the deaths of almost 2,000 people.

Mulan was a groundbreaking entry into the Disney canon in a few ways – not least in that it featured the first Asian lead for the studio. This had been on the cards for some time, but one early plan for the film would have been much less progressive. Before the team decided to adapt the legend of Hua Mulan, they had been planning a straight-to-video film called *China Doll.* The basic outline of this original idea is almost the opposite of everything *Mulan* came to offer. In it, a young girl living an oppressive and unhappy existence in China would have been offered a chance to escape and find love in England with a handsome British prince.

Thankfully, the studio opted instead to adapt one of China's most beloved folktales. The decision came at a fiscally useful moment: Disney was in the midst of a diplomatic falling out with the nation, having recently released the latest Martin Scorcese film, *Kundun*, under their Touchstone Pictures banner. Written by *ET* writer Melissa Mathison, the film tells the story of another kind-hearted character who is unable to go home: the Dalai Lama. Recognising that the Chinese Communist Party would not look kindly upon a major Hollywood feature that highlighted their ongoing issues in Tibet, Disney did their best to bury the film.

Mulan made big steps to repair the relationship, even though Chinese critics were unimpressed with the film's deviation from its source material (in traditional versions, Mulan doesn't reveal that she is a woman until she has returned home from over a decade of war). Still, opting for a story of the nation's greatest hero was definitely an improvement over choosing one about an oppressed woman finding love with a white saviour.

The prolonged military service Mulan undertakes in Chinese mythology means that she faces up against a huge number of nameless foes, necessitating one major addition to Disney's version: a true villain. Shan Yu fills the spot – a relatively straightforward figure, despite early plans to give him a mystical connection with his falcon, whose vision he would be able to share. Ultimately, this element of the character was dropped for pacing reasons. As a result, the most interesting thing about Shan Yu in the final film is the method of his demise: launched on a rocket into a tower of fireworks.

It's one of the more explosive deaths in the Disney canon and one that definitely benefits from animation's ability to make even the most horrific of endings palatable for young children. Shan Yu's exit is short, loud and colourful, barely giving the audience a moment to think about third-degree burns. Fourth-degree burns? I'm not sure how bad burns can get. The poor man dies in the middle of a stockpile of fireworks. He might be a pioneer in 360-degree burns.

Disney's writers and animators often seem to relish the chance to kill off a villain in the grimmest possible fashion. In *The Black Cauldron*, mystical forces pull the evil Horned King into the titular pot. His flesh is ripped from his bones; his very core turns to a white-hot flame. It is, in all honesty, the only interesting thing about the whole film.

The studio is only a little kinder to *Tangled*'s Mother Gothel, who is hit with a double whammy: first, she begins to age rapidly, like the Nazi in *Indiana Jones and the Last Crusade*, or perhaps just an avocado with a face. And then, for good measure, she falls out of a window. Only her cape reaches the ground – the rest has already decayed into dust.

These are perhaps the most gruesome of the Disney deaths, only partly softened by the animator's hand. Other villains are sent off in far more ludicrous ways – the sort of death only possible in a cartoon. *The Little Mermaid*'s Ursula is stabbed in the side by a full-sized galleon. *Atlantis*'s Rourke is transmogrified into a monstrous crystal man and then shattered by a propeller. And then there's the silliest of all: in *Wreck-It Ralph*, Turbo is turned into a giant bug and lured to his death by the light of a gigantic Mentos/Diet Coke explosion.

The most common way to go, though, has to be falling. From *Snow White* to *Beauty and the Beast*, half a dozen Disney villains have lost their lives to gravity. It's rare that we see a good splat, though – usually, the bad guy disappears into fog or darkness. In the case of *The Great Mouse Detective*'s Rattigan, this may mean no death at all – rats have been known to survive falls from great heights. Only the criminal underground of rodent London can say for certain whether Rattigan survived to see another day.

Disney's darkest death of all would come shortly after the release of *Mulan* when Tarzan took on the furious Clayton in his own 1999 film. During a heated chase scene in the middle of a lightning storm (several of the above deaths endure similarly poor weather), Clayton gets tangled up in the vines of the jungle. He hacks away at the plants in an attempt to free himself, and even Tarzan tries to intervene as one particularly thick vine hooks itself under his chin. Finally, Clayton makes one too many slices, and both he and Tarzan plummet through the rainforest canopies. Tarzan lands on the ground. Clayton does not. As a harrowing final touch, flashes of lightning cast a stark shadow in the background: the lifeless legs of a man, suspended from the ground, swinging.

It makes one long for a quick, fiery death at the hands of Mulan and a couple of hundred kilos of gunpowder.

Chapter 37

Welcome to the Jungle, We Got Soft Rock Ballads

Tarzan • 1999 • Chris Buck, Kevin Lima

When Disney embarked on their feature-length adaptation of Edgar Rice Burroughs' classic novel *Tarzan of the Apes*, their head of feature animation, Thomas Schumacher, commented with surprise that theirs would be the first version to approach the story in the animated medium. It made perfect sense, he reasoned, to explore a story this way when it would be so difficult to reproduce in live action faithfully. After all, a great deal of the story follows a teenage boy growing up among gorillas. Even ignoring the risk of unexpected tantrums that both species might present, their pairing in real life would result in a uniquely pungent Hollywood set.

Disney's animated adaptation certainly made the most of the format, bringing to screen a Tarzan who could connect more intimately with his new family. He is held closely by his adoptive mother, Kala. He stands toe to toe with the dominant silverback, Kerchak. At the same time, animation frees our hero from the tiresome shackles of on-set health and safety teams. Disney upgrades Tarzan's skillset from the classic vine swinging he got up to in live-action films dating as far back as 1918. Inspired by the sporting endeavours of supervising animator Glen Keane's son, Tarzan also slides across the moss-laden trees of the jungle with moves that emulate skateboarding and surfing.

Another key benefit of animation is that when your lead actor can't deliver a convincing take on Tarzan's signature call, somebody else can step in and help out. In this case, it was veteran British actor Brian Blessed who offered up the goods. Widely renowned for his booming vocal delivery, Blessed's primary role in the film was as the villain, Clayton.[1]

Buck and Lima's film is an enjoyable entry into the Disney Renaissance era, even if it lacks the narrative scope of *The Lion King* or *Mulan*. Minnie Driver offers a likeable addition to the ever-popular trope of 'posh Englishwoman is an enthusiastic adventurer falling for an unconventional man', even if that specific

1. In the original novel, Clayton is Tarzan's cousin, and has (unknowingly) usurped his position as Viscount Greystoke. But the original novel is also a sort of allegory for the author's white supremecist and pro-eugenics views, so we aren't going to be making any sort of a case for a more faithful adaptation here.

cinematic archetype had peaked just a month earlier with Rachel Weisz's star turn in *The Mummy*.

But a quarter of a century down the line, it's clearer than ever who the real star of *Tarzan* is: Phil Collins. In the immediate wake of *The Lion King*'s unprecedented success, Chris Montan, a music executive at Disney, suggested the studio should bring Collins in to act as a songwriter during the development of their new project. It was clear from the start that the process would need to be a little different from that undertaken by Elton John and Tim Rice. Director Kevin Lima couldn't envision his protagonist belting out pop bangers while wearing nothing but a loincloth. It was decided that bar a brief lullaby between Kala and her newly adopted human baby, characters would not sing in *Tarzan*. Instead, Phil Collins himself would step up to the plate.

And step up to the plate he did. There are four great songs across the *Tarzan* soundtrack (and one genuinely annoying one – 'Trashin' The Camp', which appears to riff on the then-inescapable success of dustbin percussionists Stomp). Collins was never known for his subtlety, and his pop music relied on big emotional melodies and hard-hitting lyrics that often felt a little on the nose. Which makes his music absolutely perfect for a children's film.

Take 'Son of Man', which rattles along at a breakneck pace during a scene in which Tarzan learns how to be more ape-like. It's one of several montages that feature in the film – perhaps the only real criticism that can be targeted at the Collins-focused soundtrack. With songs playing a prominent role in a film where the characters don't sing, the animators had to find ways to fill the screen wordlessly. 'Strangers Like Me' is another grandiose pop song filled with catchy hooks and emotive key changes ready-made for a montage – in this case, of the growing friendship between Tarzan and Jane as the former discovers what it is to be human.

But the stand-out song of the piece – and the one that earned Collins his Academy Award – barely features in the main narrative. Sung briefly by Glenn Close as her character, Kala, soothes the baby Tarzan, Collins quickly takes over and introduces us to a gentle, almost soporific version of 'You'll Be In My Heart'. The whole scene runs for just over ninety seconds.

Imagine teasing your best song – not only of the film, but of the entire decade – and then not returning to it until the end credits rolled. But boy, does it work. Tarzan and Jane stand in front of a sprawling African jungle, and the former delivers an iconic call that would have killed lead actor Tony Goldwyn off but is roughly equatable to a medium yawn for Brian Blessed. The screen cuts to black, and the title slams across the darkness: *TARZAN*. And then: the strings.

'You'll Be In My Heart' is textbook anticipative songwriting. From the very first bars, the song begins a slow and steady build to the chorus. It's nothing unexpected, nothing the audience hasn't heard a thousand times before. But this familiarity allows the listener to connect instantly with the song. Here we are, they think, at the tail end of the 1990s. We have come to the cinema for two things and two things alone: a summer blockbuster movie and an accompanying ballad that goes as hard as any piece of music that has ever been released.

And so the song builds – Collins reiterates the lullaby we heard an hour earlier, a lyric that was written not for the baby among the apes but for his own 10-year-old daughter, Lily.[2] The words speak directly to the listener, mothering us, comforting us. The chorus lands and cements the song's reassuring message – only for the second and third verses to up the stakes by delivering a new 'us against the world' attitude.

And that chorus. My god. Disney's films are not short on memorable songs that catch in the head and demand to be sung. Hell, for twenty years, they released a whole series of home video compilations specifically called 'Disney's Sing-Along Songs'. But even so, after almost ninety years of animated features, few songs have the sheer emotional magnitude as 'You'll Be In My Heart'. All there is to do is throw our heads back and belt out the chorus in unison.

For all the brilliant songs on the *Tarzan* soundtrack (and, again, the one absolute disaster that is 'Trashin' the Camp'), you get the sense that this is the song that Disney was hoping for when it hired their songwriter for the film. Because sometimes a choice is presented to us that makes so much sense, the only possible response is not to ask why nobody has done it before. It's simply to sit down and do it yourself. When Thomas Schumacher realised that *Tarzan* would work best as an animated film, he didn't shrug his shoulders in confusion and wait for another studio to take the lead. And when Chris Montan realised that Phil Collins's love of big melodies and emotive lyrics would work phenomenally well in a Disney movie, he didn't waste time wondering what it might sound like: he brought Collins in and delivered one of the greatest movie ballads of all time.

2. Lily Collins would later leave her own mark on Disney, playing the title role in the studio's live action remake of *Cinderella*.

The Post-Renaissance Era

Chapter 38

Rhapsody Mk. 2

Fantasia 2000 • 1999 • James Algar, Gaëtan & Paul Brizzi, Hendel Butoy, Francis Glebas, Eric Goldberg, Don Hahn, Pixote Hunt

Walt Disney's 1940 masterpiece, *Fantasia*, was never intended as a singular moment in cinema. From the very beginning, Walt envisioned an evolving film that would be re-released each year with segments dropped and new pieces brought in. The idea was that, for the relatively low cost of one or two animated shorts each year, audiences would flock back to cinemas to see the new *Fantasia*, and marvel at its wonders all over again.

Except, of course, it didn't quite work out like that. A number of factors – including the limited release brought about by Disney's technological demands – meant that the initial release of the film was something of a flop for the studio – and amid the economical strife of World War II, Walt's vision for annual *Fantasia* re-releases was dropped.

This isn't to say that the idea was forgotten about completely. In Package Era films *Make Mine Music* and *Melody Time* audiences were given glimpses of the format – music-led shorts tied together, albeit without the thought or consistency of *Fantasia*.

In 1980, Wolfgang Reitherman and fellow animator Mel Shaw started developing *Musicana*, which would be a spiritual successor to the film, drawing on music from various global cultures. The project never came to fruition, and glimpses at relatively clichéd cultural stereotypes in early concept art suggest this may have been for the best. Nevertheless, the cancellation was a disappointment for Reitherman, who retired shortly after, the second longest-reigning of Walt's Nine Old Men.

But a new *Fantasia* remained an ambition of Walt's nephew, Roy E. Disney, who was chairman of the studio's animation department between 1984 and 2004. Throughout his time in the role, ideas were bandied about: a Beatles version was proposed at one point. Eventually, in 1991, *Fantasia Continued* was greenlit with a 1997 release date. A few delays and a couple of name changes later and *Fantasia 2000* came out, its wide release debuting exclusively in IMAX cinemas on the first day of the new millennium.

Walt's vision hadn't quite come to pass, but the legacy of his most thematically ambitious feature was at least upheld. A third film, *Fantasia 2006*, never made it to our screens – but I hold out hope that somewhere down the line the studio will have the ambition and the courage to experiment with the format once again. Here are a few lessons the directors of future *Fantasia* films might pick up from this turn-of-the-millenium sequel:

1. **A balance of the familiar and the unexpected is key.**
   Though the original *Fantasia* featured some instantly recognisable pieces, some of the most iconic sequences in the film featured music not widely known outside of classical concert halls. Notably, the one segment that features in both the original movie and *Fantasia 2000*, 'The Sorcerer's Apprentice', was one of these.
   This sequel, too, balances the familiar ('Rhapsody in Blue', Beethoven's 'Symphony No. 5' and 'Pomp and Circumstance') with pieces that are less recognisable to lay audiences, like Ottorino Respighi's 'Pines of Rome'. Both films benefit from the sections introducing new audiences to magnificent classical pieces.
2. **Not everything needs a clear narrative.**
   Compared to its predecessor, *Fantasia 2000* is much more reliant on narrative pieces that have clear-cut beginnings, middles and ends. Unfortunately, these are often the weakest of the pieces – 'Rhapsody in Blue' is accompanied by a mish-mash of plotlines (and occasionally questionable stereotyping), and 'Pomp and Circumstance' soundtracks a drab Donald Duck short (unflatteringly placed directly after Mickey's iconic *The Sorcerer's Apprentice*).
   The more abstract narratives are far more enjoyable – transcendent whales, and a sprite's struggle with the titular 'firebird' of her segment. Standing above them all – and frequently doing so on only one leg – are the flamingos in the *Carnival of the Animals, Finale* segment. Perhaps fittingly, this piece was first suggested by Joe Grant, the only person to have worked directly on both *Fantasia* films.
3. **Don't fix what isn't broken.**
   Walt always wanted the ever-changing version of *Fantasia* to retain older segments within its running order – and *The Sorcerer's Apprentice* remains one of the best pieces in *Fantasia 2000*. Originally Roy E. Disney had intended to carry over half of the original segments, and *The Nutcracker Suite* remained on the bill until only a few months before the film's premiere. It was replaced by *Rhapsody in Blue*, a short film already developed as a standalone release.
   I reckon *Night on Bald Mountain* would be a stunning addition to a future *Fantasia*. And to carry across from this film? *Carnival of the Animals, Finale*, obviously. But why not also the mesmerising *Pines of Rome* segment, which had been in development for the film since 1993.[1]

1. The code that stops the CGI whales from bumping into one another was also used in *The Lion King*'s stampede scene, both having been in production at the same time.

4. **One host was enough. A dozen is overkill.**
   The biggest change between the two films has little to do with the music. Though *Fantasia 2000* opens with recordings of Deems Taylor's original introduction to the series, the rest of the pieces are presented by a range of different celebrities and musicians.
   Of these, there are a few who excel in their role (Steve Martin is charming and silly, Quincy Jones is informed and, if anything, overqualified) and those who feel superlative and increasingly out of place as the film ages (Penn and Teller and Bette Midler are both grossly misplaced). Deems Taylor was a wonderful choice the first time around – knowledgeable and serious without being drab. Should a third *Fantasia* materialise, we can only hope that Taylor's natural successor has been made apparent.
5. **There's room for new music amid the classics.**
   The strange thing about the original *Fantasia* is that many pieces we view as integral parts of the classical canon weren't all that old when the film was released in 1940. Tchaikovsky's 'Nutcracker Suite' and 'The Sorcerer's Apprentice' had been around for less than half a century. Stravinsky's 'The Rite of Spring' debuted in 1913, just twenty-seven years before the film's premiere.
   The gap between *Fantasia 2000* and its music is a little wider. There are two 76-year-old pieces ('Pines of Rome' and 'Rhapsody in Blue'), and the most recent of those featured is Shosakovich's second piano concerto, which was composed in 1957. Any future film would benefit immensely from recognising some of the gorgeous music released since, you know, the Cold War. I'm not asking for Brian Eno's 'Music for Airports', but why not give Max Richter a look-in?

In many ways, we're lucky to even have a *Fantasia 2000*. It seemed for the longest time like it was a dream held onto only by the last member of the Disney family to still work in a significant role within the company's creative teams. The film echoed its predecessor on release – instead of Walt's 'roadshows', it was limited to IMAX screens for its first four months. It ultimately made $90 million on an $80 million budget – which meant it was a loss for the studio after marketing costs were factored in. Echoing the term used for *Snow White* over sixty years earlier, the film was described by the studio's CEO, Michael Eisner, as 'Roy Disney's folly'.

But still, I hold out hope that someday, the Disney studio will find itself under the leadership of another creative mind willing to take a chance on what remains a daring and experimental format, over eighty years after its first instalment. And I'll save that person some time, too. Here are the ten pieces I would feature in a third *Fantasia* film:

1. *The River – I. The Spring* – Duke Ellington[2]
2. *Pines of Rome* – Ottorino Respighi (from *Fantasia 2000*)
3. *Teekonzert I. In fröhlicher Gesellschaft* – Gerhard Winkler[3]
4. *The Sorcerer's Apprentice* – Paul Dukas (from *Fantasia*)
5. *Night on Bald Mountain* – Modest Mussorgsky (from *Fantasia*)
6. *Symphony No. 1 in E Minor: I. Allegro ma non troppo* – Florence Beatrice Price[4]
7. *The Carnival of the Animals, Finale* – Camille Saint-Saëns (from *Fantasia 2000*)
8. *The Space Travelers Lullaby* – Kamasi Washington[5]
9. *Destino*[6]
10. *The Four Seasons* – Vivaldi, recomposed by Max Richter[7]

---

2. Every *Fantasia* film needs an abstract introduction to demonstrate to audiences the way music can be visualised without a narrative. Ellington's gorgeous River Suite might follow a river from source to sea, but this evocative opening section captures the orchestra in all its splendour.
3. I honestly don't know much about this piece, except that it is the most upbeat piece of music in all of existence. An early suggestion Eisner made for the *Pomp and Circumstance* would have had various Disney princesses appear at a college graduation in which their offspring were all appearing. It was shot down by at least one appalled colleague. But hear me out: there is no piece of music on the planet that screams 'Disney princess' more than this.
4. The first symphonic work by a Black woman to have been played by a major American orchestra, this piece was written by Price to reflect her experiences as a Black woman raised in the post-Civil War South at the turn of the 20th century. Tell me that wouldn't make good cinema.
5. A thoroughly modern piece of music, 'The Space Travelers Lullaby' is one of the most lush compositions by American jazz saxophonist Kamasi Washington. Neither *Fantasia* film has yet explored the infinite potential of the cosmos. Consider this your opportunity, Disney.
6. Though not built around a widely known piece of music, *Destino* is a natural fit for a *Fantasia* film. Originally storyboarded between 1945 and 1946, the short film represented a collaboration between Disney and surrealist artist Salvador Dali. The film was put on hiatus as the studio sought to recover from the financial impact of World War II, before being rediscovered by Roy E. Disney as he prepared *Fantasia 2000* for release. It was completed in 2003 and found its way onto DVD and Blu-ray releases of the film as a bonus feature. It has since been made available to view on the Disney Plus streaming service. Let's give it the place in the animated canon that it deserves.
7. The sweeping climax draws on an approach to classical music utilised in both *Fantasia* and *Fantasia 2000*: the dramatic restructuring of iconic pieces to fit a short format film. Like the *Night on Bald Mountain* and *The Firebird* sequences before it, Max Richter's evocative recomposed 'Four Seasons' would offer a dramatic and emotional finale that takes audiences through an entire year in just fifteen minutes or so.

Chapter 39

One of Our Disney Films is Missing

Dinosaur • *2000* • *Eric Leighton, Ralph Zondag*

Here's a curious little anomaly in the animated canon that hardcore fans in Europe might spot: the line-up in this book excludes the 2006 film *The Wild*, which was marketed as the 46th animated classic on the east side of the Atlantic. It's never been particularly clear why Disney decided to include it in the canon in favour of the earlier *Dinosaur*. Still, given how relatively bland and slight the narratives for each film are, I'll do *The Wild* a small favour and allow it to piggyback here, too.

No film in this book took as sharp a turn from conception to final product as *Dinosaur*. The film was originally conceived on the set of 1987's *Robocop* by legendary special effects artist Phil Tippett. Frustrated with the delays on set as the crew wrestled with the Robocop costume, Tippett suggested to director Paul Verhoeven a project that he thought would be significantly simpler to produce: a stop-motion dinosaur epic.

Tippett had form in this field, having directed a ten-minute short called *Prehistoric Beast* a few years earlier.[1] His dinosaur film would follow a similar design, presenting its stars in a wordless narrative more akin to a nature documentary than standard Hollywood fare. Given this, it's perhaps a little surprising that Verhoeven took the idea to a man who sat at the heart of one of Hollywood's biggest studios: Jeffrey Katzenberg.

Disney immediately went about sanding the edges off of the initial script that Tippett and Verhoeven had commissioned from Walon Green (whose best work had been 1969's *The Wild Bunch*, and whose worst work was the impenetrable sci-fi sports movie *Solarbabies*, which is about fascist governments, aliens, and a fictional sport that looks a lot like lacrosse on roller skates).

Green's script was never going to work at Disney. Much of the plot focused on an epic journey across a barren landscape attempting to reach a safe haven, but the film had a deeply nihilistic finale. Though the styracosaurus protagonist would defeat his t-rex nemesis and find safety in his promised land, it would all be for

1. Incidentally, if you'd like to watch an animated film that is about as far removed from the Disney classics as it is possible to be, Phil Tippet's 2021 stop-motion nightmare *Mad God* is your point of call. It is eighty minutes of wretched horror and wide-eyed wonder, and it is absolutely wonderful.

nothing: the movie would end with a comet wiping out the dinosaurs just as the film's hero finally found peace.

As plot points like this were cut from the film, Tippett and Verhoeven left the project, freeing the former up to work as a special effects supervisor on *Jurassic Park* and allowing Verhoeven to focus on other family-friendly projects like *Basic Instinct* and *Showgirls*.

At Disney, project development continued for the next decade. As the studio acquired computer effects companies, they found themselves better placed to deliver the animation necessary to make its first CGI film. Still, the team's ambitions for life-like scenery outpaced their tech, so *Dinosaur* became the film in the Disney canon that most relies on live-action footage. Though all the characters within the movie are computer animated (and, frequently, this is *very* obvious), the backgrounds are shot on location in Hawaii, California, Florida, and a handful of other nations, including Jordan and Samoa.

As a result, *Dinosaur* makes for one of the most curious oddities in the Disney canon – a film in which nothing ever looks quite right. Unfortunately, the plot doesn't redeem the uneven nature of the visuals. Devoid of the Verhoeven and Tippett darkness, *Dinosaur* rounded out into a by-the-numbers children's film that bears a lot of similarities to the studio's 1990s output. Aladar, the iguanodon lead, has an origin story that strongly recalls that of Disney's *Tarzan*, released less than a year earlier. The sweeping music has distinct echoes of *The Lion King*'s soundtrack – both make liberal use of the talents of Lebo M. Beyond the studio's back catalogue, *Dinosaur* was also accused of nicking its ideas from Don Bluth's *Land Before Time* series, which released its seventh instalment later that same year. It's certainly true that the film bears many of the same plot points as the first film in the franchise: a dinosaur finding a new family after being separated from its mother; an arduous journey to find a sheltered valley that remains a haven amid the dangerous prehistoric landscape. However, Tippett, Verhoeven, and Green had already hashed out these elements of Dinosaur's plot in 1987. *The Land Before Time* wasn't released until late in 1988.

These criticisms of *Dinosaur* make it an unlikely bedfellow of the film that would later attempt to replace it within the Disney canon. Another movie about an epic journey, *The Wild* was also heavily lambasted by the press for seemingly ripping off an earlier non-Disney project.

Released in April 2006, *The Wild* reached audiences a little under a year after Dreamwork's *Madagascar*. Both films feature a lion living in a New York zoo, both see characters shipped overseas in containers, both feature a motley crew of unlikely friends, and both are, if we're entirely honest, not very good.

Actually, scrap that. *The Wild* is an *awful* film. During the process of writing this book, I have rewatched every one of the Disney classics, and a number of adjacent films. I have felt it necessary to keep notes while watching, too. Small thoughts that occur. Ideas or themes that might be worth drawing out.

Here is the complete list of notes taken during my first watch of *The Wild* in fifteen or so years:

- This is terrible.
- I hate this.
- Did they steal this soundtrack from the worst episode of *Scrubs*?
- Everything is SO LOUD
- Everything is so ugly!
- Borderline racist representation in the pigeons there
- The shallowest characters I think I've ever seen
- I have never hated the concept of a silly snake so much.
- And I *love* Richard Kind. He's a delight.
- I hate it I hate it I hate it I hate it
- This squirrel belongs on a register.
- You would have thought it easier to just write a good script rather than invent a time machine, travel to a point in time when rudimentary generative AI technology was widely available, and input 'write me the worst screenplay possible'.
- Why are the dung beetles German?
- This is the longest film I have ever seen

Like *Dinosaur* before it, *The Wild* has perhaps been unfairly criticised for its similarities to another studio's films. After all, in this case, the movie is more or less a twin to *Madagascar* – a phenomenon often seen among Hollywood releases and not uncommon even among the Dreamworks/Disney rivalry.[2] Both *Dinosaur* and *The Wild* are more heavily indebted to *The Lion King* than anything else, though. The earlier *Dinosaur* aims for the scope, the grandeur, and the inspirational tale of an individual overcoming adversity. *The Wild*, meanwhile, is hung up on nicking the smallest of details – a lion cub who hasn't found his roar or a villain who is ultimately turned on by the henchman he has misled along the way.

Where *Dinosaur* manages to take bold decisions and make them blandly inoffensive, *The Wild* makes the blandest possible decisions and makes them boldly offensive. What if we have a snake who is incredibly stupid except for the one moment that matters? What if we make this cute koala extremely crude? What if – *what if* – we make this six-inch tall squirrel a certified sex pest who harasses a giraffe for the entire film because he is convinced she loves him? And what if, at the film's end, we justify his actions by revealing that she does?

There is a simple reason why *The Wild* isn't included as an animated classic in this book: it wasn't produced by Walt Disney Animation Studios. Instead, the film was animated by C.O.R.E. Feature Animation in Canada, who had previously worked on CGI for live-action Disney films like *Flubber* and *Dr. Dolittle*.

2. See also *Antz/A Bug's Life* and *Shark Tale/Finding Nemo*.

But really, part of me is glad that the film does not qualify because, frankly, *The Wild* does not deserve to be an animated classic. There are other films in the Disney canon that offer tired plots and uninspiring characters – *Dinosaur* is a great example. But generally speaking, even these films are boldly experimental and don't shy away from trying new things. The only thing *The Wild* tries is my patience.

Chapter 40

Llama Drama

The Emperor's New Groove • *2000* • *Mark Dindal*

Trudie Styler is roaming the halls of Disney's animation studios with a small team of documentarians by her side. As part of a deal to secure her husband, the rockstar Sting, as songwriter for their latest movie, Disney has given Styler permission to follow the production process over the coming months. Little do either party know that work on the new animated classic in question, *Kingdom of the Sun*, will be among the most tumultuous the studio has ever seen. There will be so much toxicity, in fact, that Disney will refuse to give Styler's documentary a full release.

The story of *Kingdom of the Sun* started long before Styler and Sting joined the party, though. In 1994, director Roger Allers was looking for a new project after the completion of megahit *The Lion King*. The studio encouraged him to look at ancient South American cultures for ideas, and Allers soon began to put together an outline for a film inspired by Anthony Hope's 1894 adventure novel, *The Prisoner of Zenda*. Like the book, his story would echo the classic *Prince and the Pauper* model, with a young, arrogant prince swapping places with a lookalike. Being a Disney film, there would be other elements in play, too: a villainous adviser with a plot to destroy the sun, a love story between the fake prince and his counterpart's fiancée, and a sentient rock, voiced by Harvey Fierstein. Oh, and the prince would get turned into a llama.

Allers was seen by senior leaders at Disney as one of the guiding lights that had turned *The Lion King* from a small side project into a blockbuster success. They were happy to let the director take the lead on his ambitious new project with little oversight – at least initially. Owen Wilson was cast in the lead role of the peasant who switches places with the prince. The villainous Yzma was to be voiced by Eartha Kitt (best known as the singer of 'Santa Baby' and for her role as Catwoman in the 1960s Batman series). Comedian David Spade was cast in the relatively minor role of Manco, the selfish prince. During this period, Allers approached Sting, asking him to write songs specific to various moments throughout the film.

Everything was going great, with actors recording their lines and Sting writing eight songs for the soundtrack. But then the Disney executives began to get cold feet. Allers had pitched the project as an epic musical drama in the mould of *The Lion King*. But recent releases that had attempted to do something similar had underperformed. Nobody could claim that *Pocahontas* and *Hunchback* were failures.

But they weren't *The Lion King*, and that's what Disney wanted. Producers brought on a co-director, veteran animator Mark Dindal, whose job would be to insert more comic moments into proceedings. Once again, production trundled along peacefully.

But by the summer of 1998, concerns were reaching new heights. Executives were unimpressed with progress and had begun to worry that the film would not be ready for its release date just two years down the line. They began to pressure producers, threatening to close down the entire production. This heightened pressure also brought new attention to the increasingly unwieldy mechanics of the plot. In an unprecedented move, Disney executives Thomas Schumacher and Peter Schneider split the *Kingdom of the Sun* team into two, encouraging each section to brainstorm ways to salvage the film. Styler's documentary, named *The Sweatbox* after the screening room in which editorial decisions are made about works in progress, begins at this crucial moment. We hear from Disney animators as they wait patiently in the halls of the feature animation department, wondering just how much of the last four years of work is about to be cut.

The answer: almost everything. Having been split in half, the creative team had come up with two very different proposals for *Kingdom of the Sun*. Allers, unwilling to kill his darling, had made some small changes, attempting to whittle the surplus elements down until they were more manageable. Dindal's team, on the other hand, proposed turning the epic drama into an irreverent comedy. Owen Wilson's character was gone, replaced by an older family man peasant. The talking rock was out, too. There was no *Prince and Pauper* switcheroo and no more love story. Instead, David Spade's arrogant prince would become the film's star, and Yzma, voiced by Eartha Kitt, would have a simpler plot in mind: murder. Only one other element of the original plot would remain: failing to kill the prince, Yzma would instead turn him into a llama.

It was a huge change – not least because the studio refused to move the release date. The team had less than two years to reboot the movie completely. And they would do it without the original mastermind, Allers, who stepped back after his vision was decimated by the changes.

Dindal became the sole director of the project, retooling it as a comedy and making various changes, big and small. In some cases, all that needed adjusting was a single word – *Kingdom of the Sun* became *Kingdom in the Sun*. Other elements needed a more significant shift. *The Sweatbox* captured the phone call in which it was revealed to Sting that more or less everything he'd written for the film had been scrapped. His songs, so closely interwoven with the Allers plot, were now irrelevant. Sting takes it in good stead, probably because he knows his wife is recording the whole thing, but promptly heads off to the Himalayas to do whatever it is that Sting does to blow off steam. I don't know, gong bath therapy, something like that.

By the time the dust had settled, there was barely a year left to go until the film's proposed release date. John Goodman had taken on the peasant role of Pacha, and Sting had returned from the mountains to deliver just two songs for the film. The first of these was a big number that would introduce audiences to Spade's spoiled prince. Disney suggested that Sting sing it, and the musician countered by suggesting that a younger artist take it on. In the end, neither got their way: 'Perfect World' was performed by a bombastic Tom Jones, who is eleven years older than Sting.

There was one area in which Sting finally got his way, though. The film's conclusion sees the prince finally learn about the fairly basic concept of 'kindness', agreeing not to build his holiday home/water park on top of Pacha's village. Originally, Dindal and his team planned on having him build it directly next to Pacha's village instead, decimating a patch of rainforest to do so. Sting, who has a long history of championing the rights of Indigenous people, was furious. *The Sweatbox* shows him reading out a letter of dissent that he has just written before cutting to the production team as they read it. One of them cheerfully agrees that the rockstar has a valid point, while the rockstar's wife has a camera pointed at him. Still, faced with Sting's threat to resign from the film, the team made a small change to the finale – now the prince simply holidays in a small shack alongside the rest of the village's residents.

As the release date came around (albeit pushed back, at last, by six months), there were some final changes to be made. The prince was renamed Cuzco after the production team discovered that 'Manco' sounded more or less the same as the Japanese equivalent of the rudest word you know. Yes, that one. The film's title changed again, too, settling on *The Emperor's New Groove*. It was a divisive choice, particularly among critics, who thought it was broadly meaningless while alluding to the story of *The Emperor's New Clothes*, a classic fairytale that has absolutely nothing to do with the film's plot. And it's a fair comment. If you don't know anything about *The Emperor's New Groove*, the title doesn't make any sense at all. However, if you've seen the film, the title is... well, still pretty abstract.

The Emperor's New Groove came out in December 2000 and promptly bombed – at least by Disney's expected standards. Its box office was less than half of Dinosaur's, which had taken the summer slot vacated by the film as production dragged on. The delays had been costly – not only had the budget ballooned to $100 million, but the postponed release date had also put the film up in direct competition with two major family film releases – *How The Grinch Stole Christmas* and Disney's own live-action sequel, *102 Dalmatians*.

To make matters worse, in March of the same year, Jeffrey Katzenberg's Dreamworks also released a buddy comedy set among an ancient South American civilisation. *The Road to El Dorado* (another relative flop) was set in the last days of the Aztec empire. It marked a point of contention at Disney, not the first time Dreamworks had released a film that bore at least a passing resemblance to a project being developed during his time at the studio.

For a while, it looked like all of the internal battles during the creation of *The Emperor's New Groove* had been in vain. But Disney hadn't counted on the influence of the still fledgling internet. The irreverent comedy Mark Dindal brought to the film was ahead of its time – filled with surreal moments and the breaking of the fourth wall. In the years that followed, young audiences would connect with these gags, and before long, the film had become a cult sensation in certain circles. To this day, it remains one of the funniest films in the Disney canon and, alongside *Lilo & Stitch*, one of the few bright spots of the Post-Renaissance Era.

Disney has refused to release *The Sweatbox* in full, editing it significantly for a DVD bonus feature and allowing an approved edit to be screened only in a few industry-related situations. It's a shame because it offers real insight into the ongoing battle between Hollywood's creative and corporate sides, showing both as capable of making mistakes. It also has another effect, enhancing audience appreciation for the film at the heart of all the conflict. Amid all the stress behind the scenes, audiences think to themselves, how on earth did they end up making a film this fun?

Chapter 41

Mirror, Mirror

Atlantis: The Lost Empire • *2001* • *Gary Trousdale, Kirk Wise*

A steampunk adventure inspired by the novels of Jules Verne. A plucky young genius with strawberry blonde hair and big round glasses. A lively love interest who wears a magic crystal around her neck. And, of course, the mystery and majesty of the mythical lost city of Atlantis.

All of these things can be found in the 1990 anime series, *Nadia: The Secret of Blue Water*. Also, they all turn up a decade later in the final film from Disney's powerhouse directorial duo of Trousdale and Wise.

Atlantis: The Lost Empire turns up in the heady rush of Post-Renaissance films that hit big screens at the beginning of the new millennium – the fourth new animated classic to land in cinemas in just 14 months. And while it isn't a patch on the directors' past two films, *Beauty and the Beast* and *Hunchback*, it holds up pretty well today.

Atlantis is an adventure, after all – and it really feels like it thanks to ambitious plotting, impressive scope, and a surprisingly big death toll.[1] The gawky Milo Thatch is a boiler engineer with a dream: to discover the sunken city that his grandfather so firmly believed in. Like all dreams that involve people dying in submarines in the deepest of oceanic crevices, Milo's is funded by a crackpot millionaire.

The film signposts much of its plot pretty clearly. There's an overtly sexual German woman who appears to be equal parts Jessica Rabbit and Alison Doody's "Surprise! She's a villain!" character from *Indiana Jones and the Last Crusade*. James Garner voices a captain who is unafraid to hint heavily at his planned deception even while still standing in the dock. But audiences won't mind, because the action keeps moving, the animation is vibrant and diverting, and the characters are (mostly) likeable.[2]

1. Youtube film statisticians Film Theory estimate as many as 35,000 deaths in the film. Most of these come from tying the destruction that sinks Atlantis to a volcanic eruption covered in Plato's *Critias*, but given the film itself opens with a quote from the text, that seems fair game. Even without the eruption's involvement, the film has an impressive 185 onscreen deaths, thanks mostly to a disastrous encounter with a leviathan. The Disney film with the most deaths, however, came out just over a year earlier: the meteor in *Dinosaur* is estimated to kill off hundreds of thousands of lemurs. Points for the most onscreen deaths go to Mulan – both the film, and the individual character, who manages to single-handedly wipe out over a thousand soldiers during the avalanche scene.
2. Well, all except the one-dimensional Moliere, who is one the most irritating characters to feature in a Disney film since *The Black Cauldron*'s Gurgi.

One of the biggest creative undertakings for the film was the creation of a whole new language – Atlantean. Originated by linguist Marc Okrand specifically for use in the film, Atlantean was designed to be a fictional mother language, with roots that could have inspired many of the dialects in use around the world today. Whopping great nerds among you may know Okrand already, as creator of the Klingon language in *Star Trek*.

Given the tremendous effort made to create a breathtaking and immersive new civilisation, it was a surprise to many when, in the wake of the film's release, some viewers suggested a raft of similarities with *Nadia: The Secret of Blue Water*.

The series, which ran for thirty-nine episodes, is now mostly forgotten outside of its native Japan but was hugely influential in its time.[3] On a broad level, the plot varies greatly from *Atlantis*. Where Disney's film deals with a trip to the bottom of the ocean and pitches the mythical citadel as peaceful, much of *Nadia* occurs at or above sea level and has the (Neo-)Atlantean people act as the show's primary antagonists. But those earlier comparisons are hard to miss – particularly the powerful crystal and distinctly steampunk themes.

However, *Atlantis* wasn't the first time a Disney film had been accused of plagiarising an anime series. In 1994, even as *The Lion King* was breaking box office records, several newspaper and magazine articles highlighted the similarities between the film and another Japanese series, *Jungle Emperor* – which had been released in the United States under the name *Kimba the White Lion*.

Based on a popular manga from the early 1950s, the original 1965 run of *Jungle Emperor* was Japan's first colour-animated TV series and became a cultural phenomenon across the country. It was even broadcast overseas, dubbed into English and shown in the United States in 1966. In fact, the show's protagonist wasn't even called Kimba until the English dub was recorded. In the original Japanese show, he's known as Leo, but to avoid copyright issues, the name was changed. Initially, the name Simba was considered, but again, copyright fears intervened. 'Simba' is literally the Swahili word for 'lion'. It seemed safer to create an altogether new name. Kimba was born.

Like *Nadia* and *Atlantis*, a quick look over the plots of *Jungle Emperor* and *The Lion King* reveals more differences than similarities. Yes, both lions have lost their fathers. Still, Kimba takes on his newfound responsibility and attempts to bring peace immediately, where Simba moves from arrogant little nepo cub to self-absorbed and focused on self-preservation. There is also a very prominent human presence in *Jungle Emperor*, something that is entirely missing from Disney's story.[4]

3. The series also comes from a remarkable pedigree, having first been conceived some 15 years earlier by Hayao Miyazaki. Since Walt Disney's death, no animator has made as great an impact on the artform as Miyazaki, who is best known for his work with Studio Ghibli, where he has directed films including *Spirited Away*, *My Neighbour Totoro* and *The Boy and the Heron*. His early film *Laputa: Castle in the Sky* also makes liberal use of the ideas first compiled for the early treatment of *Nadia*.
4. While we're at it, another surprisingly big element of the *Jungle Emperor* plot is that after the death of Kimba's father, the animals somehow manage to retrieve his hide. As a result, Kimba

And yet, some similarities have been hard to ignore. Kimba's late parents appear to him in the sky to impart wisdom. Certain visually striking scenes seem to be replicated closely in the later film, including the stampede and elements of *The Lion King*'s climactic fight. One frequently cited piece of evidence is a piece of early Disney concept art in which Simba appears white. I'm not even going to *try* and secure the rights for that in this book, but your internet search engine of choice will dig it up in no time at all.

Disney has long been adamant that any similarities between the two films are purely coincidental, though some point to comments made by animators on the project who claim to have brought up the resemblance to the original anime during production. Others highlight the fact that co-director Roger Allers worked at a Tokyo animation studio between 1983 and 1985 – though, as far as my research can tell, the show wasn't being broadcast in Japan during that period. In fact, it was aired in the United States in 1984 – so if anything, there's a case to be made that Allers was the one person working on the project who *hadn't* had an opportunity to watch the original anime. A remake was released in Japan in 1989 but didn't make it to North America until almost a decade later, long after *The Lion King*'s release.

Disney's argument concerning the great Kimba vs. Simba debate has usually gone something like this: we made a cartoon about a lion and set it in Africa. *Jungle Emperor* is a cartoon about a lion in Africa. Of course, there are similarities. Mandrills, lions, and hyenas will always make for interesting characters.

It's very possible that there was some purposeful replication of *Jungle Emperor* in *The Lion King*. But that's all: small reflections that pay tribute to an iconic anime series that bears no significant resemblance besides these brief homages. Several hundred people worked on the film – why wouldn't one want to slip in a sly nod to the show? After all, art is the culmination of our influences: even the creator of *Jungle Emperor* spoke of how Disney's *Bambi* shaped his original manga series.

With *Atlantis*, the source of the reflection is even clearer, and it absolutely does come down to a theft of sorts – albeit a very loving thievery, and not from *Nadia*. Instead, almost every similarity between the two projects seems to stem wholly from their mutual love of Jules Verne's fantastical novels and, in particular, *Journey to the Centre of the Earth* and *Twenty Thousand Leagues Under the Seas.*[5] These books feature terrifying sea beasts, magnificent crystals and, of course, the lost city of Atlantis.

---

regularly chats to the skin of his dead father, and on several occasions he and his friends *wear* it as a disguise. I'm honestly grateful that Disney didn't nick this plot point for *The Lion King*. Though it might have made *The Lion King 1½* a tad more interesting.

5. You heard me: it's 'Seas', not 'Sea'. In fact, while we're at it, what direction do you think those 20,000 leagues take? I'll give you a clue: it isn't down. 20,000 leagues is around 60,000 miles – enough to travel directly through the earth from one side to the other more than seven times over. The Nautilus – Captain Nemo's ship in the book – just goes down into the sea a little (that's the under bit), and chugs along nicely for 60,000 miles (which is still more than twice the planet's circumference.)

For thousands of years, we have relied on forms of plagiarism to inform our storytelling. The myths of ancient civilisations mirror each other endlessly. Three of the planet's biggest religions are built around the same stories of the same god. Shakespeare stole liberally. *Harry Potter*, *Star Wars*, *The Hunger Games*, and *The Wizard of Oz* are just a few of the hundreds of stories that follow the 'hero's journey' pattern. *Cars* is just *Doc Hollywood* with hubcaps. *Rebel Moon* is *A Bug's Life* is *The Magnificent Seven* is *Seven Samurai*. And even then, *Seven Samurai* was heavily influenced by the cowboy films of John Ford.

We are overwhelmingly fortunate to live in a world swamped with stories – but we shouldn't deceive ourselves into thinking that any tale is truly free of outside influence. We are right to champion new voices and defend the rights of others to receive credit for the stories they have shaped. But there is a balancing act: when does influence become theft? When does theft become homage? When do we accept that the world is better for having both Liam Neeson's *Taken* and Pixar's *Finding Nemo* even if they are both – and you know I'm right here – the exact same film?[6]

6. Both of the film's lead characters lose a child to abduction! Both travel around the world to save them! Both are wildly overprotective single fathers! And that's not even getting to the scene in *Taken* where Liam Neeson accidentally attends a vegan support group, or the deeply aggressive phone call that Marlin makes to an Australian dentist's office, rambling on about his 'particular set of gills'.

Chapter 42

Close Encounters of the Merch Kind

Lilo & Stitch • *2002* • *Dean DeBlois, Chris Sanders*

A few years ago, while visiting family in Brazil, I stumbled upon a strange phenomenon. We were in a beach town a few hours north of Rio de Janeiro, escaping the afternoon heat by flitting from shop to shop along the beachfront. The stalls were small, and their facades were each completely open; an attempt was being made to coax in both avid customers and the cool sea breeze. Some of the shopkeepers were selling local crafts – handmade necklaces, caipirinha-making sets and small sculptures of fishing boats, anchors and other maritime fare. There were Havianas, of course, and colourful towels in varying designs. And then there were T-shirts. Stacks and stacks of T-shirts. And in every store with a stack of T-shirts, there was one repeated motif: the sweet little shrug of Marie from *The Aristocats*.

I couldn't get my head around it. *The Aristocats* is hardly the most iconic of the Disney classics, and Marie isn't exactly the most likeable character in the film. In fact, she's frequently an entitled little telltale. A spoilt posh girl who seemingly has only two interests: romance, and falling off things. Why then, I thought, are the Brazilians so enamoured with her?

As it turned out, it was not just Brazilians. A year later, I spotted her in European clothing stores, and before long, her pristine little face was emblazoned across T-shirts and pyjama sets in UK shops, too. After a while, I came to realise that while *some* of the people buying these items must be die-hard *Aristocats* fans, for many, it didn't matter at all. Marie is, if not anything else, a pretty and feminine cartoon character. Though she can be an absolute tyrant in the film, she looks innocent and harmless on a 7-year-old girl's T-shirt. It's the perfect apparel for someone whose parents are still stuck in the 1970s mindset when it comes to gender norms.

In recent years, though, another Disney character has staked a claim in the same spots that Marie once called her home. A little blue alien invader has become more ubiquitous than anyone might have expected – particularly given that he represents more or less the exact opposite of innocent old Marie.

* * *

In so many ways, *Lilo & Stitch* feels at odds with much of the Disney canon. Its characters don't sing songs – instead, audiences are treated to a number of Elvis

Presley classics, as well as two non-diegetic originals sung in 'Ōlelo Hawai'i, the native language of the film's island setting. There's no love story, at least not in the romantic sense. Even the artwork is a distinct step away from the usual Disney style, instead reflecting the fuller figures favoured by artist Chris Sanders, who pulls quadruple duty on the film as writer, director, concept artist and star (Sanders voices Stitch, a character he first conceived of in the mid-1980s).

It was a conscious effort by Disney to try something new. Recent big-budget films had been box-office disappointments. In response, one of the animation studio's most senior figures, Thomas Schumacher, suggested a smaller project that wouldn't need to be a huge hit to qualify as a success. It was an approach the studio had taken in the 1940s, when *Dumbo* served as a simple project after the elaborate run of *Snow White*, *Pinocchio* and *Fantasia*.

Tasked with taking on this low-budget film, Sanders revived an old idea he'd had for a children's book about an alien lost and alone among the creatures of a remote forest. Before long, the premise evolved into *Lilo & Stitch*'s exquisitely balanced plot, which effortlessly juggles kitchen-sink family drama with outlandish sci-fi adventure.

Every element of *Lilo & Stitch* is perfectly realised. The film was animated in Disney's Florida studios, which were seen by many as second tier, being based in the middle of a literal theme park where guests could pass through and see the artists at work on the film's unique characters and stunning watercolour backgrounds.[1] For Sanders, though, the underdog reputation of the studio meant the staff there were always eager to prove themselves. He was reminded of Walt's studio as they toiled towards *Snow White* while the rest of Hollywood jeered outside.

Hidden down in Florida, the *Lilo & Stitch* team was able to fly under the radar. While Eisner gave notes on projects being developed in the Hollywood studios, Schumacher went to lengths to keep the film out of sight until it was in a state where he knew it would get the right reaction.

It meant that Sanders and his co-director, Dean DeBlois, could take the approach they felt was necessary to tell the story. They could develop a leading lady, in the 6-year-old Lilo, who was unlike any Disney protagonist who had come before. She looks and acts like a real child, small and stumpy and prone to outrageous and nonsensical behaviour. She yells at her sister, Nani, and Nani yells back. The Hawaiian actress Tia Carrere plays this older sibling. Alongside Jason Scott Lee, another actor in the film who grew up in the state, Carrere was integral to bringing authentic voices to the characters. Hawaiian Pidgin sneaks into the dialogue throughout the film. In recent years, Disney has been at pains to ensure that its work is a true representation of the cultures featured. In 2002, Sanders and DeBlois were well ahead of the curve, and *Lilo & Stitch* is all the better for it, offering meaningful

1. Many of the curious tourists that Lilo photographs and keeps on her wall are based on the theme park guests who visited during production.

echoes of the difficulty of life in Hawai'i during the economic downturn at the beginning of the new century.

* * *

It might be tempting to think that Stitch's ever-growing merchandise presence simply results from his being the star of what is – and I do not say this lightly – very possibly the best film among all of Disney's animated canon. *Lilo & Stitch* was, after all, a huge success at the time of its release – it easily made back its budget and even gave the Steven Spielberg/Tom Cruise smash *Minority Report* a close run at the box office.[2] It was nominated for an Academy Award and only lost out to the revelatory Studio Ghibli film *Spirited Away*.[3]

Equally, audience members who first fell in love with it as children are now adults who have disposable income to spend. Stitch is, after all, not limited to t-shirts. He appears on phone cases, lamps, picture frames, soft furnishings and kitchenware. In early 2024, retailer Primark opened a Stitch café in one of its UK stores – not content with selling Stitch fidget toys and make-up sponges, the store added Hawaiian-themed waffles and sandwiches.

Ultimately, though, I suspect Stitch's popularity comes down to the exact same thing as Marie's; it's all about what he stands for. And Stitch fits much better with modern sensibilities than a clean-cut kitten. He captures our messiness, our chaos, and our inherent desire to do better. It helps too, of course, that he is very, very cute.[4] The only slight disappointment in the whole merchandise affair is that, presumably because Stitch is blue, and for some very drab folk, 'blue' means 'boy', Disney has frequently paired him on t-shirts, mugs and bags with a pink equivalent named Angel. Within the *Lilo & Stitch* canon, Angel is the Experiment 624 to Stitch's 626, first seen in the film's spin-off TV show.

It's a shame that, potentially by sheer virtue of being pink, Angel has taken such a significant spot in the *Lilo & Stitch* merch. Not least because the film features two of the more well-written and realistic women seen within the entire Disney canon. Maybe Nani isn't an obvious choice for the side of a mug. But Lilo – sweet, stocky Lilo with her wide eyes and her stubby little fingers – is surely worthy of a spot? Someone let Primark know: the best character in the Disney oeuvre is sitting right there, and it's a crime of intergalactic proportions that I can't get her on a T-shirt.

---

2. In 2025, the film's live action remake upset expectations by out-performing Cruise's final Mission: Impossible movie on their opening weekend.
3. The lead character of *Spirited Away*, incidentally, was voiced by the same actress who played Lilo, Daveigh Chase. Talk about hedging your bets. Chase has one other iconic role to her name, though it's much less family-friendly. In the American remake of *The Ring*, it's the voice of Lilo who drags herself from the well and crawls out of the TV screen.
4. Stitch's design is echoed in another iconic character of early 2000s animation: *How to Train Your Dragon*'s Toothless, who was also designed by Chris Sanders.

Chapter 43

2002: A Space Odyssey

Treasure Planet • 2002 • Ron Clements, John Musker

The story of *Treasure Planet* is one of dogged determination and faith in an idea, even when nobody else believes in it. Can you think of anything more Disney?

Like *Alice in Wonderland* before it, *Treasure Planet*'s journey to the screen was decades in the making. For the longest time, the passion project of the directing duo Ron Clements and John Musker was little more than an ambition that the pair refused to let go of. The directors pitched the film four times over the course of eleven years before they would finally get their way – wearing down studio execs like two children refusing to let their parents rest until they give in and bring home a puppy. The only problem was that this puppy was going to cost $140 million.

Musker and Clements' first pitch for the project came in 1985 while they were still in production for their first collaboration for the studio, *The Great Mouse Detective*. Knowing that Paramount Pictures was developing a *Star Trek* take on Robert Louis Stevenson's novel, the studio's then-CEO, Jeffrey Katzenberg, shot down the pitch. It wasn't all bad news for the directors, though; another idea floated by them at the same meeting was greenlit instead – *The Little Mermaid*. That film was a huge smash, and as the new decade dawned and the pair found themselves responsible for Disney's biggest hit in years, Clements and Musker pitched again. Disney still wasn't interested, and they got to work on another new project.

How do you follow up a film like *The Little Mermaid*? Easy. You knock out *Aladdin*, change the voice-acting landscape of animated cinema forever, and begin to make all those directors who struggled for decades to make a successful Disney film look like they weren't even trying. Surely, this time around, their pitch for *Treasure Planet* was a surefire thing?

Well, no. It turned out that Katzenberg had an outright animosity towards the idea of Treasure Island in space, and for a third time, the pair's ambitions were shot out of orbit. At this point, you'd think it was time to give up on the film – especially when, in 1995, Disney bought the distribution rights to another version of the story: *Muppet Treasure Island*.

But Clements and Musker refused to give up on their dream, and while directing *Hercules* they managed to get things underway at last. Making the most of a contract renegotiation (and taking advantage of Katzenberg's departure from Disney), the directors finally began work on *Treasure Planet*.

Now for the plot twist: after seventeen years of being told that their film wasn't good enough for the studio, of fighting to deliver their vision and to prove its worth to the studio execs who had doubted them from the start, *Treasure Planet* was released on 27 November 2002.

And it was an instant failure.

Upon release, *Treasure Planet* was – by some margin – Disney's biggest flop to date, making just $109.6 million at the worldwide box office on a budget of around $140 million. In the years since there's been a great deal of discussion about what exactly went wrong. Some have pointed to a downward trend in Disney's releases at the time – the fallout, perhaps, from the hugely successful Dreamworks film *Shrek* that came out a year previously. Others blame the film's lacklustre script or the curious mix between clean-cut computer-generated scenery and ugly, lumpy hand-drawn aliens (the film's main villain, Long John Silver, is actually a hybrid of the two, with his mechanical arm rendered by a computer and added to the traditional animation later).

Others still argue that sci-fi adventure animations were always doomed to fail, pointing at the disappointing box office performance of *Atlantis: The Lost Empire* and Don Bluth's *Titan A.E.* in 2000, a film that did so poorly that Fox Animation Studios folded just a week after its release.

Maybe Disney was right not to have believed in *Treasure Planet*. But, also, maybe that lack of belief helped fuel its failure. After all, one of the three films that out-performed *Treasure Planet* on its opening weekend was Disney's own *The Santa Clause 2*. It's one thing to lose a cut of your audience to *Harry Potter and the Chamber of Secrets* and another thing entirely to lose them to a sequel released by your parent company just a few weeks earlier.

The more interesting question around *Treasure Planet* is not what went wrong in 2002 but what has gone right in the two decades since the film's release. Because while the film might not have the lasting merchandise pull of *Lilo & Stitch*, which came out just five months earlier, it remains perhaps the most talked about film from this relatively dark patch in Disney's history. After fighting for years to get it made and then watching it flounder at the box office, Clements and Musker have finally seen their film find a dedicated and passionate audience.

TikTok absolutely loves *Treasure Planet*. Stumble upon the right corner of the app, and you'll find film bros rhapsodising about the film's stunning visuals – the hybrid scenes that combined groundbreaking CGI with traditional hand-drawn animation. You'll watch fan edits that capture this same beauty and pair it with cuts of Long John Silver's moving speech about taking charge of your own destiny. There are a fair few people who appear to have had a sexual awakening while watching the semi-feline Captain Amelia, as voiced by Emma Thompson. At least one person feels the same way about David Hyde Pierce from Frasier and his man-dog Niles-in-space character, Doctor Doppler. That one is not a choice I wish to examine in any great depth, but it is a choice that has been made nonetheless.[1]

1. I also have a theory that the popularity of Jim Hawkins among Gen Z audiences is at least in part responsible for the current prevalence of the undercut hair-style favoured by the character.

What does this say about *Treasure Planet*? What does this say, even, about Gen Z, who continue to fawn over this ambitious hodge-podge of ideas and its unfulfilled glimpses at a complex tale about father figures and their role in our development? Honestly, nothing.

All that we should take from the growing popularity of the film is that over twenty years have passed since its release, and the adult voices we now hear celebrating *Treasure Planet* were once the children for whom the film was made in the first place. These are the opinions of those who watched *Treasure Planet* at their sixth birthday party and were blown away by an intergalactic pirate adventure. Roger Ebert may not have understood the appeal in 2002, but these kids did. And now they're here to tell us why we're wrong about it.

And are we wrong about it? Well, not entirely. We are, at least, a little justified when we imply that the film was rightly a flop. Because this is a phenomenon that echoes through every era of Disney's output. It is a reappraisal fuelled by nostalgia. If you've ever revisited a film you loved as a child – the sort of movie you watched over and over again on VHS or DVD – you'll know that the experience can go one of two ways. Maybe you'll find what you always found: comfort incarnate, unbridled joy and warm familiarity. Or maybe you'll wonder what you ever liked about it. So many movies we loved in our youth turn out to be charmless chores later in life.

As far as I can tell, what determines your adult feelings about a childhood favourite varies from person to person. Art is, after all, subjective, and what opinion lies further from object reality than "*The Black Cauldron* is a fun film that is easy to follow and totally suitable for young children"?

The films we grow most attached to, of course, are those that we are exposed to most in our formative years. And this is perhaps part of the reason, too, for the phenomenal growth in adult Disney fans over the past two decades. For many years, Disney's films were hard to come by – limited to short theatrical runs and occasional re-releases, and television screenings that relied on a child's physical presence in front of the screen at the moment of broadcast.

In the 1980s, home video releases empowered children to claim individual films as their own for the first time, and video recorders enabled television screenings to be captured on VHS to be rewatched until the scenery wobbled and Baloo spoke with a strange metallic distortion, like a drunken animatronic at Disneyland. I can still tell you exactly which films were recorded onto which tapes – the ritual of rewatching scorched upon my mind. *Dumbo* into *Mary Poppins*. *Robin Hood* into two minutes of ITV adverts into *The Sword in the Stone*.[2]

2. Disney executives were initially deeply resistant to the idea of releasing their animated classics on VHS. Cinematic rereleases were a core part of their strategy, and they were wary of cutting this revenue stream. As a result, one of the first classics to make it to market, *Dumbo*, was sold at a ludicrously high price of $84.95 – around $280 today, adjusted for inflation. In 1985, Disney's head of home video, Bill Mechanic, experimented with a (somewhat) cheaper release. A $29.95 *Pinocchio* VHS promptly sold out 1.7 million copies. Disney quickly embraced the new medium, though they would continue to create scarcity in the decades to come, only releasing films for short periods before withdrawing them once more.

Children of the 1990s had a stronger connection to Disney films – old and new – than any generation that had come before them. Suddenly, sixty years of animated classics were discoverable, either in limited-time-only official releases or captured off the telly on Boxing Day morning.

The children who were watching *Treasure Planet* in 2002 lived in a period where these films were also shown regularly on the Disney Channel. It's no wonder so many adults today feel such a strong connection to the studio – their childhoods were awash with Disney's films and television programmes. As they move through their grown-up lives, their encounters with these characters are saturated with nostalgia.

So we look back now on *Treasure Planet* as it approaches a quarter century as part of the Disney lexicon. We can openly receive it as another animated classic that might not rank among the studio's greatest achievements but will always have a stronghold of fans ready to drop anchor at a moment's notice and settle themselves down to watch some pirates muck about in space. It took forty years to get here, but at last, somebody else truly appreciates Clements and Musker's vision.

Chapter 44

And the Winner is…

Brother Bear • *2003* • *Aaron Blaise, Robert Walker*

The 76th Academy Awards were among the most one-sided ceremonies in film history. Peter Jackson's landmark *Lord of the Rings* trilogy had recently come to a close. Feeling guilty about relegating the previous two films to technical and musical wins, the Academy decided to offer the final instalment, *The Return of the King*, as many statuettes as could fit in Jackson's arms. The film won every single one of the eleven awards it had been nominated for, tying for the record with *Titanic* and *Ben-Hur*.

Honestly, it must have been a little boring on the night. The same announcement, over and over again: 'And the winner is…'.

By the time Robin Williams took to the stage – hiding behind master of ceremonies Billy Crystal to deliver an unconvincing ventriloquism bit – the audience must have been thrilled for a change of pace. After all, Williams was here to announce the winner of Best Animated Feature – one of the few awards for which *The Return of the King* had never had a look-in.

The Best Animated Feature award has a shorter history than you might think – it was only inaugurated in 2001, when the rise of studios like Dreamworks meant that there was some actual competition to be had. For much of the Academy's history, members had not seen adequate reason to create the category – Disney was the only studio regularly releasing features that might have actually warranted an award. And yet, there was little room for Walt or his predecessors in the running of more prestigious categories either. Despite *Snow White*'s instant success and universal acclaim in 1937, the film was not nominated for Best Picture. Instead, Walt took home an honorary Oscar statuette (and seven miniature ones). The studio had seen only one of their animated features enter the running for Best Picture: *Beauty and the Beast*. The film lost out to *The Silence of the Lambs*, another movie about a serious-minded woman forced to get along with a monstrous man.

And so the 76th Academy Awards marked only the third occasion that the accolade for Best Animated Feature had even been on the table. And so far, Disney had yet to win in the category. The inaugural trophy had gone to *Shrek*, and its genre- and Disney-defying fairytale upending. Disney had not even had a direct nomination that year, settling instead for a nod in favour of Pixar's *Monsters Inc.* The following awards ceremony had been only a little better – both *Lilo & Stitch* and *Treasure Planet* had been nominated, but the prize had gone to Studio Ghibli's anime masterpiece *Spirited Away*. Surely it would be third time lucky.

The number of nominees for Best Animated Feature has historically varied from year to year, depending on the quality of the films released. Since 2011, we've consistently managed the maximum number of nominees possible – five. But in 2003, only three films made the cut; each neatly representing the transitional state of the animation industry at that distinct moment in time.

Brother Bear represented the old school of American animation, a traditional Disney cartoon complete with talking animals and meaningful life lessons. Most of the artwork had been hand-drawn, even if it was digitally coloured and featured CGI sequences. The story was set in Alaska, some 10,000 years ago, and followed a young Inuit named Kenai who was taught a lesson in empathy by the northern lights. Turned into a bear, Kenai set out on a journey to attempt to return to his human form, but along the way, he developed a kinship with an orphaned bear cub.

It's all so elementary, so generic, that it's actually surprising to realise that *Brother Bear* is only the second animated classic to transform its lead character into an animal for the duration of the film.[1] Thomas Schumacher declared an early plot treatment as 'the idea of the century', which was a pretty bold claim to make when pre-production started in 1997, when the century in question had more or less run its course and seen the invention of the internet, aeroplanes, television, modern computers and instant ramen. But by all means, the human-turns-into-animal story tops the bill.

The second nominee, *Finding Nemo*, only served to further put the film's old-fashioned approach under the spotlight. Pixar had already been on a tremendous run of hits, starting with 1995's groundbreaking *Toy Story* and continuing up to *Monsters Inc.* the year before. But *Finding Nemo* stepped the studio's game up to an entirely new level. Thus far, Disney had managed a single CGI film in *Dinosaur*, while Pixar sat at the forefront of the technology. Each new film showcased phenomenal new effects – for *Monsters Inc.*, the studio had developed a tool that could animate over a million hairs on the lead character, Sully. *Finding Nemo* saw Pixar build upon early techniques for creating realistic computer-animated water.

It didn't help that *Finding Nemo* had a more interesting and original plot than *Brother Bear*. It still dealt with familiar themes – overprotective parents, fear of the unknown – but it did so with elan and creativity. Its stars – from the diminutive Nemo to the amnesiac Dory – were instantly iconic. Try walking through any aquarium

1. Disney had begun the transformation of Pinocchio into a donkey, but never saw it through beyond the ears and the tail. Beast is already turned long before Belle shows up, and Arthur's exploits in *The Sword and the Stone* are brief and voluntary. In fact, it wasn't until *The Emperor's New Groove* that a character's change was the heart of the film. The phenomenon occurs only once more in the canon to date, in *The Princess and the Frog*, but there are plenty of examples in other releases by the wider Disney company, from Pixar's *Brave* and *Turning Red* to live-action features like *The Shaggy Dog*.

without hearing some small child gleefully exclaim that they've seen Dory. Few children are getting hepped up at zoos because they've just spotted Kenai or Koda.

And, as a final blow to Disney, *Finding Nemo* had come out during their very public separation from Pixar. In part due to concerns around the direction of Disney, and perhaps in part because Eisner had very publicly commented on the perceived piracy-encouraging nature of the Apple iPod, Pixar chairman (and Apple CEO) Steve Jobs had refused to extend the studio's working relationship with Disney while Eisner remained in charge. *Finding Nemo* came out amid a long period of uncertainty regarding Disney and Pixar's relationship. Robin Williams (himself nursing his long-standing grudge against Disney's corporate ruthlessness) even alluded to the situation as he introduced the category during the Oscars, addressing Eisner directly while in character as a cigarette-smoking French Minnie Mouse.

And Williams wasn't the only French voice criticising Disney at the time. The third nominee on the roster in February of 2004 was an independent film called *Les Triplettes de Belleville* (translated directly to *The Triplets of Belleville* in the States and renamed *Belleville Rendezvous* in the UK and Ireland). An international co-production between companies in France, Belgium, the UK and Canada, the film has a distinctly French vibe – which is to say there's a lot more smoking than in other animated films of the period, and the whole plot is built around the kidnapping of a Tour de France cyclist.

Les Triplettes de Belleville also stands out visually. While it echoes the animation techniques Disney was using at the time – mostly hand-drawn with elements of CGI to simplify complex elements – it couldn't look any different. Director Sylvain Chomet delivers a gritty, brownscale style filled with grotesque characters. The kidnapped cyclist is occasionally genuinely unpleasant to look at, equal parts sinewy limbs and bulging muscle. A truck that follows the cyclists as they race is topped with a grinning accordionist whose teeth are filled with the bugs that fly into her face.

Animation has never been an exclusively American endeavour, and the new Oscars category finally offered an opportunity to highlight films made elsewhere. International animation functions similarly to international filmmaking as a whole: with Hollywood acting as such a dominant force, the movies that break through are often the most distinctive, the most original. The most unlike anything a major American studio might think to create. To date, only two international animations have won Best Animated Feature – *Spirited Away* and another Studio Ghibli release, *The Boy and the Heron*. But tucked among the last two decades or so of nominations, you'll find a treasure trove of innovative, daring and occasionally deeply strange films. *Loving Vincent. My Life as a Courgette. I Lost My Body.* Some of the most political feature films ever nominated at the Oscars have made their way in via this category. *Persepolis* is a coming-of-age story set against the backdrop of the Iranian Revolution of 1979. *Flee* is a deeply moving documentary about a refugee from Afghanistan.

By comparison, *Les Triplettes de Belleville* has less to say – except in one specific area. It's clear that Chomet has some qualms about the studio that continued to dominate the animated world even as it slumped into one of its occasional creative fallow periods. Disney is the target of a few jibes in the film – most notably a visible Mickey Mouse-shaped turd floating in a toilet in the background of one scene and, later, a photo of a character at a theme park. They are wearing Mickey ears and holding a huge lollipop that has a word printed onto it: SUCKER. Disney was still something of a controversial entity in France, where their Paris theme park continued to underperform.

Anyway, Robin Williams continues to avoid the task at hand for almost as long as I have, but eventually remembers why he's onstage. He makes a big show of opening the envelope, and announces the recipient of the award. And the winner is… *Finding Nemo.*

Brother Bear never really had a chance, squeezed into a category alongside two far more original, far more interesting prospects. In fact, as Disney continued to flounder and the world of animated cinema exploded with new and exciting talent, the studio's animated classics would continue to be trounced year after year. Eventually, a full decade later, Disney would win their first Best Animated Feature statuette for *Frozen*. In the intervening years, Pixar would win no less than six times, Michael Eisner would be ousted, and Steve Jobs would sell his studio to Disney for over $7 billion. But that was some way off, and after the release of *Brother Bear*, it would be five full years until Disney would even get another nomination. All of which is to say: we've got a rough few chapters ahead.

Chapter 45

A Discouraging Herd

Home on the Range • *2004* • *Will Finn, John Sanford*

There are some truly inspired vocal pairings in Disney's animated canon. Nathan Lane and Ernie Sabella as Timon and Pumbaa. Kristen Bell and Idina Menzel as Anna and Elsa in *Frozen*. The entire cast of *The Emperor's New Groove* effortlessly bounce off each other. Who would have had Eartha Kitt and Patrick Warburton as one of the most iconic duos in cartoon villainy?

Anyway, here we have a film where Roseanne Barr, Jennifer Tilly and Dame Judi Dench play a trio of cows attempting to apprehend a yodelling cattle rustler. I suppose some films have casting directors, and others have a guy in a back office pulling names out of a bucket of shredded press releases.

Home on the Range is often derided as the film that killed off Disney's 2D animations. This isn't fair for a number of reasons – not least the existence of *The Princess and the Frog* and *Winnie the Pooh*, both of which were released long after the stench of manure had left cinemas.

It's also important to recognise that, in the studio system, decisions are rarely made off the back of one failure. Disney's move away from traditional hand-drawn animation had been made long before Will Finn and John Sanford's film reached cinemas.

Walt Disney Animation Studios had been on a hell of a ride in the two decades since Michael Eisner joined the company as CEO in 1984. Back then, Disney's animated films had been performing so poorly that Eisner and Frank Wells had considered shutting that part of the operation, keeping it open solely because Roy E. Disney had wanted to take up the challenge.

The remarkable run that followed, with releases including *The Little Mermaid*, *Beauty and the Beast*, *Aladdin* and *The Lion King*, had turned the company around. Leading Disney's film division throughout this period was Jeffrey Katzenberg. He had frequently rankled staff across the organisation, but his work rate – and eye for a hit – had made a significant impact.

After the tragic death of Wells in a helicopter incident in 1994, things began to fall apart. Wells often acted as a mediator between Eisner and Katzenberg, and without his input, key relationships across the company began to crumble. To make things worse, Katzenberg believed he had been promised Wells' role should the latter leave the company. When he was denied this position, Katzenberg left the organisation. Some hoped this would allow the company to regroup, and others (including Roy E. Disney) felt that Katzenberg hadn't been as instrumental to the company's recent successes as the press had made him out to be.

Regardless of where you stand on the question of Katzenberg's role in Disney's success, it's clear that he had a big part to play in their stumbling steps into the new millennium. In the immediate wake of his departure, Katzenberg founded a new studio with partners Steven Spielberg and David Geffen. A direct competitor to both Disney's animated and live-action studios, Dreamworks' impact was quickly felt. Though early animated releases *Antz* and *The Prince of Egypt* did not come close to Disney's output (the same year included *A Bug's Life* and *Mulan*), in 2001, Dreamworks hit gold. Their second computer-animated release, *Shrek*, significantly outperformed *Atlantis* and completely turned the Disney fairy-tale model on its head.

Here was a raucous, silly and frequently crude kid's film that captured young imaginations in a way that Disney had been failing to do. Though *Brother Bear*'s Academy Award competition highlighted Pixar's dominance in the field, Dreamworks was fast becoming a major threat in its own right. It was fast becoming clear that CGI would play a dominant role in animation going forward. In March 2002, with their most recent film *Atlantis* having underperformed at the box office, there were lengthy discussions about a decision to transition Disney's primary animation studio at Burbank into a CGI operation. Four more films followed, and regular hand-drawn production ended with the release of *Home on the Range*.

If there's one compliment we can pay *Home on the Range*, it's that the film does a terrific job of highlighting all of the problems Disney's films were facing at the time. It's curiously old-fashioned. There are several musical numbers that are scattered throughout, though none of them have any of the charm present in Renaissance era soundtracks. At the same time, the script feels desperate to keep up with *Shrek*'s irreverence. It's rumoured that the 'brief mild rude humour' that earned the film a PG rating in the States refers to a line in which Roseanne Barr's character, Maggie, chastises the audience for staring at her udders.

The film's fatal flaw, though, is its weak writing. The South American package films aside, only two of Disney's pre-millennium classics were based on original stories: *The Aristocats* and *The Lion King*. And even the latter of those leant heavily on Shakespeare. By comparison, *Home on the Range* was the sixth original story the studio had released in only four years. Though Disney would find a way to make their in-house ideas work,[1] this shift in approach was clearly still a work in progress.

This isn't to say that *Home on the Range* is a bad film. In fact, it has some very funny moments, some gorgeous animation, and a minor twist to enjoy. But the problem is, it also isn't very good. Where the studio spent years at the cutting edge of animation, breaking boundaries and reimagining what cinema could look like, *Home on the Range* spends its runtime just trying to keep up. And worse still, it doesn't even manage to do that.

---

1. At the time of writing, the last nine of the studio's films are either original concepts, or sequels to original concepts. *Moana* and *Encanto* are among the best films the studio has released.

Chapter 46

Clucking Hell

Chicken Little • *2005* • *Mark Dindal*

When *Home on the Range* was released to a lukewarm reception in 2004, it must have seemed like the shift to CGI had come at the perfect time. Pixar had already turned animated cinema on its head, and Dreamworks' *Shrek* had subverted fairy tale movies – the very genre of film that Disney had relied on time and time again to revive their ailing fortunes.[1]

In *Chicken Little*, the studio could finally rejoin the zeitgeist with a vibrant, irreverent computer-animated movie that was also – oh, this doesn't feel like it was part of the plan – the worst thing they'd made in two decades.

If *Treasure Planet* presents a case for the redeeming power of nostalgia, then *Chicken Little* offers a strong counter-argument. However much love we might hold for the films we grew up with, we should always be open to accepting that possibly – just possibly – we were wrong.

It can be difficult to cast a critical eye over the magical stories of our youth – I'm aware even in writing this book that I am willing to overlook glaring flaws in earlier Disney releases. Problematic elements of films like *Peter Pan* and *The Aristocats* can be diluted by rich animation or irresistible songs.

The recent phenomenon of the Disney Adult has become tied very closely to the idea of somebody who is uncritical of the studio in any way – be it their politics, business practices, or simply the quality of their films.

This isn't a unique attribute within the world of fandoms, where supporters of a celebrity or brand can take their passion to extreme levels. An unwillingness to critique media, or even accept that others may not share their views, has spilled over into the real world on more than one occasion. In 2020, an overwhelmingly positive review of Taylor Swift's album *folklore* (which gave the record an 8/10) was deemed to be too ungenerous by Swift's phenomenally engaged fanbase. Within an hour of the piece being published, the author was receiving hateful phone calls

---

1. Mike Myers has a habit of doing this. Much like *Shrek* made it difficult to take stories about beautiful princesses seriously, his *Austin Powers* films had shone a light on just how silly the Bond films were. Whether the issue needed a light shone upon it, I'm not sure. The films themselves were frequently a great big neon sign advertising their own flaws. But it's certain that Myers was part of the process that led to Daniel Craig's grittier reboot. A few years later, he would achieve the feat once again, *The Love Guru* being so bad that the very specific genre it killed off completely was: Mike Myers films.

and seeing her contact details being shared widely online so that others might join the harassment.

As best I can tell, there have been no real examples of Disney Adults engaging in similar behaviour. Nobody has yet rampaged against The New York Times because they've been so-so on *Strange World*. There has been no pitchfork-wielding mob baying at the doors of Bob Iger's corporate naysayers – and this despite *Beauty and the Beast* providing the fandom with the perfect song for the occasion.

And yet, the very concept of Disney Adults instils a certain sense of revulsion among those familiar with – but not engaged in – the sorts of activities the phrase evokes. In the same way football fans have often been caricatured as violent throngs of chanting hooligans, and lovers of country music have been accused of fostering a borderline-erotic relationship with their pick-up truck, Disney Adults must deal with their own clichés. These stereotypes might accurately define a small, noisy corner of the subculture – but to assume any Disney fan fits the following description perfectly is akin to assuming that every insect is a bee. They might all have six legs, but there's a whole lot more going on. With that noted, these are the factors that define a prototypical Disney Adult:

- Disney Adults have a passionate and mostly uncritical love of all things Disney. Now, what 'all things' actually entails is up for debate. Do subsidiary properties like Marvel, Star Wars and The Muppets count? In short: they can, but they don't have to. It's possible to be a Disney Adult and not spend your time shipping Hawkeye and Agent Coulson. It is generally assumed, though, that a Disney Adult will have a wide-reaching knowledge of the animated canon.
- Disney Adults will often be as passionate about the parks as they are about the media. In fact, Disneyland and its global counterparts are the backdrops to most encounters the average layperson might have with the fandom. This is because it's much easier to share a fun photo of your trip to The Magic Kingdom than it is to accurately capture the fact that you know every lyric to *Moana*'s 'You're Welcome'.

  Some of the most mocked examples of Disney Adults are social media posts showing extreme reactions to the parks. One famous example is a 2022 video of a millennial woman breaking down in tears as she meets Goofy in person (or should that be 'a person in Goofy'?) for the first time. This reminds me:
- Disney Adults are overwhelmingly millennials, though there are plenty of Gen Z participants too. We've already seen how Disney sparked this particular fire by making children of the 1980s and 90s the first generation to have regular access to their films.
- Disney Adults are fully grown human beings who dress up as their favourite characters to visit Disneyland.

This one isn't even technically true; Disney's parks don't allow outright fancy dress. Fans instead engage in 'Disneybounding' – dressing in clothing that reflects elements of a character's look. Somebody might wear a red and white polka dot dress to evoke Minnie Mouse's style without donning a literal costume. A green shirt, tie and pair of chinos will give an air of Zootopia's Nick without requiring the purchase of full furry gear.

- And finally: Disney Adults spend far too much money on the corporation. The £80 it costs to subscribe to Disney Plus for a year pales in comparison to other expenditures. An over-eager fan might spend thousands on trips to Disney parks, staying in branded hotels, or holidaying on one of the company's five themed cruise ships. Other merchandise – clothing, toys, ornamental pieces of plastic with oversized heads and undersized charm – can easily add hundreds more to that figure. An entire industry exists beyond the corporation's reach, taking its own cut of the pie through unofficial means. Hello, welcome to my book, I hope you're having fun.

This final cliché that haunts the fandom is one of the bigger points of contention among outsiders looking in. There is a sense on the wider internet that Disney Adults fit within a very specific demographic. Their age is a part of it, yes, but so are their ethnicity and wealth. Many of the faces one sees under the fandom's hashtags are white. There is an assumption of class privilege, too – surely nobody struggling to get by is going to spend hundreds of dollars on tickets to a theme park, or even twenty bucks on a limited edition Funko Pop.

And yes, it is true that the demographics skew heavily in this direction – a 2024 New Statesman article found that roughly 88% of self-identifying Disney Adults were white, while 58% of those surveyed spent between $1,000 and $10,000 on company products and services in any given year. Only 2.8% spend less than $100, though this cut-off point is notably below even the cheapest annual subscription to Disney Plus.

Much of the vitriol against the Disney Adult comes down to second-hand embarrassment. There are two common arguments that are seen in the comments of viral posts online. First, there is a sense among many that there is something morally wrong – or at least inherently weird – about an adult liking media that is intended specifically for children.

There's nothing new about this way of thinking – goodness knows that the average Victorian thought childhood should last strictly as long as it took to read *Alice's Adventures in Wonderland*. After that, the child – ideally still no more than three feet tall – was considered to be of working age and was promptly stuffed up a chimney.

Nowadays, adults looking to cling to their childhood in even the most inoffensive of ways are often decried in the media as being somewhat suspect. It is normally the right-wing media that carries out this shaming – a demographic that has a long history of stirring up moral panics over anything they don't understand, from heavy metal to video games.

And this is what sits at the heart of this particular critique of the Disney fandom: a lack of understanding. Overwhelmingly, critics who argue against adults enjoying children's media understand neither what Disney is nor what life is like for those within the fandom. Because first and foremost, Disney has never been solely for the kids. From the very beginning, Walt's animations have been intended to be enjoyed by adults and children alike. A promotional poster for *Snow White* featured a review recommending the film to 'children, young folks, men and women'. The studio set up a whole art department in World War II specifically to provide men on the front with cartoon characters that could be used as insignia on their military vehicles.

At the same time, these critics are usually of an older generation than the younger-skewing Disney Adults. Their values differ, but so do their lived experiences as adults. With homeownership more unachievable than at any moment in recent history, and wages stagnant amid spiralling costs of living, Disney connects fans to a simpler time. It takes them, for one brief moment, away from a world in which they might be worrying about rent, or having to come up with a plan for dinner even though they've already done that six times this week. Their experiences with Disney can also offer a way to connect with the ones they love, be it friends and family who engage in the fandom with them, or loved ones who have since been lost.

The woman who went viral for crying when she saw Goofy at Disneyland wasn't overwhelmed by his sheer charm – though it wouldn't be our place to judge even if that had been the case. Goofy had been her late grandfather's favourite character. In a place that is geared towards making individuals as happy as possible, it's no stretch to imagine so sweet a memory bringing anyone to wistful tears. When so much of our daily life is a struggle, it is a hard-hearted person who outlaws so harmless a form of escapism.

But this is what arguments like these seek to do, even if the cases presented in order to deliver the verdict are fundamentally hypocritical themselves. The second major polemic approach against the Disney Adult is that the very concept of fandom is inherently a bad thing. That to commit any amount of one's self to a movie studio, or a popstar, or the spindly ethereal form of Timothée Chalamet is to admit to a weakness in character; an inability to form a personality of one's own that doesn't rely on an external factor.

This is, of course, nonsense. Sports fans are not treated like this for their lifelong devotion to a singular team. They might be endlessly mocked if they have chosen to support, say, Tottenham Hotspur or the New York Mets – but their very character isn't usually called into question for the simple fact that they have chosen a team to follow in the first place.

Sometimes, you will hear religious preachers decrying fandom as the misguided reaching for a spirituality that the person is otherwise missing in their life; the idea that what the individual is really aching for is an encounter with God and not a handshake from Chip and/or Dale at at a restaurant in EPCOT. But this accounts neither for the number of religious people who also have a deep connection with Disney nor for the fact that *Oliver & Company* is both significantly shorter and significantly funnier than the Bible. It features less incest too, for that matter. And more Billy Joel.

Fandoms may form a part of an individual's identity, but there's no harm in that. Identities have to be formed of *something*, or else we would all be little more than pod people wandering aimlessly around in circles until we keeled over from sheer boredom. So why not make 'enjoying Disney' a part of that personality? Is it really all that different from being passionate about coffee, or reading, or telling people to try Huel?

Perhaps you identify as a Disney Adult. I suppose, with the publication of this book, I should finally succumb to the label myself. The problem I've always had with the term – and by 'always' I mean for the roughly three years that it has existed – is that it implies an all-encompassing fidelity to the brand. An absolutist approach that cannot co-exist with other facets of a personality, and that leaves the fan devoid of an ability to think critically about what they are consuming. But this isn't true. It is possible to be a Disney Adult and, at the same time, a good friend, or a passionate tennis player. An avid learner, and a talented home cook. And it is possible to be a Disney Adult and to accept that not everything the studio does is perfect. That it has treated staff poorly in the past. That it has engaged in racist stereotypes in its films. And, less importantly, but no less true: that *Chicken Little* is absolute garbage.

Chapter 47

The Bare Necessities are the Mother of Invention

Meet the Robinsons • *2007* • *Stephen J. Anderson*

It takes more than paper and pens to pioneer long-form animation. Walt Disney knew this from the start. So many of the landmark releases within his lifetime are not only artistic achievements but also technical ones. For Walt, the imagination had a thousand uses, and as disparate as they might seem, ideas could always find a way to interact with one another.

Early on, this meant taking the bare bones of *Alice's Adventures in Wonderland* and connecting them with hybrid live-action cartoons. Later, Walt took the burgeoning concept of talking pictures and combined them with his cartoon mouse. The addition of sound gave Mickey Mouse a launching pad that would enable him to become a worldwide cultural phenomenon – but in return, the bounce and verve of Walt's characters enabled audience and industry alike to understand the potential of the new technology.

Ambition begat innovation. Walt sought to achieve the impossible, so he set his team on a mission to redefine what could and could not be done. Though he might originally have believed the creation of a feature-length cartoon would be no more difficult than the creation of ten animated shorts, Walt learnt as he went and adapted as necessary.

For *Snow White*, this included the development of a new multiplane camera that could imbue two-dimensional drawings with a sense of depth and, thus, reality. In simple terms, a camera is positioned, looking down upon multiple layers of glass planes. Between each of these planes, a different cel of animation can be placed, allowing operators to move one sheet without disturbing the others. The effect for the audience is a foreground that can move separately from the background, giving the illusion of depth perception.

The Disney multiplane was not the first on the scene. *The Adventures of Prince Achmed*, one of those forgotten animated features that predate Disney's first, had used an early version back in 1926. Later, Walt's old pal Ub Iwerks built the first multiplane camera to deliver the three-dimensional effects it would become associated with. Iwerks had founded his own studio by this point, so Disney called upon inventor William Garity to develop one for use in the production of *Snow White*.

Garity filled an interesting position at Disney. Though Walt was championed as the great innovator, scientific minds such as Garity were the creative forces behind many of the studio's most famous developments. Fantasound, the early stereophonic surround sound system used in *Fantasia*, was another of the projects developed by Garity during his time at Disney.

As Walt's business grew, so did his ambition. With each new development, there was a need for more experimentation and innovation. When Walt's attention drifted to Disneyland in the 1950s, that's where the studio's brightest technical minds found themselves, too. Walt created a new business to develop his theme park, which was an unpopular project among Disney shareholders. The team he formed to design rides and theming was quickly given a nickname: the Imagineers.

Even today, some of the most inventive work done by Disney is that of the Imagineers (the studio bought Walt's secondary company when the theme parks turned out to be even bigger money-spinners than their films). Early animatronic characters have taken on new life in recent years – in Tokyo Disneyland, Belle and the Beast dance together as guests move around them. The Avengers Campus in the Disney California Adventure park has a Spider-man animatronic that is flung from a rooftop. While completely airborne, it completes programmed moves before landing safely out of sight to be prepared for the next slingshot moment. In 2024, Disney revealed its latest invention – the work of Lanny Smoot, a modern-day Garity. The HoloTile floor is a surface that moves underfoot in any direction it needs to. Users can walk on the spot or be turned around as they stand still.

There's still innovation happening in the animation studios – programmes to create more realistic art for Disney's films, but more than anywhere else, the spirit of Walt Disney's passion for innovation is alive among the Imagineers.

Meet the Robinsons is an attempt to pay tribute to this ambition. The film was the first released by Disney after John Lasseter's arrival as the new chief creative officer of Disney's animation studios, but it was mostly developed before his arrival. In this sense, you'd be forgiven for thinking of it as a 21st-century *Black Cauldron.* After all, both films are enthusiastic if chaotic affairs conceived amid a creative dirge at the studio. Notably, though, *Meet the Robinsons* differs from *The Black Cauldron* in one important way: it's actually enjoyable.

It isn't *great*, mind. But that's because the film is stuffed with so many ideas that it has a tendency to overload the viewer. *Meet the Robinsons* seems, above all else, to have two goals: it wants to celebrate the great innovators who never give up, and it wants to be a zany fantasy film set in an unfamiliar world, like *Alice in Wonderland* and *Peter Pan* before it.

It enjoys partial success in both. Closing with a Walt Disney quote that reveals the origin of the Robinsons' family motto, the film attempts to position Walt as an innovator who is broadly comparable to boy genius Lewis. Except there is one glaring issue here. It's not that Lewis's peanut butter and jelly gun is infinitely less practical than two jars and a knife. It's that unlike Lewis, Walt's greatest innovations were not the work of one great mind, but rather a huge collaborative effort in which many of the most important and inventive figures are broadly unknown today. In this sense, *Meet the Robinsons* would have made a stronger case if it leaned in on the way Lewis's family empowered his success or, better still, if the film simply made more references to great minds like William Garity.

At the same time, Stephen J. Anderson's movie attempts to take the audience on a whirlwind tour of an unexpected world where nothing quite makes sense. Here, young orphan Lewis is transported into the future, where he explores the madcap house of the Robinson family. The introductions to these individual family members account for more or less the entire plot of the book that the film is loosely based on, *A Day with Wilbur Robinson* by William Joyce.[1] In the film's second most obvious influence, *Alice in Wonderland*, the world is intended to be one led by nonsense, and to that extent, it seems almost logical that we should be subjected to an ongoing parade of certified weirdos. But in *Meet the Robinsons*, Lewis is simply transported to the then-distant future of 2037.

Now, upon release in 2007, this might have been a sticking point. Why, in a world that is essentially meant to be our own, just thirty years down the line, does every single person in the Robinson household appear to be an eccentric wildcard, living the strangest possible life? The elderly Bud walks around with his clothes back-to-front and a smiley face drawn on the back of his head. His brother Fritz is married to a sock puppet. Uncles Spike and Dimitri apparently live in plant pots at the front of the house, fighting an eternal battle over which of the entrance's two doorbells guests should ring. Even Franny Robinson, who appears to be one of the more reserved family members, is generally preoccupied with her lifelong passion: teaching frogs to sing.

But it isn't 2007 anymore, is it? We're almost twenty years into the film's thirty-year leap, and suddenly, the characters' descents into absurd obsessions make absolutely perfect sense. Think of all they've seen so far: the rise of social media, the extreme tonal shift of America voting in its first Black president and then, just for fun, a really racist one that just won't go away. There's been war, climate catastrophe, a global pandemic. Hell, the film's villain is essentially just AI headwear gone rogue. Hat GPT, if you will. Even the multiple doorbells make sense – one was probably there when the family moved in, and the other is a Google doorbell that the tech-savvy Lewis insisted on adding a few years later. Anyway, the point is that the world is making less sense by the day, and it's entirely possible that we'll all be hiding in plant pots by the time 2037 rolls around.

1. Initially, Disney intended on basing the character design in *Meet the Robinsons* on Joyce's artwork for the book. But in 2005, Blue Sky Studios released their animated feature *Robots*, on which Joyce had been a key artistic voice. Though they are stylistically different, both films share a certain wacky spirit. In 2019, the studio was bought by Disney as part of the acquisition of 21st Century Fox assets. Why not enjoy *Meet the Robinsons* and *Robots* as a William Joyce double bill on Disney Plus?

Chapter 48

His Bark is Worse Than His 'Good Morning! Oh, and in Case I Don't See You, Good Afternoon, Good Evening, and Goodnight.'

Bolt • *2008* • *Byron Howard, Chris Williams*

Animated cinema has often been an effective way to introduce children to difficult subjects, from the death of a loved one to the difficulties of growing up. An in-depth examination of the existential crisis was, frankly, long overdue by the time *Bolt* rocked up in 2008 with its canine take on *The Truman Show*.

Our heroic pup is a Swiss White Shepherd with a head-to-body ratio of roughly 1:1. An overloaded opening sequence whizzes the audience through a world of competing exposition: Penny picks Bolt up from a rescue centre! But five years later, Penny's father has been kidnapped! And now, for reasons unexplained, evil forces want Penny! But Bolt has been genetically altered and now has superpowers! Which the evil forces do not seem remotely interested in! They only want the 10-year-old girl! Penny is cornered and escapes, thanks to Bolt headbutting a car! Penny is cornered again but escapes because Bolt's super bark has the explosive power of a small nuclear warhead! And then – a twist just ten minutes into the film: it's all just a TV production.

Bolt's entire life is a lie – kept from him so that he can offer a believable performance as his beloved Penny is put in peril time and time again. It's an extremely complex set-up for what is essentially a very familiar plot – *Bolt* doesn't just remind the viewer of Jim Carrey in *The Truman Show*, discovering that his entire life has been a ruse created for a reality TV programme. It also recalls the aliens in *Galaxy Quest* finding that their heroes are just third-rate sci-fi actors, or Buzz Lightyear in *Toy Story* finding out that he is not an intergalactic warrior, but a toy.

Though *Toy Story* is the only one of the above films that does not feature actors (unwitting or otherwise), it's probably the film that most closely influenced *Bolt*. In 2006, Disney finally acquired Pixar. It was a move two decades in the making: Michael Eisner had turned down an opportunity to buy the nascent company in 1986, but the feature animation department had worked closely alongside John Lasseter and his team for the rest of the decade. Eventually, Pixar signed a deal to produce three films for Disney, starting with *Toy Story*. The phenomenal success of the first feature CGI animation meant that the collaboration continued until the 2006 purchase. By that point, Pixar were arguably the most innovative animators on the planet – and the reason films like *Chicken Little* were so widely derided. This is why, upon purchasing Pixar, Disney promptly placed its central figures – Lasseter and the studio's co-founder Ed Catmull – at the head of all their animation units: Walt Disney Animation Studios, Pixar Animation Studios and Disneytoon Studios.

Bolt was the first animated classic to be produced under the watch of Lasseter, now Disney's Chief Creative Officer. His eye for simple storytelling plays a key role in the final film. Initially conceived by *Lilo & Stitch*'s Chris Sanders, the original premise for the film was similar but unwieldy. The famous TV dog was still present – stuck in an unfamiliar situation with a cynical cat. But there were also two characters that, for reasons lost to history, were both radioactive. One was a gigantic rabbit. The other was a 'cookie-selling Girl Scout zombie serial killer'.[1] Actually, I could be convinced by this.

Lasseter toned it all down, though – the action was moved from the American Southwest to a cross-country adventure. The radioactive rabbit became an over-eager hamster based on Lasseter's own chinchilla, who joined the animators on a retreat during production, whizzing around the place in a plastic ball.

The cast of *Bolt* is arguably among the most unhinged in the Disney canon.[2] The title character is voiced by the then 54-year-old John Travolta, who, even accounting for dog years, is roughly two decades older than his counterpart.[3] Mittens, the cat reluctantly dragged into proceedings, is played by Susie Essman – best known for playing the deeply awful Susie in HBO's *Curb Your Enthusiasm*. Her onscreen husband, Jeff Garlin, would steal her thunder by appearing in Pixar's latest classic, *WALL•E*, that same year. Even with Lasseter on side, Disney's old frenemy kept outshining them. As much as *Bolt* was a significant upgrade for the studio, it paled by comparison to Pixar's masterpiece *WALL•E*, which would go on to win the Academy Award for Best Animated Feature.

Travolta and Essman's performances entered the long history of talking animals in Disney films. There are, broadly, four main categories of talking animal movies.

1. **Films in which animals and humans co-exist, and animals can talk among themselves.**
   This is the biggest category and where *Bolt* fits in. In these films, the animals can generally understand human languages but cannot directly communicate with them. Humans are almost always the antagonists here – which is fair. As a species, we're mostly awful. From *One Hundred*

1. 'Creativity Inc.: Overcoming the Unseen Forces That Stand in the Way of True Inspiration' (Ed Catmull, Amy Wallace, Random House, 2014)
2. After, of course, *Home on the Range*'s Roseanne Barr, Cuba Gooding Jr, Jennifer Tilly and Dame Judi Dench.
3. *Bolt*'s release fell in the middle of Travolta's third wave of cinematic success, sandwiched between remakes of *Hairspray* and *The Taking of Pelham 123*. He would return to the Hollywood sidelines the following year after the flop of a film whose title might also aptly cover his work here: *Old Dogs*.

and One Dalmatians to *The Aristocats* and *Lady and the Tramp*, these films generally represent a world where being a pet is a really cushy deal – until one awful person decides to ruin the fun.

2. **Films in which animals can talk to humans, but for some reason, only choose to bother with one specific person.**
There are very few films where animals can talk to any human they like – by my count, only *Pinocchio* and *The Adventures of Ichabod and Mr Toad* would count. Usually, the animals are far more selective. *The Rescuers*, for example, can clearly communicate in English with humans. For some reason, they only choose to converse with small children who are in trouble. The logic is beyond me: children are terrible conversationalists, and those in troubling situations are incredibly single-minded in what they want to talk about. 'That man bought the last Kinder Surprise', they say tediously. 'That man opened the egg and retrieved the toy inside, and made it, and is now looking at me and pointing at his toy in a way that can only be meant to hurt my feelings', they'll go on. Shut up, kid. I'm trying to play with my tiny Hot Wheels car.

Anyway, this, to me, is the most interesting version of the talking animal movie. Why do Bagheera and Baloo only talk to Mowgli? Could they not use their linguistic abilities to convince the man village to be less awful or to help them in their plight against Shere Khan? The answer, of course, is that the animals in *The Jungle Book* and its thematic cousin *Tarzan* haven't learnt to speak human languages. Mowgli and Tarzan have learnt to speak like animals.

This doesn't hold for Bernard and Bianca in *The Rescuers*, though. They're just masochists who enjoy wasting their English-speaking skills on children so dumb they can't even manage not to get kidnapped.

3. **One specific animal can speak to humans.**
This is a smaller category, with just five characters fitting the bill: Archimedes in *The Sword in the Stone*, Iago in *Aladdin*, Cuzco in *The Emperor's New Groove* and Tiana and Prince Naveen in *The Princess and the Frog*.

The eagle-eyed reader might have spotted that both Cuzco and the *Princess and the Frog* characters are not, in fact, animals by birth, but rather humans who have been magically cursed into taking on an animal form. This raises the question: what's the deal with Archimedes and Iago? It's very plausible that they, too, were once human. Both characters are exactly as grumpy as I would be if I lost my opposable thumbs and had to spend the rest of my life on the shoulder of an incompetent wizard.

Only one film acts as a direct mirror to this, in which one specific human can talk to all animals. Step forward Antonio, the youngest member of *Encanto*'s family Madrigal.

4. **Anthropomorphic animals live in a world without humans.**
   This might be the sweet spot – normal human life, except everybody is cute and fluffy. *Robin Hood* was the original title in this category, and a similarly lusted-over fox continued the tradition four decades later with *Zootopia*. The fundamentally terrible *Chicken Little* also fits in here – and has a fox character to boot – though the fact that a cinema in that film's animal world is screening a live-action *Indiana Jones* film does raise some very confusing questions.

   Do *The Lion King* and *Dinosaur* count here too? Both feature talking animals that display some human characteristics (like acting as hyena bait while wearing a Hawaiian grass skirt) but exist in worlds that could plausibly belong to any of the previous three categories. Without humans around to interact with, we'll never know.

Back to *Bolt*, and Chloë Grace Moretz was originally cast as our lead character's owner, Penny. Moretz was on the rise as a young actor but was still a couple of years away from breakout roles in *500 Days of Summer* and *Kickass*. Though she had recorded all of her lines for the film, at some point a decision was made to bring in one of Disney's biggest young stars of the time – Miley Cyrus, who was gaining widespread popularity among the film's target audience with her starring role in the Disney Channel TV show *Hannah Montana*. Cyrus re-recorded Penny's dialogue, and only one scene remains with Moretz playing the character – the opening, in which Bolt is plucked from rescue shelter obscurity to become a star.

Though *Bolt* sits at the end of the Post-Renaissance Era of Disney classics, it fills a similar role to the one that *The Great Mouse Detective* held in the mid-1980s. With new creative talent guiding the studio forward, the film was a testing ground for a reinvigorated approach to storytelling. It marks a studio settling into new animation techniques, and finding its footing for another remarkable run of films in the years ahead.

The Revival Era

Chapter 49

In Black and White

The Princess and the Frog • 2009 • Ron Clements, John Musker

The Princess and the Frog drew a great deal of attention when it was first announced in 2006. There had, historically, never been a great deal of Blackness in the Disney back catalogue. There was, of course, an overwhelming amount of whiteness – a term that we use here specifically to denote a view of the world that has been overtly shaped by the white people who have generally acted as the primary producers and gatekeepers of mass media in the United States.

The studio didn't have a long-term Black artist on their books until 1957, when Floyd Norman was hired to work on *Sleeping Beauty*. To date, the only animated classic with a Black director is *Fantasia 2000*, in which Pixote Hunt takes credit for just one of the eight segments. In short: almost every non-white character to have featured across the first half century or so of Disney films was conceived by white writers, artists and directors. And this skewed view of non-white experiences inevitably impacts the way that audiences – both young and old – come to understand what it is to be Black, or Asian, or any number of other caricatured peoples. It impacts the views of white audiences, and it impacts those of the people being portrayed.

A precedent was set from the very first Disney feature, in which the princess' greatest asset was that she was the 'fairest' in the land. By the 1940s, this white-centred worldview had expanded, and racist caricatures became a staple in Disney's films. A famous scene in *Fantasia*, since cut out of home releases, featured young Black centaurs in subservient roles. One is shown shining the hooves of a white centaur.

The following year, *Dumbo* featured a gang of singing crows who were very heavily inspired by Black entertainers of the era (and, certainly, the blackface minstrel shows that would remain popular in the United States until at least the 1960s). In 2019, the aforementioned animator Floyd Norman defended these crows, describing the criticism they have received in recent years as 'PC nonsense'. Walt Disney wasn't a racist, he claimed. Yes, the gang's leader was originally named 'Jim Crow' after the segregation laws that remained in place across the Southern United States at the time, but this was intended as a joke at the expense of racists. After all, the crows are among the kindest and smartest characters in the whole film. Norman made no mention, however, of the film's faceless Black labourers, who toiled in the rain, raising tents for the circus. These characters sing a song in which they profess their illiteracy and their tendency to throw their money away the moment they're paid. The lyrics describe one of the 'roustabouts' as an 'ape'.

The most famous example of racist tropes within the Disney back catalogue comes from outside the animated canon. 1946's *Song of the South* has proven so controversial in the decades since its premiere that it has never seen a home video release in the States. The film is the epitome of Black lives framed through a white lens, featuring an idyllic take on plantation life in the years immediately after the American Civil War. The film is based on the white folklorist Joel Chandler Harris' retellings of stories from the Black-American oral tradition. These stories were written in a dialect that Harris thought was representative of the language used by Black Americans in the Deep South. Though Harris' stories were distinctly set in the post-Civil War era, Disney never explicitly states this in their adaptation. The Black workers are folksy and cheerful, and seem pleased with their gentle existence serving the plantation's short-tempered white owners. Perhaps the only clear sign that the Black characters in *Song of the South* are not enslaved comes when Uncle Remus (who has recently been wrongfully chastised by his white boss for the third time) decides to leave and faces no punitive repercussions. Nevertheless, Remus' decision is made not out of a sense of self-respect but rather out of shame. His eventual return comes not from a personal realisation but instead from a sense of duty to a young white boy who was indirectly injured as a result of his leaving.

By framing every encounter through a white lens, Disney created a sense of otherness around characters who aren't white or are not white-coded. Sometimes, a film draws humour from this otherness – think Shun Gon in *The Aristocats*, who plays his piano with chopsticks and sings lyrics that read like a Chinese takeaway menu. Often, though, this same otherness denotes something far more sinister, like the Siamese cats in *Lady and the Tramp*, who are presented as duplicitous and sly in their short time on screen, during which they sing in broken English through buck teeth.

Some efforts were made towards inclusivity during the Renaissance era, in which Quasimodo fell for a Romani woman, and the studio made its first films about non-white princesses with *Pocahontas* and *Mulan*, respectively. But still, Black characters were rarely presented as more than side characters. Those that did appear were often presented with deeply stereotypical traits, from the Rastafari crab Sebastian in *The Little Mermaid* to the gospel-singing Muses in *Hercules*.

At the turn of the millennium, The Disney Channel's television programming finally started to present Black voices in less cliché-laden ways. Young Black women took the lead in both the animated series *The Proud Family* and the live-action *That's So Raven*. Another cartoon series, *Fillmore!*, presented audiences with a witty police procedural spoof in which a Black hall monitor took on the crimes and mysteries of his middle school.

And yet, there were still no Disney animated classics with a Black lead. Even *The Lion King*, a film set entirely in Africa with a lead character whose parents were voiced by James Earl Jones and Madge Sinclair, cast two white men to play that lead: *Home Improvement*'s Jonathan Taylor Thomas and Ferris Bueller himself, Matthew Broderick. *The Princess and the Frog* was an opportunity – whether on purpose or not – to atone for this absence of Blackness. And, perhaps unsurprisingly, there were issues right from the start.

When Disney first announced the film, there were some relatively small but key differences that immediately caught the eye of Black Disney fans and prominent cultural voices. The protagonist was named Maddy, which was criticised both for being an uncommon name within the Black community and for sounding a little too close to 'Mammy', an outdated term once used to describe matronly Black women who looked after white children, usually while enslaved. It didn't help, either, that Maddy was a maid within a white household.

To their credit, Disney was quick to respond to these criticisms. Maddy was renamed Tiana and took on a new job as a waitress. The white family she originally would have worked for now become wealthy friends – who she knows because her mother worked for them. On the outside, the film presents itself as an empowering story for Tiana. She is passionate and hard-working, driven by her ambition to run her own restaurant. Refreshingly for a princess movie, she doesn't even have her eyes set on a man. This, instead, is the preserve of her exhausting white best friend, Charlotte, who also claims an important first for a Disney film: never before had the studio featured a supporting character so clearly under the direct influence of cocaine for their entire screen time.

Scratch under the surface, though, and the film still has plenty of flaws in its portrayal of Blackness. Not least among these: Tiana is actually green for more than half of her screen time.

As it happens, Tiana's actual screen time was the most of any Disney princess at the time of the film's release – just shy of forty-five minutes.[1] But for twenty-three of those, she appears in frog form. It was one of several indignities foisted upon Tiana over the course of the movie. In her searing thesis 'Almost There, Indeed: Disney Misses the Mark on Modernizing Black Womanhood and Subverting the Princess Tradition in The Princess and the Frog', April Callen highlights a number of these – why, she asks, is Tiana the sole princess whose (eventual) love interest is stone cold broke? Why is it that Disney felt comfortable making her the victim of off-screen sexual harassment by that love interest, and why must it be played for laughs?

Much of this may come from unconscious bias inherent in the predominantly white team behind the film.[2] Black women have historically been overly sexualised within cinema. Though Prince Naveen's ethnicity is unclear, white society has long used false narratives about irresponsible spending to maintain control over non-

1. *Sleeping Beauty*'s Aurora is on screen for less than eighteen minutes, and Jasmine – the first non-white princess, but also the only one not to be the titular star of her film, features in *Aladdin* for less than twenty minutes.
2. Directors Clements and Musker, previously behind *The Little Mermaid* and *Aladdin* are both white. Of the five men with screenplay or story credits, only Rob Edwards is Black.

white groups. Given Naveen's inherent lack of money, it's also particularly jarring that the film withholds from Tiana the ability to own and run her restaurant until she marries.

Callen also notes that Tiana is the first princess not to marry a prince of her own race. Outwardly, perhaps, a positive message about love not being limited by skin colour. But why save this distinction for the first Black princess in a film released at a time when the desirability of Black women was a common talking point in mainstream (white) media? Callen suggests that having two Black leads may have parked the film firmly in the public consciousness as a 'Black movie', impacting the film's reach.

Frustratingly, the more you watch *The Princess and the Frog*, the more issues arise. The Black villain is a voodoo practitioner. The white best friend spends most of the film as the only possible salvation for Tiana. Much of Tiana's virtue is presented by her willingness to work hard in order to achieve social mobility that will allow her to become a successful member of society. And, of course, the biggest fantasy of all in a film rife with magic: 1920s Louisiana reimagined as a world free of segregation and the horrific actions of groups like the Ku Klux Klan. This is perhaps the most significant example of the white gaze within the creation of *The Princess and the Frog*. The only moment of outright racism in the film is a snarky comment from a banker regarding the ability of a person from Tiana's background to run a business successfully. This at a time when lynchings were common across the state. It might seem ambitious to expect Disney to include such abhorrent acts in their film, but they were the ones who chose to set the plot of their first Black-led film in this place, in this period. There's no way that the studio was unaware of the racism that ran rampant across the Southern states at the time. The film is set two decades before the release of *Song of the South* – a film that premiered in three states over, in Alabama, without its biggest star present because segregation laws barred him from participating.

And yet Disney still treats *The Princess and the Frog* as a triumph in representation: the first Black princess. A story about working hard and achieving your goals. And, in some ways, the film really did make a significant difference. Young Black children (and in particular girls) could finally see themselves in a Disney movie. The Black population of New Orleans was represented at a time when they had felt disproportionately ignored in the wake of Hurricane Katrina. It's understandable, perhaps, for Disney to hold onto the film. *The Princess and the Frog* was clearly created in good faith, and its flaws result mostly from an approach to inclusivity that was very much of its time – telling untold stories but not necessarily asking the right people to tell them.

Disney has, in the years since, become far better at giving marginalised voices an opportunity to be heard. 2021's *Raya and the Last Dragon* featured the studio's first Southeast Asian princess, with a screenplay by writers from American-Vietnamese and Malaysian backgrounds, respectively. When Clements and Musker began production on their next film – this time set in the Pacific Ocean, they took their time to research Polynesian culture in-depth. They formed an Oceanic Story Trust that acted as consultants around the film's cultural accuracy and sensitivity to the peoples it portrayed. *Moana* presents a very different Disney princess who isn't tied to a love interest at all.

The public has come to realise that companies don't undertake objectively good projects because it's the right thing to do. Michael Eisner was famously quoted as saying that a film studio has no obligation to make history, art, or any sort of a statement. The only objective is to make money. But in the same breath, he also acknowledged that the way to make that money is to entertain the audience. And in entertaining the audience, inevitably, there will be times when history is made. Art is created. A statement is delivered.

It is the persistence of audiences that has shaped the media we see today. Everything we see in cinemas, theatres, television, or literature was created so that people can enjoy it. And so, in a sense, it is on us to ensure that better films get made. That there is representation for every corner of society. This doesn't take accountability away from the studios. It simply defines who the studios are accountable to. Once upon a time, Disney felt comfortable releasing a film like *Song of the South*. Not anymore. Now, even the most indirect remnants of the film are fading from pop culture, preserved only as historical documents to remember a different era. In 2023, both California's Disneyland and Florida's Magic Kingdom closed Splash Mountain, a ride inspired by the animated segments of *Song of the South*. Both rides reopened a year later with a new theme and a new name: Tiana's Bayou Adventure. *The Princess and the Frog* isn't perfect, but it's one hell of an upgrade on what came before. Times change, and art evolves. We've had one Black Disney princess. Now it's time to see what the studio could do with a second.

Chapter 50

Big Hair, Don't Care

Tangled • 2010 • Nathan Greno, Byron Howard

Disney got back to their roots – in more ways than one – for their fiftieth animated classic. *Tangled* is a return to Disney's winning fairy tale formula. Its star, Rapunzel, was the tenth Disney Princess to be added to the studio's ever-growing roster of sellable leading ladies. *Tangled* is also the first of the Princess films to be computer animated – a big leap after the decision to revert to traditional animation for *The Princess and the Frog* the previous year.

So there are plenty of big landmarks to revel in there. At the time of its release, Disney made a great deal of noise about them, and rightfully so. Would Walt ever have thought it possible that his animation studio would reach *fifty* films? Could he have anticipated that seventy-three years after *Snow White*, that milestone would be reached by another movie based on one of the Brothers Grimm fairy tales?

One thing I suspect Walt would never have foreseen is the other achievement that *Tangled* holds on to, even today: it is the single most expensive animated film in cinema history.

In fact, at the time of its release, the film's estimated budget of £260 million made it the second most expensive film ever made. Only the third entry in Disney's *Pirates of the Caribbean* series cost more.

Even today, the film sits very comfortably in the top thirty, a full $10 million above the next animated movie on the list.[1] How is it, then, that a children's cartoon cost more to make than many of Marvel's biggest blockbusters, all but two of DC's superhero movies, and 90% of the *Fast & Furious* films – a franchise whose sole purpose seems to be to find the most ludicrously expensive cars in the world and drive them off tall objects?

There are several contributing factors. This should surprise no one – it's very, very difficult to rack up a bill of $260 million with a single big purchase unless you're Elon Musk and you're buying a dying social media platform as a joke.

The first proposal for *Tangled* came in 2001, when long-standing Disney animator Glen Keane pitched a modern retelling of *Rapunzel.* By the time the film was announced two years later, it had already taken on an unconventional approach

---

1. 2019's remake of *The Lion King* which, despite widely being referred to as 'the live-action *Lion King*', is almost 100% computer animated. Only a single shot – the sunrise that opens the film – features any live-action footage.

that would distance it from movies like *Snow White*, *Sleeping Beauty* and even Renaissance-era films like *Pocahontas*.

It's clear that Katzenberg's Dreamworks, and their recently released *Shrek*, had shaken Disney to the core. *Rapunzel Unbraided*'s truly terrible title feels like it belongs to the straight-to-DVD rip-off films you'd find in service station newsagents in the early 2000s. The plot would have echoed a live-action Disney film of the period, *Enchanted*. Set in modern San Francisco, the story saw two teenagers transported to a fairytale realm. The teenagers would have been turned into Rapunzel and her prince, and then *those* characters would have been turned into a squirrel and a dog. The whole thing sounds thoroughly exhausting, and it's probably for the best that the film's release was pushed back so that it could be rewritten as a more traditional take on the story.

Delays to production and the subsequent rewrites and changes that they precede will always add costs to a film. And so it was no help whatsoever when, in January 2006, the film was shut down completely, only to be restarted a few weeks later when Pixar's Ed Catmull and John Lasseter took charge of Disney's animation studios. More rewrites would follow, alongside another round of storyboarding, with even more changes occurring two years later when Keane and his co-director left the project, and *Bolt*'s Byron Howard and Nathan Greno stepped in.

All of this is enough to ramp up the costs of any animated film significantly, but it doesn't quite account for a budget that rivals the GDP of Kiribati. What *will* take up a little space on the bank statement is development costs for software that will enable you to animate seventy feet of hair smoothly.

Tangled sits at the cusp of the Revival Era, the first CGI Disney film of the 2010s. It still feels alarmingly contemporary – if you want to break a millennial, tell them that *Tangled* is fifteen years old and watch their brain malfunction in real-time. A huge part of this temporal dissonance has to come down to the film's quality – it is the first animated classic to look like a contemporary CGI film. Unlike *Bolt*, which came out just two years earlier, *Tangled* looks more or less as impressive as films made a decade later. And this came at a cost.

Disney's proprietary hair simulation software, dynamicWires, had actually been created for use in *Bolt*. It added a layer of reality to the fur of the three animals at the heart of the film, as well as human characters like Penny. But it is one thing for a piece of software to animate the small movements of hair on a dog as he pounces into action; it is another thing entirely to animate 140,000 strands of hair, each of which is almost the length of a tennis court.

And so dynamicWires received some significant upgrades for *Tangled*, and a team of five animators focused their energies on delivering hair simulation for Rapunzel that balanced realism with aesthetics. They spent months adapting how their software worked to create the subtlest of details for the film – the way it piled up on the floor, the impact that areas of hair not currently on-screen had on those that were visible. As well as trying to deliver believable hair, the animators worked to add a little fantasy logic to the visuals. There is, after all, no way that a real-world Rapunzel would be able to run so quickly while dragging so much hair behind her.[2]

The benefit of spending so much on the film's animation software is that future films won't require similar levels of investment in the same area. Perhaps this is why the studio greenlit *Zootopia* – the sheer amount of fur involved was an opportunity to make the most of their program.

It was money well spent, though – the film still holds up a decade and a half down the line. After hesitancy in translating their princess films into a CGI world, Disney delivered a beautiful cinematic experience. From Mother Gothel's tumbledown tower in a hidden clearing to the ethereal lantern lighting at the heart of the story, *Tangled* frequently matches up against the animation in later-Renaissance era films.

The rest of the movie, though, feels like a modernisation of the princess film. *The Princess and the Frog* acted as a transition piece for the genre, pairing more nuanced characters with traditional visuals. *Tangled* feels more fully refreshed. Flynn Rider, the roguish anti-hero, is a charming change of pace. His character design even represented a concession to the female gaze: Greno and Howard held a 'Hot Man Meeting', gathering female employees together for a marathon review of what they did – and did not – find attractive in men. Rider's final appearance was hugely influenced by what these women found appealing. He is, of course, still a man in his early twenties who falls in love with a teenager – but I suppose some concessions need to be made to avoid alienating the lucrative 'creep' demographic.

Talking of creeps – Mother Gothel is among the very best of Disney's modern villains. Sure, she kidnaps a child so that she can make it comb her hair and sing to her, but when she returns the musical favour, she delivers one hell of a show-stopper. *Tangled* isn't short on great songs (or reprises – there are two in the film and a bonus one on the soundtrack album), but none compares to 'Mother Knows Best'. It's a playful, sinister Broadway number that sits at odds with the rest of the music in the film, which was mostly inspired by 1960s folk rock. The whole song is essentially an anthem for narcissistic mothers everywhere, a clever musical framing of the character's toxic relationship with Rapunzel. After all, whenever the pair express their love for one another, Mother Gothel has to have the final word – their refrain has her telling Rapunzel that she loves her most, though it always looks suspiciously like the words are actually being delivered to Rapunzel's youth-giving hair. But hey, who can blame her? That hair cost tens of millions of dollars. And that's before we even think about how much Mother Gothel is spending on conditioner.

2. There are varying estimates to precisely how much Rapunzel's hair would weigh. The Liberty Science Centre in New Jersey claims it'd come in at just nine kilograms. Kelly Ward, who worked specifically on the problem for *Tangled*, has a doctorate in the computer animation of human hair. She reckons it'd weigh around twenty-seven to thirty-six kilograms. I'm inclined to side with Ward, though either way it's a hell of a push to imagine the princess having the strength to pull it around everywhere. Frankly, given she's spent 18 years confined to what just about constitutes a fancy studio apartment, you'd imagine her legs would give in less than a mile into her journey, with or without hair.

Chapter 51

Hunny, I'm Home

Winnie the Pooh • 2011 • Stephen Anderson, Don Hall

The Ashdown Forest isn't like other forests. For one thing, there's a conspicuous lack of trees. It's heathland really. Not a forest at all. Some ten square miles of rolling hills and dusty brown shrubs, with seasonal flourishes of vibrantly purple heather.

I grew up in a small village on the edge of the forest. My family and I weren't so close that we would pass through it each day, but we were near enough that the bus would skirt its edges on the way into town. We could easily dip into the forest for an hour or so on a sunny weekend, running up the short grass by Gills Lap car park as we attempted to catch our kite upon the wind.

On those days, as our family made short treks across the heath, my sister and I were encouraged to keep our eyes out for hoofprints embedded in the cracked dirt paths. These were, according to my parents, Eeyore's footprints. It made perfect sense to us, even as we stepped out of the way of horses and their riders, who left their own tracks behind them. We'd long known that the Ashdown Forest was better known to most as the Hundred Acre Wood – home to Christopher Robin, Winnie the Pooh, and all of their friends. Why would it matter to us that Eeyore, a cuddly toy donkey, would not even have horseshoes?

In 1925, A.A. Milne bought Cotchford Farm to use as a country home. The timber-framed building sits just north of the forest, a few moments' walk from the village of Hartfield. The area's natural beauty had an instant impact on Milne, who soon began writing stories about his son's toys. Pooh Bear had, by this point, already made an appearance of sorts in a 1924 poem that referred to him as Edward. But now, with the uniquely beautiful Ashdown Forest (and, in particular, an area of the nearby Buckhurst Park estate known as Five Hundred Acre Wood) on his doorstep, the world of Pooh was transplanted to East Sussex.[1]

I suppose many people grow up in areas that have famous literary connections. But, to me, there has always been something special about growing up with Winnie the Pooh as a neighbour of sorts.

1. Cotchford Farm continued to inspire Milne for the rest of his life. He died while staying at the house in 1956. Twelve years later, it was bought by Brian Jones of The Rolling Stones. Shortly afterwards, Jones was expelled from the band. In July 1969, he was found dead in the house's swimming pool.

There are not many characters whose fame outweighs that of the location itself. *The Hunchback of Notre Dame* may be intrinsically tied to Paris, but the city will always be more well-regarded for its romance than anything else. Even the cathedral is more widely known than the story's title character. It is, after all, *The Hunchback of Notre Dame* and not, say, *Quasimodo's Gaff.*

With Pooh, many people aren't even aware that his home has a very real location in the world. He simply belongs to the Hundred Acre Wood, an idyllic place in which there are no roads and no buildings. Where, until the final chapters of *The House at Pooh Corner*, there is almost no intrusion from the outside world at all (bar a near-endless supply of balloons).[2]

So, to come from that place – or as near to it as any child might hope to – tints your view of the world a little. Exploration is (and this is a little sentimental, but then so is everything in the world of Pooh) a little less scary when, no matter where you travel, you are likely to stumble across a friend from home.

As a child, there was always a flutter of familiarity that ran through me when I came across Pooh Bear in the wild, so to speak. I might have been in a toy store in the United States or a stationery aisle in a French supermarket. Heck, I might just be walking down the street in a small town somewhere overseas. But I'd catch sight of Winnie the Pooh – a branded teddy bear, or on the cover of a magazine, or on the t-shirt of a passerby – and I would be reminded of home, if only for an instant.

There has always been a sense of security in the world of Pooh. The stories are gentle, well-meaning and funny. There are no real antagonists unless you count Rabbit (who is, let's face it, an absolutely awful bigot). This 2011 sequel – the first and only to be added to the animated canon since 1977's *Many Adventures of…* – is the perfect example of this. It is a serenely gentle film in which the biggest villains are the Backson (an imagined beast who is responsible for spoiled milk and stopped clocks) and the concept of homonyms (the sublime knot/not sequence is one of the silliest gags in the entire animated canon).

Directors Anderson and Hall perfectly capture the spirit of the 1977 original – no mean feat after three decades of wilful misinterpretations and commercialisation. From the live-action fearmongering of the 1980s after-school special to the increasingly generic Disneytoon Studios films of the late 1990s, it often seemed like Disney had forgotten what makes Pooh and his friends so enduring.[3]

---

2. If we're being pedantic – and I'm something of an amateur Pooh scholar at this point, for lack of a better phrase, so I certainly will be pedantic: Pooh does not live in the Hundred Acre Wood. Pooh, and almost all of his friends, live *near* the Hundred Acre Wood. Only Owl actually abides in the woods themselves.
3. The most recent rebrand, 2023's *Me and Winnie the Pooh* continues this trend. The series, aimed at preschoolers, recasts all of the voice actors with American children, which has exactly the effect you think it will. Worse still, Eeyore is positively chipper in this version. If you ever need evidence that *Me and Winnie the Pooh* fundamentally misrepresents the characters, look no further than its eighteenth episode, entitled 'Eeyore's Morning Affirmations'.

Not so here. Future Frozen songwriters Kristen Anderson-Lopez and Robert Lopez do a fantastic job of capturing the Sherman Brothers sound, modernising just slightly with little tricks like using the grumbling of Pooh's stomach as percussion.[4] Actress Zooey Deschanel helps out, too, singing the classic theme (which now includes Tigger, too) and several other tracks, as well as writing a song for the end credits.

The crisp animation also subtly upgrades the familiar look of the original film. Eeyore, in particular, is a stand-out – the funniest character in a film filled with funny characters. The forest itself, once again minimally realised so as to reflect an illustration on a page, is captured with the tranquil other-worldliness it requires while somehow still looking like the Ashdown Forest itself. This is the result of a trip the directors took to East Sussex in preparation for the film, their head of story and art director among those along for the journey. Anderson and Hall also asked Burny Mattinson, an animator who had worked on the studio's previous shorts, to deliver the film's storyboards. The result is a film that feels intricately connected to a place that most people aren't aware actually exists.

The plot echoes the storybook structure of *The Many Adventures of Winnie the Pooh*, combining three more stories from Milne's books into one distinctly less episodic narrative. Some critics complained that, at just sixty-three minutes, the film was too short. Still, given the accessibility of the story to the youngest of cinema-goers (and the way the film gleefully breezes along), it's a very welcome runtime. Whisper it, but 2011's *Winnie the Pooh* might actually be slightly better than the 1977 film.

It's a shame, then, that it remains a relative unknown among the Disney canon. It was absolutely trounced in cinemas, releasing on the same day as the final instalment in the *Harry Potter* franchise. But, as both a joyful recreation of the earlier Winnie the Pooh shorts and the last 2D animation among the animated classics to date, the movie is well worth a revisit.

I don't get down to the Ashdown Forest too often these days. I've settled now, further up the country, in another place with a famous fictional resident: Nottingham. Like Pooh Bear, Robin Hood lived with his friends in the forest. And like Pooh Bear, Robin Hood is known around the world. But all the same, Winnie the Pooh has the stronger hold on me. After all, I've never used my archery skills to take on corrupt officials or rob people in the middle of the woods. But I have been a small boy, dragging his favourite toy across the Ashdown Forest, leaning over the edge of Poohsticks Bridge, waiting to see which twig will emerge first.

4. These grumbles are what earns Robert a space in the end credits under 'Additional Voices'. His wife, Kristen, supplements her songwriting work with a role of her own – she's the voice of Kanga here.

Chapter 52

Playing to the Crowd

Wreck-It Ralph • *2012* • *Rich Moore*

The first time I watched the *Indiana Jones* trilogy, it all felt very familiar. I was still young – maybe seven or eight years old – but I found that I already spoke the film's language. I wasn't fluent yet. I couldn't keep up with all the nuance of the dialogue, and I wasn't picking apart the mise en scene to find the hidden symbolism. But the very plot itself was filled with scenes that I instantly recognised. Scenes that were etched into my consciousness like the fairy tales of the Brothers Grimm. Not because I was literate in the history of motion pictures but because I watched *DuckTales*.

Pop culture references have been turning up in films and television shows since the very dawn of the art form. A knowing wink towards another piece of intellectual property builds a sort of camaraderie with the audience, an opportunity to draw the viewer in. This film gets me, they'll think. This film, too, has seen *Reservoir Dogs*.

In animated cinema – in films that are overtly targeted towards families – they can serve an important role. Children very rarely have the disposable income to pay for a cinema trip or a digital download for a movie night at home. They simply do not have the work ethic. And so throwing in gags that appeal to the adult making these purchases might edge a decision in favour of your film over, say: *Caillou 2: Electric Boogaloo*.

Over the years, the occurrences of pop culture references appear to be on the rise. The vultures in *The Jungle Book* were a clear nod to The Beatles, but were a relatively rare example of the phenomenon. Cut to the 90s, though, and we have Pumbaa quoting *In The Heat of the Night* and Robin Williams delivering a performance that is roughly 70% references. In 1990, Disney released *DuckTales the Movie: Treasure of the Lost Lamp*. It was the first animated theatrical release the studio had distributed that wasn't produced by the feature animation team – in other words, it wasn't part of the official Disney canon.

What it was, though, was a joy – a rollicking adventure with a very distinct poster. Front and centre is Scrooge McDuck, running to escape an ancient ruin. On his head: a brown fedora. By his side: a leather whip. The poster was even designed by Drew Struzan, the iconic artist behind the *Indiana Jones* one sheet. That there wasn't a single reference to the series in the movie itself seems unimportant – the image is there, burned into the audience's minds.

Not that there weren't plenty of overt references to Indy in other media, too. My childhood was filled with mine-cart chases, hair's-breadth escapes from tumbling boulders, and last-minute retrievals of rogue headwear. And so, by the time I finally watched *Raiders of the Lost Ark* for the first time, I was a ready-built fan, committed to a cause that I was only just learning even existed.

I wonder if this is the path taken by children who have watched – or will watch – *Wreck-It Ralph*. The film is set within the machines of a classic American arcade and is overloaded with nods to video games past and present. In many cases, these references will be as inexplicable to young audiences as I once found the concept of a gigantic boulder set to run on a distinct path with the sole aim of crushing a person. In fact, the very idea of an arcade will feel alien to many children growing up outside of the United States. In the UK, these gigantic machines dedicated to singular video games are generally found in one of two places: in large bowling alleys, next to the bit where you trade in your shoes, and roughly one-eighth of a mile out to sea, at the end of a pier.

But the magic of references is that while they might trigger a warm flush of nostalgia through the heart of one person, they will appear completely benign to somebody uninitiated with the source material. And so we can imagine teenagers today playing their first *Street Fighter* title and briefly pausing during their first fight to think: 'Hey! Isn't that the fella from Wreck-It Ralph's bad guy support group?' And yes, it is. But unfortunately, that moment of wonder was a rookie error in the midst of battle, and I'm afraid Zangief has now thrown you into a screw piledriver so powerful that it sent a small shockwave out across the arena. Also: you're dead.

Wreck-It Ralph is smart, in that its references never overpower the plot in the way that broader approaches by films like *Shrek* or *Boss Baby* might.[1] In fact, the nature of the film means that director Rich Moore and his team could organically fit in a stunning amount of winks to the history of gaming, from instantly recognisable characters like Sonic and Bowser to more niche figures like Bentley Bear from 1983's *Crystal Castles*.

Every inch of *Wreck-It Ralph* is considered, with three disparate fictional video game worlds capturing the variety offered in any given arcade. Ralph's home game, *Fix-It Felix*, is a classic 8-bit platformer. Even when off-duty, the game's denizens move with a charming stutter. By comparison, *Hero's Duty* is an overwhelming first-person shooter, a state-of-the-art game with the most complex design seen within the film. Candy-coloured racing game *Sugar Rush* is bright and cartoonish, with clear nods to *Mario Kart*.

Equally well-designed is the voice cast, which draws on its actors' strengths to deliver one of the strongest ensembles in any Disney film. It might not be a stretch to ask Sarah Silverman to play immature and scatological, or Jack McBrayer to

1. *Boss Baby*'s references are exhausting, but admirably varied. Among the films that are knowingly spoofed are: *Apocalypse Now*, *Glengarry Glen Ross*, *Mary Poppins* and, of course, *Raiders of the Lost Ark*.

deliver wholesome and naïve, but there could be no better choice for Vanellope and Felix. Jane Lynch is equally obvious a choice for the tough-but-damaged Calhoun. All three feel like the only choice that could have been made. As the titular Ralph, John C. Reilly may have been a less clear choice – but his vulnerability becomes the very heart of the film – a good guy in spirit, but a bad guy in code.

Wreck-It Ralph felt like a distinct change of pace for Disney when it was released in 2012. Even today, it feels like the film most rooted in our world, most distinctly tied to our culture. But films like this can play a meaningful role in growing up. So many animated movies teach young people the value of friendship or integrity. This one teaches them the otherworldly power of UP UP DOWN DOWN LEFT RIGHT LEFT RIGHT B A START.

Chapter 53

Top of the Ice Pops

Frozen • *2013* • *Chris Buck, Jennifer Lee*

Here is a definitive ranking of every song featured in the 53rd Disney animated classic, *Frozen*:

10. 'For the First Time in Forever (Reprise)'

Since *Beauty and the Beast*, no Disney film has been so indebted to Broadway musicals as *Frozen*. This is, generally speaking, a very good thing: the film is jam-packed with music that is both memorable and varied. Husband and wife duo Robert Lopez and Kristen Anderson-Lopez were behind the songs, their second gig in the Disney canon, following on from 2011's *Winnie the Pooh*.

This track, written by Anderson-Lopez over the course of just twenty minutes, is the exception to the rule – and arguably the most Broadway-esque song on the soundtrack. But it's a half-hearted reprise of a much better song, and it serves wholly for exposition. There's too much talking and an overwhelming sense that it simply doesn't need to exist. But hey, doesn't every big musical have at least one song that bores the audience rotten?

9. 'Frozen Heart'

Poor 'Frozen Heart' is the only song on the film's soundtrack that does not make it into the inevitable Broadway adaptation. The problem is that it doesn't add much to the story. The song is essentially a brief and ominous introduction both to the very concept of ice, and of the dangers of a 'frozen heart'. It's replaced onstage with a Greek chorus-style narrative track that brings the audience directly into the story.

8. 'Vuelie'

The only song I'm including here not to have been written by Lopez and Anderson-Lopez; you can make your case for it being part of the score if you like. But the striking vocals are the first piece of music the audience hears, replacing the traditional glimmer of 'When You Wish Upon A Star' for the studio's logos. 'Vuelie' was written by the film's composer, Christophe Beck, and the Sámi musician Frode Fjellheim, and draws on Nordic folk music – including the distinctive Sámi joik. Anyway, it's brief, but it's absolutely gorgeous, and it draws the audience into the film's world as well as any other opener.[1]

7. 'For the First Time in Forever'

The first version of this song on the soundtrack, 'For the First Time in Forever' briefly attempted to make history as the first Disney song to directly reference vomiting, until the studio stepped in and the lyric was changed to be about eating chocolate. It was the coward's way out, but at least the version that made the film does manage to keep a line about being gassy. And look: I know it's crude, but given the heightened levels of coeliac disease in Nordic countries, it's nice of Disney to abstractly acknowledge it by giving one of their leading characters gastric problems.

6. 'Love is an Open Door'

From here on in, every song is a certified banger, which is perhaps why *Frozen*'s soundtrack is one of the most consistent of all the Disney films. The lover's duet between Anna and her charming, definitely-not-a manipulative-man-using-her-for-power prince Hans is bright and silly. It draws on the lively and irreverent songwriting Robert Lopez had brought to musicals like *Avenue Q* and *The Book of Mormon*.

Occasionally, Anna's quirky naivety in the film comes across as an echo of *Tangled*'s Rapunzel – but the character comes into her own in musical numbers like these.

5. 'Reindeer(s) Are Better Than People'

The biggest crime on the *Frozen* soundtrack is not its behemoth showstopper, no matter what some people will try to tell you. It's that Jonathan Groff, a talented Broadway actor who had been among the original cast of *Spring Awakening*, is given just one song. The acoustic ditty (and really, this is the sort of composition for which the word 'ditty' was invented) runs to just fifty seconds – but charms endlessly nonetheless. Groff duets with himself as Kristoff, and Kristoff's impression of his pet reindeer.

4. 'In Summer'

The *second* biggest crime on the *Frozen* soundtrack is that another great Broadway actor, Josh Gad, is also relegated to a single song. Gad, who originated the role of Elder Cunningham in *The Book of Mormon* (and thus had form for delivering Lopez's wry lyrics), makes the most of 'In Summer', a song that acts both as an introduction to Gad's broadly likeable snowman Olaf, and a mildly threatening science lesson for younger audience members, who may lean into their parents and ask precisely what snow does do in summer.

1. Other openers that absolutely smash the brief and drop the audience right into the middle of a very specific place: 'Overture' from *The Jungle Book*, 'Once Upon A Time in New York City' from *Oliver & Company*, and 'Circle of Life' from *The Lion King*.

3. 'Do You Want to Build a Snowman?'

Frozen takes just eight minutes to blast through its first two songs and leap straight into the third, 'Do You Want to Build a Snowman?'. Audiences already know they're in for a musical treat, but this track really solidifies that, with a melody that lingers in your head for weeks. It was almost dropped from the movie for being too sad, and there's a case to be made. The song shows the growth of an emotional rift between two sisters who had, just minutes before, been playing joyfully together. Ultimately, the song proved too popular with Disney staff to be dropped, and the film is all the better for it. Though it still features animal sidekicks and a blissfully ignorant snowman, *Frozen* is among the more mature Disney films. That might make its popularity with preschoolers all the more baffling – but it also means it has more emotional resonance for the parents forced to watch it over and over again.

2. 'Let It Go'

Look, you should consider yourselves lucky that the song makes it this high in the chart. When I envisioned this chapter, I pictured the song ranking going from first to last place, with 'Let It Go' sitting squarely at the bottom of the pile. The scourge of children's birthday parties and an aggressive karaoke favourite for the most toxic member of the hen-do? It's no wonder this song has become as divisive as it has.

But then I revisited *Frozen* for the first time in almost a decade, and good god, 'Let It Go' is an absolute tune. Hitherto relegated to a minor singing part on 'For the First Time in Forever', Idina Menzel leans fully into the number. It's a powerhouse performance of a song written specifically for Menzel, a musical theatre veteran who had first appeared in the Broadway debut of *Rent* before originating the role of Elphaba in *Wicked*.

It's fitting that 'Let It Go' should be the song that most lingers in fan's heads; its very existence shaped *Frozen* into the form we know. Initially, the movie was a more traditional take on the classic Hans Christian Andersen fairy tale, *The Snow Queen*. Elsa's role would see her descend into full-on villainy, with a show-stopping song to mark the transition. Directors Chris Buck and Jennifer Lee didn't anticipate their songwriters not just stopping the show, but redirecting it altogether.

Lopez and Anderson-Lopez approached the bookmarked villain song from an unusual angle – empathy. In possibly the most Disney move possible, they took the time to consider the character and understand where she was and what she was feeling at that moment in the film. And, in doing so, the icy Snow Queen began to look a lot more human. The result was a shift that moved Elsa away from villainy and warranted a rethink of the entire plot.

At the same time, the empowering anthem to self-expression made it malleable to any number of personal situations. The powerful refusal to deny one's true self any longer has made it a popular coming-out anthem among the LGBTQ+ community, a celebration of the choice to feel where once they concealed. It's also something of a coming-of-age song; Elsa's burgeoning ice powers are a metaphor for either her personal growth into an adult in her own right, or simply for the physical changes any teenager might go through.

For many commentators, the big question was how this song, with its myriad mature readings, became the anthem of a generation of kindergarteners. It's a question that seems obvious to me. Perhaps everybody else was laden down by a critical eye swollen from over-analysing everything, so here's my take on why 4-year-old Susie loves 'Let It Go'.

It. Is. A. Banger.

'Let It Go' is an unrelenting epic that cannot and will not be resisted. And that's it. It was the first big Disney anthem since the invention of YouTube, meaning that tech-savvy toddlers could bring it up on a screen with just a few awkward smashes of their little cocktail sausage fingers and revisit the catchiest Disney song in twenty years as much as they pleased. It's a simply huge song, soaring above the mountains of Arendelle, shattering icicles with its ridiculous climax – a dazzling finale from Menzel, who actually asked that the song be placed into a higher octave so that it sounded more youthful and less sultry.

Is it perfect? No, not at all. Though Menzel's vocals are incredible, the instrumentation feels unsophisticated and occasionally sounds like its own karaoke backing track. And for all the perceived meanings the song has taken on, it ultimately delivers emancipation to its female singer through the time-tested method of: a makeover.

These are forgivable sins, and honestly, a little time away from the cultural phenomena that the song briefly became will do wonders for the cynics. 'Let It Go' is, after all, something of a spiritual sequel to 'Defying Gravity', another song first delivered by the *wickedly* talented Idina Menzel.

1. 'Fixer Upper'

But look, you can't convince me otherwise. 'Fixer Upper' is an absolute *bop*.

Chapter 54

Parental Leave

Big Hero 6 • *2014* • *Don Hall, Chris Williams*

Compared to the floundering Disney of the early 1980s, or the Disney of the 1940s that seemed perpetually on the brink of financial collapse, the studio's 21st century operations are positively streamlined. The arrival of Michael Eisner and Frank Wells at the tail end of the Bronze Era galvanised a corporate revival at Disney. It more than equalled the creative one that began at the same time.

A series of mergers, starting with television company ABC and taking in Pixar, Marvel, Lucasfilm, 21st Century Fox and, most recently, Epic Games, has left Disney as one of the largest entertainment companies in the world.

Today, Disney's theme parks still claim to be the happiest place on Earth, and their boardrooms may just be the most synergistic. Not satisfied with rebooting Star Wars, Indiana Jones, and The Muppets, launching the Marvel Cinematic Universe (MCU), and bringing The Simpsons to streaming via Disney Plus, we've also begun to see a series of crossovers between their various intellectual properties.

Not all of these have been successful: The Simpsons have frequently been employed for animated shorts that riff humorlessly on Marvel, Star Wars, the Disney Princesses and – in one particularly self-congratulatory clip, the first anniversary of Disney Plus itself.

Big Hero 6 sits at the other end of this spectrum. While working on 2011's *Winnie the Pooh*, director Don Hall found himself poring over the database of properties belonging to the recently acquired Marvel. He uncovered a short run of comics called *Big Hero 6* and saw potential in the property. Where the MCU frequently came up against the wrath of comic book fans frustrated at the way Disney played fast and loose with beloved characters, this arc – barely known to even the most ardent of readers – was obscure enough that Hall felt safe taking liberties with the established lore.

And take liberties he did. By the time *Big Hero 6* reached our screens, it barely resembled the source text at all. Hall and his co-director Chris Williams had shifted the action from Japan to 'San Fransokyo', a hybrid of San Francisco and Tokyo that imagined the former had been rebuilt by Japanese immigrants after the 1906 earthquake.

Another big change was a central member of the team: Baymax. In the comics written by Steven T. Seagle and Duncan Rouleau, Baymax was a robot bodyguard who could transform into a dragon. In the film, he becomes a benign healthcare assistant; still a robot, but now much cuddlier. He looks like the youngest member of the Michelin Man/Stay Puft Marshmallow Man acting dynasty.

Baymax, it should be noted, is the heart and soul of *Big Hero 6*. His expressionless blundering – gentle and well-meaning – is endlessly fun. Whether he's attempting to squeeze his impractical form through small spaces or simply wandering into traffic, Baymax is deeply endearing. This may be due to Hall and Williams' efforts to find a perfect animation reference. The waddle of a penguin was considered, but ultimately, the decision was made, and Baymax's distinct movements were settled: his walk would reflect that of a toddler with a full nappy.

The family history of Hiro, the film's main protagonist, also differs from the comics. In Seagle and Rouleau's original work, Hiro was building Baymax when his father died – the robot's AI was programmed using his late father's memories. Disney, seeing an opportunity to ramp up the grief for young Hiro, decided that in their version of the story, *both* of his parents would be dead, and he would be living with his aunt and brother. And then, just for good measure, they'd kill off the brother mid-movie, too.

Loss of a family member has been a trope within the Disney canon since the first frames of *Snow White*, in which the title card informs us that the Queen is her stepmother. Things were made more explicit still just a few films later when Bambi's mother was killed off-screen by a hunter.

Like Snow White, Cinderella is also an orphan left in the care of a wicked stepmother. In 2014, veteran Disney producer Don Hahn told Glamour magazine that these frequent missing parents – and in particular, the maternal absences – had two very different factors influencing them.

On the one hand, Hahn suggested that the loss of a parent is a very effective way to push the plot forward. This is especially important in animated cinema, which tends to have shorter running times than its live-action equivalent. Once Bambi's mother dies, he has no choice but to step up. The loss of Hiro's parents in *Big Hero 6* ensures that both he and his brother, Tadashi, are independent spirits who can look after themselves from the very beginning of the film. Hiro is even, perhaps, a little too independently-minded. It is only after Tadashi dies at the end of the first act that he is drawn further into the plot and given a chance to grow.

The other reason Hahn offered is much sadder. In the autumn of 1938, Walt and Roy Disney convinced their parents, Elias and Flora, to move south to join them in California. The brothers pitched in together to buy a bungalow in North Hollywood that would act as their parents' new home. It was a kind but ill-fated gesture: less than a month after moving in, a leak in the furnace filled the house with noxious gas. When a housekeeper discovered them the next day, Elias was unconscious, and was ultimately revived. Flora was less lucky.

Both Walt and Roy blamed themselves for their mother's death. Hahn believes it accounts for the frequent absence of mothers within the Disney classics, though I'm less convinced. *Snow White* had already been released at the time of Flora's passing – the profits from the film would have enabled the brothers to splash out on a house for their parents. *Bambi* had already been selected as a feature at the time of the incident, and the death of the deer's mother is also part of the original novel. This is, of course, also true for *Cinderella* and, if you really want to push the theory, both *The Sword in the Stone* and *The Jungle Book*, which were the only other features Walt worked on where the protagonist's mother was conspicuously absent.

Though the canon is filled with movies in which parents die or are simply never around to begin with, the overwhelming majority of occurrences actually come from the Renaissance era or later. The big hitters of that period almost all featured parents who were absent for one reason or another. Only Ariel's father is around in *The Little Mermaid* – and they're diametrically opposed throughout the film. This is also true for both Pocahontas and *Aladdin*'s Jasmine, a film in which the titular character is also an orphan. In *Beauty and the Beast*, Belle has a much more positive relationship with her father, who promptly gets kidnapped. Her mother is, of course, dead.

In a brutal run for Disney's infant protagonists, Simba, Quasimodo and Tarzan all lose at least one parent during the opening act of their respective films. Even *The Rescuers Down Under* features a child protagonist whose father has died. Across the entire run of Renaissance films, only Mulan and Hercules have living parents. Mulan is a constant source of disappointment to hers, and Hercules grows up believing himself adopted, separated from his birth parents by a rule that, frankly, you'd think his father would be in a position to change.

There are plenty more dead and missing parents as we enter the 21st century, too. *Atlantis*, *Lilo & Stitch*, *Chicken Little*, *The Princess and the Frog* and *Frozen* are by no means a complete list. A good deal of *Meet the Robinsons* is set inside an actual orphanage. Moana's gran dies in a relatively abstract way, turning into a magical sea turtle. And, though it isn't explicitly mentioned, it's probably fair to assume that the parents of more or less the entire cast of *Home on the Range* ended up on a barbecue somewhere.

Talking of barbecues, *Big Hero 6*'s Tadashi is cooked by a particularly eager flame grill when his university suffers from an explosive fire. Also seemingly lost to the disaster is his professor, Callaghan. Later – twist! – Callaghan is revealed to not only be alive, but also acting as the mysterious villain of the piece. A smart subversion of our expectations reveals that he, too, has lost a loved one.

For Hiro, the parallels he can draw between his own grief and that of the murderous Callaghan allow him to recognise how unhealthily he has been mourning. In his darkest moment, his attempt to turn the affable Baymax into a brutal killing machine puts his late brother's friends in mortal danger. And these friends are, of course, his route to salvation.

Disney may have a cruel fondness for murdering the families of their characters, but they always offer a surrogate option that can fill the hole left behind. Simba finds Timon and Pumbaa; Lilo finds Stitch. Quasimodo finds kinship in the entire population of Paris, and Belle finds a hirsute prince and an Ikea catalogue of friends.

Ultimately, and perhaps just a little tritely, Hiro gathers his new team – Big Hero 6 – around him. He is able to realise that a chosen family can be just as valuable as a real family. Also, he has an aunt who has been raising him since he was four years old. But best not get too attached to her, just in case the studio needs a little plot impetus for a future sequel.

Chapter 55

A Brave New World

Zootopia • *2016* • *Byron Howard, Rich Moore*

One of my wife's biggest gripes with life in the UK is how difficult it is to dress appropriately for a visit to the shops. In the winter, the streets are freezing cold, and one must always be prepared for an unexpected torrential downpour. In the summer, the dry British heat can be surprisingly unbearable, and one must always be prepared for an unexpected torrential downpour. Our shops, meanwhile, have some universal agreement in place to remedy whichever season currently has a hold. In the heat of summer, when customers are likely to be wandering in off the streets wearing light dresses, t-shirts, or shorts, the air-conditioning is turned up to full blast, and it is entirely possible to freeze to death while standing in the queue for the tills. In the winter, when the weather outside is frightful, and customers have dressed accordingly in heavy knitwear and waterproof coats, the stores ramp their heat up until the boiler is fit to burst. Walk into your nearest department store and witness hordes of middle-aged women lying on their backs like toppled tortoises, defeated by the sudden heat and their eighteen layers of thermal clothing.

Have pity, then, for the denizens of Zootopia, where each district has wildly different climates. You might leave your house in the desert region of the city, commute into the snowy tundra, and spend your evenings at a karaoke bar in the stagnant heat of the rainforest quarter. I'm not sure how one is meant to dress accordingly in a place where the daily forecast features a presenter standing in front of a map, broadly waving their arms over the whole thing and simply saying: 'All of the weather, everywhere.'

It's one of the many questions the audience might reasonably find themselves asking when watching a film like *Zootopia*. Any time a film creates a completely original world so different from our own, it is bound to create difficult problems that must be fixed for the film's setting to make sense. In films intended for adults, it is not uncommon for a great deal of time to be put into meaningful world-building. There are entire books dedicated to Pandora, the planet at the heart of James Cameron's *Avatar* films. The fantastic *Mad Max: Fury Road* doesn't explain a thing, but nevertheless shows its audience a fully realised post-apocalypse where even the weirdest elements have been clearly thought through.

Children's films, however, don't tend to have this committed approach to world-building. Kids are less likely to ask about the practical side of building a city out of twelve distinct ecosystems. They are more likely to ask why the elephant doesn't want to serve the fox an ice cream.

I, however, despite several major indicators suggesting otherwise, am not a child. I am an adult man who is writing a book about Disney movies. And I. Have. Questions.

Because first up, how does this multi-ecosystem city even work? Was the metropolis founded on this particular spot because of some unique phenomenon that created an icy landscape directly beside a sprawling jungle? It seems unlikely. During our brief initial tour of the districts, it is heavily implied that the Rainforest District's humidity is controlled by an elaborate (and presumably hose-pipe-ban-defying) sprinkler system. Similarly, we see giant puffs of snow shot out of the ground in Tundratown. Property taxes in Zootopia must be through the roof.

While we're at it, what happened to the birds? Though the residents of the city are all mammals, we do see a few insects (Are they sentient? Do any of the mammals care?) and catch a glimpse at a fish market, which answers one question (What are the predators eating?) and asks several more (Where are the fish coming from? Are *they* sentient? Do *any* of the mammals care?). The only mention of birds in the film, though, is in the lyrics to in-world pop banger 'Try Everything' by Gazelle.[1] So, *what happened to the birds*? There are two obvious answers: first, birds were excluded by the animators to keep things simple. Director Byron Howard says this is the case, pointing out that the team went so far as to omit any mammal that did not fit neatly into the predator/prey binary. But this doesn't fix the 'Try Everything' lyric. The second answer, then, is far more compelling: big old bird war.

Of course, none of this really matters. Children's films have free reign to be as silly as they like, and creating nonsensical worlds is a part of this. *Zootopia* is certainly a great deal more considered than Pixar's *Cars*, in which the main protagonist travelled from town to town inside the belly of another character, tractors were farmed as cattle, and the animators couldn't even put the eyes in the headlights, which any 5-year-old could tell you is *obviously* where they go.

One of the joys of *Zootopia* – and there are many – is seeing the playful ways the animators engage with the challenges of this multi-species metropolis. Trains have doors of different sizes, and juice bars have built-in dumb waiters to lift their drinks to giraffe height. These touches extend to international releases, too: the moose newsreader that appears in most English language versions was replaced by a koala in Australia, a jaguar in Brazil, and a raccoon dog in Japan.

1. *More* questions! Gazelle is a gazelle, so is it like a major popstar in our world simply being called 'Human', or is it viewed more like actual popstar H.E.R. – a stylised name that plays on the language? Whatever the case, I was ready to critically call out how thicc Disney made Gazelle until I discovered that Shakira, who voices her, had been unimpressed with the more true-to-nature original character design and asked for more curves to be added. This doesn't mean I'm not still judging Disney. I'm just also judging Shakira now. I tell you one thing – those people who complain about the live action Little Mermaid being Black are very rarely commenting on how huge the gazelle's ass is in Zootopia. Read into that what you will.

The title was also subject to change overseas, albeit for less fun reasons. In some international markets, including the UK, *Zootopia* became *Zootropolis*, mostly to skirt copyright restrictions on the original title. It's a shame, because the play on 'utopia' is a much better fit for a film that is so focused on uncovering the reality behind a seemingly idyllic world.

There's no denying that prejudice is the overarching theme of the film – the message occasionally being delivered through jokes that are either a little rough around the edges (Judy Hopps informs one character that only a rabbit can call another rabbit 'cute' and later chastises her reluctant partner Nick for touching a sheep's wool without permission), or allude to a darkness that younger audiences won't necessarily recognise (Judy's fox repellent is essentially pepper spray. There are predators in every world).

But for the most part, *Zootopia* is a smart and very funny film. It's one of the highlights of the Revival Era, filled with knowing jokes. The references for children are fun and silly – particularly the pirate video salesman Duke Weaselton, whose name echoes a character from *Frozen*,[2] and whose DVDs present animal puns both on existing Disney films and a few that had not yet been released.[3] There are also a few references for adults, which are delivered smartly and subtly – a throwaway *Breaking Bad* joke is organic enough to still get a laugh over a decade after the show's end.

Ultimately, *Zootopia* is evidence that an engaging story and a funny script are far more important than a coherent world. The detective story at the film's heart – essentially *48hrs*, but more furry – is cleverly designed to subvert expectations and deliver unexpected twists. Who cares what happened to the birds?[4]

---

2. Both are voiced by Alan Tudyk.
3. *Meowana*'s inspiration came out later that same year, but *Floatzen 2*'s wouldn't arrive for another three and a half years. The third film shown, *Giraffic*, is a play on *Gigantic*, a retelling of *Jack and the Beanstalk* that would have been Disney's 59th animated classic. It was cancelled 18 months after the release of *Zootopia*, its only legacy being this brief cameo.
4. *I do*. Did Gazelle kill them? Maybe Gazelle killed them. *Zootopia 2* comes out soon, and if I don't get answers, there'll be hell to pay.

Chapter 56

Miranda, Make Way!

Moana • 2016 • Ron Clements, John Musker

Lin-Manuel Miranda seems to exist in a perpetual state of puppy-like excitement. I know that this cannot possibly be the case – that his life, like any other, will be tainted with occasional sadness, will present moments of deep and troubling anxiety. Nevertheless, Miranda remains a man who appears to be constantly in awe of his own good luck, no matter how hard he worked for it.

Given this, it's almost impossible to imagine how he took the news that Disney – a studio whose films he had grown up watching – wanted to collaborate with him on their latest animated classic. The obvious answer is that he exploded, outright, there on that spot, leaving only a scuff mark and a few stray goatee hairs. But his continued presence in the world suggests that he probably held himself together, more or less, and then knocked out three or four of the most enjoyable Disney show-stoppers since the death of Howard Ashman.

Miranda's employment at Disney owes a great deal to the groundbreaking work that Ashman had undertaken alongside Alan Menken a quarter of a century earlier. They had been the pair to bring Broadway sensibilities to the studio, starting with their work on *The Little Mermaid.* In the wake of Ashman's untimely passing, Disney began drawing on other talents from the world of theatre: Tim Rice, who was the lyricist behind *Jesus Christ Superstar* and *Evita*, had been brought in to collaborate on the unfinished music for *Aladdin* – he contributed the film's breakout hit, 'A Whole New World'. *Godspell* composer Stephen Schwartz was hired for both *Hunchback* and *Pocahontas* (he would later return to theatre to create his most enduring musical, *Wicked*).

After the mostly song-free wilderness years of the Post-Renaissance Era, the studio returned to musicals once more. *Frozen*'s husband-and-wife songwriting team included Robert Lopez, who had been responsible for the less-than-family-friendly Broadway hits *Avenue Q* and *The Book of Mormon.*

So, the hiring of Lin-Manuel Miranda was not without precedent, though it was much more of a coup than Disney had originally realised. His first interviews with the company came late in 2013 when his profile had been buoyed slightly by the success of his first Broadway musical, *In the Heights.* It seems very likely that Miranda would have mentioned other work on his plate at the time, namely an ambitious hip-hop musical about one of America's founding fathers. It's just as plausible that the Disney staffers he met with had no idea that the musical would rocket Miranda to international fame, making him a household name across the United States and a valuable marketing asset in his own right.

And so, in 2014, the notoriously prolific Miranda was juggling two projects: Disney's latest animated film, *Moana*, and soon-to-be global sensation *Hamilton*. For the former, he was part of a trio of acclaimed musicians, working alongside veteran film composer Mark Mancina and Samoan-born artist Opetaia Foa'i. As a member of Te Vaka, Foa'i has become one of the most recognisable names in Pacific music and was often treated as a superstar during the trio's research trips in Polynesia.

Moana might be based on an original story by directors Clements and Musker, but it draws heavily on the history and the folklore of Polynesian cultures. The film's central premise is inspired by a real-life mystery – why a culture that was the planet's foremost pioneer in seafaring abruptly stopped their voyages for around a thousand years. Anyone who watches *Moana* will know the answer: the chief was a real homebody.

While the directors allowed their plot to be guided by a trust of Polynesian voices, Foa'i ensured the culture's influence was felt in the songs, which frequently feature lyrics in Samoan, Tokelauan and Tuvaluan.

Miranda, for his part, brings distinctly familiar traits from his other work into the film. Many writers have themes they return to repeatedly throughout their creative output. The English novelist Graham Greene was hung up on Catholicism and the inescapable guilt that comes along with it. Steven Spielberg's films frequently return to childhood innocence and its inevitable loss. And Lin-Manuel Miranda appears to have two themes that are never far from his mind: legacy, and the role of the individual within a community. It is the latter that looms large in *Moana*. Our title character is desperate to explore the ocean but is held back by her sense of duty – both to her father, the chief she is being raised to replace, and to the residents of Motunui, who each play their part in maintaining life on their island.

The film's opening number introduces the conflict between Moana's ambition and sense of responsibility. Like Nina from *In the Heights*, she dreads the idea of disappointing those who put their hope in her. Like Alexander Hamilton, she fights for what she believes is right and ultimately does so because she wants the people of her nation to thrive. It's easy to imagine work on *Hamilton* affecting Miranda's mindset as he worked on *Moana* – he would often appear via video call in meetings, in costume as the lead character during breaks in rehearsals.

Like Howard Ashman before him, Miranda's influence on Disney films has stretched beyond songwriting – he acted as an integral part of the story team on his second project within the animated canon, *Encanto*. Again, we saw a plot that emphasised the importance of playing your role within a community, and again, we examined the fear of letting down one's family.

Productive as ever, Miranda worked on half a dozen projects for Disney in the following years, providing music for two Star Wars films and acting in both a reboot of the 1980s cartoon series *DuckTales* and a long-awaited *Mary Poppins* sequel. But the crowning achievement might well have been his work on Disney's live action remake of *The Little Mermaid.* With the original film's lyricist Ashman unable to contribute new work, it fell to Miranda to take up his duties, collaborating with long-time hero Alan Menken to create new songs.

In fact, *The Little Mermaid* meant more to Miranda than anybody might have expected – with the sole exception of Menken. Because way back in the late 1980s, Menken's niece went to school in Manhattan's Upper East Side, where she was classmates with the future writer of *Hamilton.* The young Miranda was as passionate then as he is now. Upon learning of his classmate's connection to a Disney composer, he began asking questions about Menken's upcoming project and requested an autograph. In fact, he asked so many questions that Menken recognised his name years later during the initial success of *In The Heights.*

Watching the original *Little Mermaid* was a defining moment for Miranda. During the making of *Moana*, he welcomed his first child into the world – and named them Sebastian, after Ariel's crabbiest friend.

Miranda is the only one of *Moana*'s songwriting team not to return for the sequel. Still, it's impossible to imagine that the emotional connection to Disney won't draw him back for future projects. As a first engagement with the studio, though, he could have done no better than *Moana.* It's possibly the best and brightest animated classic since the Renaissance. Clements and Musker, working on their first fully computer-animated film together, added to their remarkable successes and delivered a breathtakingly beautiful film – the water animation alone is enough to make up for my having to sit through uglier films like *Chicken Little* to write this book. The characters are instantly lovable – from Dwayne Johnson's cocksure Maui right down to Alan Tudyk's spectacularly stupid Heihei. And, at the film's heart, Moana, easily the most likeable of the Disney Princesses and, in her own way, a Pacific Islander reflection of Lin-Manuel Miranda. Young, plucky, and hungry, and prone to delivering iconic songs without batting an eyelid.

Chapter 57

The Princess Inquiries

Ralph Breaks the Internet • *2018* • *Phil Johnston, Rich Moore*

One commonly cited argument against sequels is that they leave nothing to the imagination. Desperately seeking ground to expand upon, every minor plot point is explored, no matter how unnecessary. *Independence Day: Resurgence* asked, 'What would happen if the aliens returned?' The answer (that we would win again) turned out to be the only thing less interesting than the film, which most of you will have only just remembered even exists. The fourth *Die Hard* film finally revealed what Lucy McClane, the hero's 6-year-old child in the first film, would be up to nineteen years later (being an almost entirely normal 25-year-old). The fifth *Die Hard* film then remembered that John McClane had a son, too, and filled us in on what he was doing (being an international super-spy, for some reason). So many sequels insist on answering every possible question that a fan's thoughts might have possibly considered, even once.

Not so, *Ralph Breaks the Internet*, which catches up with the star of *Wreck-It Ralph* and his best friend, Vanellope. Instead, this film *asks* questions – mainly through virtue of not really making any sense whatsoever.

After Ralph accidentally wrecks Sugar Rush, the candy-themed racing game that Vanellope rules over as a benevolent princess, the two travel into the internet in order to buy a replacement part. Immediately, we have questions – not least, how on earth did Fandango get a prime spot alongside Cisco and Snapchat as one of the first of the many, many brand names Ralph spots during his time online?

The choices that Disney had to make in order to create a film that is set almost entirely within the internet would be enough to drive anybody over the edge. Every scene leans very heavily into meme culture – which guaranteed that it would age like milk, given the fast-moving nature of internet culture. There are already some painfully dated references in *Ralph Breaks the Internet*, from jokes about Chewbacca Mom,[1] and the Screaming Goat trend,[2] to cameos from popular YouTubers. These cameos were always going to be a dangerous choice, given the frequently unhinged behaviour of some of the internet's biggest stars. Disney must have undertaken

1. A deeply charming video posted to Facebook in 2016, in which Texan mother Candace Payne absolutely loses her mind over the simple joy of wearing a Chewbacca mask with a moving mouthpiece.
2. Already a decade old by the time of the film's release, the meme was exactly what it sounds like, and was intensely annoying.

extensive checks to ensure that the YouTubers featured in their film were above board. But it's hard to escape the darkness that the internet can bring out in people. Colleen Ballinger, a comedian who briefly appears in a role that strongly resembles her character 'Miranda Sings', has since been accused of inappropriate conduct with a number of underage fans.

The studio wasn't paid by any of the companies featured in the film, and so had to make decisions over which brands to feature, and which to exclude. They attempted to factor in the longevity of each brand before deciding who made the cut. In: networking hardware manufacturers Netgear and business analytics company Purple. Out: the then-booming content factory Buzzfeed, which is instead referenced obliquely through an advert for the fictional company 'BuzzFood' and, more obviously, in 'Buzzztube', the video-sharing site that Ralph uses to make his internet fortune.[3]

The most obvious reason for the film's exclusion of Buzzfeed is its similarity to the studio's own website, Oh My Disney, which features heavily here. Ironically, while Buzzfeed's operations have been significantly cut since the film's release in 2018, it's still online. Oh My Disney, however, is long since gone, with much of its remaining content now tucked away on the Disney News site.

Vanellope's brief time at Oh My Disney – operating as an undercover pop-up ad, and presumably working at pace, lest the site be shuttered without warning – is stuffed with references to the sprawling reach of the company. It's both a testament to how far Disney has come since 1937, and perhaps to how impersonal the sheer scope of their intellectual property can be. An establishing shot features areas dedicated to the *Star Wars* and *Marvel* franchises, *The Muppet Show* (Kermit's head floats lifelessly in a beam of green light), Pixar, and – at the very centre of everything – Disney Animation. The presence of the latter threatens to create a cartoon ouroboros; we are, after all, watching a film within that very canon.

The sequence allows for a number of cameos, and product placement opportunities. *Big Hero 6*'s Baymax appears in front of a contextless advert for Disney's range of Tsum Tsum toys, moments before Vanellope is pursued by stormtroopers, running past Marvel's Rocket Raccoon, who is having a chat with *Zootopia*'s Judy Hopps.

It is the conclusion to this chase, in which Vanellope glitches her way into the Disney Princesses' backstage lounge, that poses the biggest question of all: who gets to be a Disney Princess?

* * *

Though Disney's films have featured princesses since their very inception, it wasn't until the year 2000 that the studio wrangled them together under one banner.

3. Youtube, which is the clear inspiration behind the second part of that portmanteau, definitely *does* exist in the film's version of the internet though – as does Google, even though the pair choose to search using a fictional engine named 'KnowsMore' instead.

Andy Mooney, who had recently become president of Disney's consumer products division, had attended a performance of *Disney on Ice*, and had noticed that many of the young girls in the audience had turned up in makeshift costumes. Mooney saw an opportunity and soon incorporated the official Disney Princess franchise.

In the early days, some at Disney were hesitant about the new approach. Roy E. Disney, the last representative of the family on the Disney board, highlighted the long-standing policy of not mixing characters from fairy tale films. There were fears that the characters 'individual mythologies' might be weakened. Efforts were made to ensure the integrity of each character's narrative – for years, the official Princesses would be pictured alongside each other, but would never make eye contact in any images. This approach is firmly put to bed by *Ralph Breaks the Internet*, where the current line-up of Princesses (plus Anna and Elsa from *Frozen*) chat freely among themselves while they wait to make appearances at the Buzzfeed-esque 'Which Disney Princess is your BFF?' quiz.[4]

The presence of Anna and Elsa is interesting, given that neither is a part of the official franchise. With Elsa, the reason was clear: she isn't a princess, but a queen. As of the end of *Frozen II*, which came out almost exactly a year after this movie, so is Anna. But why was she included here?

The Disney Princess line-up has always been in flux. When the franchise launched, it featured all the obvious princesses to date – you know, the ones who are legally princesses: Snow White, Cinderella, Aurora, Ariel, Belle and Jasmine. It also included Pocahontas, who is the daughter of a Native American chief and who, in real life, was described as a princess during her trip to England (a cynical move to enable her to meet with more of the influential upper class). Mulan made the cut, despite only being in a relationship with a captain from the Chinese army. And, finally, Tinker Bell and Esmeralda were included, despite one being a fairy and the other's entire storyline revolving around how separate she was from any sort of ruling elite.

These last two were quickly dumped and, over the years that followed, additional princesses were added as their films were released. Tiana, Rapunzel, Moana, and, most recently, Raya are all now official Disney Princesses.

And yet there's a very obvious exception sitting right under our noses. Our crude little hero Vanellope was revealed at the end of *Wreck-It Ralph* to be a princess herself. Pamela Ribon, a writer for the film, was working on the screenplay for *Moana* when she realised that the two had equal claims to the Disney Princess title. The sequence here, which plays around with both princess and Disney movie-making clichés, is the direct result of this epiphany. It's also easily the most enjoyable part of the film, with Vanellope introducing her fellow royals to the joys of comfortable clothing, and the princesses in return sharing their advice about the benefits of staring longingly into 'important water'.

4. Belle and I are besties, according to both Buzzfeed *and* the Disney News article that once belonged to Oh My Disney.

There have been calls over the years for another prominent (and technical) princess who falls under the Disney umbrella to be given a place on the line-up. After all, given that Disney has owned the Star Wars franchise since 2012, can Princess Leia not claim a spot alongside Moana and Mulan? After Carrie Fisher passed away in 2016, over 50,000 fans signed a petition asking just that – but to no avail.

The reasoning is not that Leia doesn't belong to the animated canon – the star of Pixar's *Brave*, Merida, is an official Disney Princess. It might be because she's not animated – but then, why does Vanellope not make the cut?

The problem the Disney Princess line-up faces is that, as the company becomes the entertainment behemoth seen in *Ralph Breaks the Internet*'s Oh My Disney pavilion, they must face up against the overwhelming numbers of princesses who have their own claims to the throne. In *Enchanted*, Amy Adams plays a princess named Giselle, who appears in both animated and live-action forms and riffs heavily on exactly what it is to be a Disney princess. TV shows for young children like *Sofia the First* and *Elena of Avalor* both feature title characters who fit the brief. Amelia Renaldi, played by Anne Hathaway in *The Princess Diaries*, never got a look in – though, like Anna and Elsa, her promotion in the second film writes her off. Kida, from *Atlantis: The Lost Empire*, is also excluded by virtue of running the gaff. But what about Eilonwy from *The Black Cauldron*? Surely she's got a rightful place on the line-up?

Like Leia, though, there are obvious candidates whose claims come via a more recent acquisition by Disney. For years, children have been getting confused about whether or not the titular star of *Anastasia* is a Disney Princess. The simple answer is: she wasn't, because Disney didn't make that film. But in 2019, the company bought Fox and its extensive film catalogue, and now she has every right to be.

That acquisition also brought another major franchise under Disney ownership. A franchise, in fact, that has literally dozens of princesses waiting to join the party (and probably devour it). After all, given that the finale of *Aliens* sees Ripley face up to a gigantic and vengeful 'alien queen', can we not claim that all of her female offspring have a rightful claim to being Disney Princesses too?

Chapter 58

Do You Want to Build a Franchise?

Frozen II • *2019* • *Chris Buck, Jennifer Lee*

Though there had already been sequels within the Disney canon, the arrivals of *Ralph Breaks the Internet* and *Frozen II* marked by far the fastest turnarounds from original film to follow-up. There had been thirteen years between *The Rescuers* and its 1990 sequel. The two Winnie the Pooh films were separated by thirty-four years. We're looking at a whopping *sixty* year gap between *Fantasia* and *Fantasia 2000*. Think about how many apprenticeships the great sorcerer Yen Sid could oversee during that period.[1]

As was the case for the *Wreck-It Ralph* sequel, *Frozen II*'s release saw the studio cut the wait for fans to just six years. It might have been even sooner had Disney not been focused on delivering a Broadway adaptation of the original movie first. All the same, by the time the film was released, fans had already been further exposed to the growing *Frozen* franchise. Screenings of Disney's live-action adaptation of *Cinderella* had been preceded by a new short, *Frozen Fever*. Pixar's *Coco* was released alongside a twenty-minute-long Christmas-themed special, *Olaf's Frozen Adventure*.

Nevertheless, for many, the new film represented the first real follow-up to the record-breaking original movie. Expectations were high across the board, and the children who fell so hard for *Frozen* were not the only ones looking to see what Disney would deliver with the sequel.

After the impact of 'Let It Go', there were many members of the queer community who were watching on hesitantly to see how Elsa's character would further develop. The show-stopping song had since been wholly adopted as a coming-out anthem about embracing one's true self and not hiding away for the benefit of others, and many fans felt it fitting that Elsa, too, should come out as gay.[2]

---

1. A quick aside here, as I feel I let you down with earlier chapters on the Fantasia films. The sorcerer's name there? Take another look, and reverse it. Hardly the most subtle of references, is it? Yen Sid was not only named after Walt, but his personality draws heavily on what it was like to work for the man, too.
2. It's worth considering, too, that in the original plans for *Frozen*, Elsa would have been the villain. This argument can fall one of two ways: perhaps Elsa has no love interest because villains generally don't have love interests, but equally, many Disney villains have been explicitly queer-coded in the past – it is very possible that there was at some point a world in which Elsa was designed with this in mind, echoing the (not-so) discrete characteristics of previous antagonists like Ursula and Scar.

Still, hopes were high that *Frozen II* would introduce a female love interest for Elsa and… well, of course, it didn't. Though Disney would be more explicit about homosexual relationships in future films, the studio was still shying away from actively putting a gay character on screen at the time of the film's release. There had been hyperbolic news articles about the first gay character in the Marvel Cinematic Universe earlier that same year – the person in question being an unnamed man who features in one short scene, talking about his male partner. Still, the absence of an overtly queer relationship for Elsa disappointed many fans – though few still hold out hope that she'll connect with a young member of the indigenous Northuldra tribe named Honeymaren. With *Frozen III* coming soon, and a fourth instalment also in development, perhaps there's time for Elsa to find a groundbreaking love of her own in future films.

Another group with their eyes on *Frozen II* were the film critics, who watched the original film's development into a franchise with wary eyes. Some bold and original ideas had fueled Disney's revival of the 2010s. There was plenty of variety, too – a city of anthropomorphic animals, the animation studio's first superhero movie, and *Moana*, which had once again reimagined the Disney Princess formula. But since that last film, there had been a small wave of sequels across both Disney Animation Studios and the once deeply creative Pixar.

At the time of *Frozen II*'s release, four of the five most recent Pixar films had been sequels – including a fourth entry in the *Toy Story* series that even fans considered wildly unnecessary after the critically acclaimed third film had seemed to offer a perfect conclusion to the franchise. Disney seemed to many to be hitting something of a creative wall – recent live-action releases included returns to the worlds of *Pirates of the Caribbean*, *Winnie the Pooh* and even *Mary Poppins*.

In some ways, *Frozen II* does manage to differentiate itself from its predecessor, to build a more fully realised world that is better placed to act as the foundation for an ongoing series. Relationships have developed off-screen since the first film – a necessity, given that Kristoff and Elsa had never actually spoken to one another until the intervening shorts. The kingdom of Arendelle has grown, too – we see more residential areas and more people. With the latter, Disney has also responded to criticism of the overwhelming absence of ethnic diversity in *Frozen*. The little citadel has opened its gates to new residents, and for the first time, we see members of Arendelle's population who aren't cursed with the complexion of a poached chicken breast.

An extension of this approach defines the plot, too. Where the first film liberally lifted from the Sámi culture, the second acknowledges them – and the very idea of colonialism. In fact, in keeping with other Disney classics of the era, there is no singular villain in the piece. Instead, there is a more complex antagonist for the sisters to face up to: the legacy of their ancestors' mistakes.

While this ambitious approach is, in some senses, welcome, Disney doesn't deliver it without stumbling over themselves here and there. The studio includes the indigenous Northuldran people as their reference to the Sámi, but somehow manages to appropriate a fictional culture by retroactively making Elsa and Anna part-indigenous themselves. The finale deals obliquely with the idea of reparations by having Anna unleash a tidal wave on Arendelle in order to right the colonial crimes of the kingdom's past. But Elsa's last-minute reprieve means that, ultimately, there is no cost to anyone. Do I want to see Arendelle washed away while the townspeople look on and nod quietly to themselves, understanding that this is the only way to make things right? No, but then I suspect the Northuldran people wouldn't either. I know it's a film for children, but there must be some middle ground – a way of saying 'sometimes we must make sacrifices to address past mistakes' without razing a kingdom, but also without reducing the impact of Anna's choice. As it is, the Northuldran people had their resources plundered and were subsequently trapped in a snowy prison for several decades, and in response, the Arendellians were briefly inconvenienced and forced on an autumnal nature walk.

For young fans, *Frozen II* remains a joy. There's another absolute belter for Elsa (and an 80s power ballad for Kristoff), and Olaf gets significantly more screen time.[3] For all its flaws, Disney was willing to take *Frozen II* to ambitious new places and forge a path that didn't rely wholly on the success of the first instalment. At times, their approach feels fairly formulaic and a little devoid of charm – but perhaps you build a franchise the same way you build a snowman. You start with a plain but solid body so that you have a foundation that you can, in time, sculpt into something with a little more character.

3. He also dies, in a scene that roughly echoes the infamous MCU Thanos snap. Thankfully, the scene is just abstract enough that when I caught the film in the cinema upon its release, its significance completely escaped most of the youngest audience members. One pre-schooler a few rows ahead of me spent the following ten minutes asking his mother where Olaf was. She, wisely, refused to acknowledge the question until the film's conclusion, when Elsa magically revives him: "There he is," she finally said, as if the whole time they had simply been playing a snowman version of Where's Wally.

The Streaming Era

Chapter 59

It's the End of Baloo as We Know Him (But He Feels Fine)

Raya and the Last Dragon • *2021* • *Carlos López Estrada, Don Hall*

Poor *Raya* – perhaps the animated classic most heavily impacted by the global pandemic of 2020. Like many Disney films before it, *Raya* made fairly significant headway with production before the studio decided some changes were in order, replacing the directors, adding new writers, and bringing in a different actress, Kelly Marie Tran, to voice the intrepid lead character. But even compared to turbulent productions like *The Emperor's New Groove*, these changes presented difficult and specific challenges – they were announced while the planet was dealing with the ongoing COVID-19 crisis.

The increased use of computers in animation has made home-working more plausible – if not the preferred practice – across the industry. Once, this was an oddity, though an occasional salvation. In the late 1990s, an employee at Pixar accidentally deleted around 90% of the progress made on *Toy Story 2*. It was only salvaged because Galyn Susman, the film's supervising technical director, had recently given birth and had been working at home for the previous few weeks. For a short and intensely stressful moment, the only surviving copy of *Toy Story 2* was on a computer that had been wrapped tightly in blankets and put in the back seat of Susman's Volvo for a trip across San Francisco Bay.

Now, in a twist of fate, a Disney film would be saved by people taking it out of the studio and into their homes. Over four hundred homes, in fact, according to a grateful note at the end of *Raya*'s credits.

The film looks impressive, then, given that it was mostly animated by people who were only dressed from the waist up or were fighting off incursions by over-enthusiastic home-schooled children.[1]

There is, perhaps, a sense of decline. Of the movement back towards one of the studio's fallow periods. *Moana* marked a peak for the Revival Era, after which Disney presented two sequels. Their return to an original story (Raya is the first Disney princess not to be based on a pre-existing character) is dampened a little by the same sense of well-meaning blandness that affected *Frozen II*.

1. Perhaps the film's infant con artist Little Noi and her monkey crime syndicate were inspired by the difficulty Disney's team had wrangling their own children while trying to deliver the film.

Raya's plot is heavily inspired by Southeast Asian cultures, much as *Moana* drew on Polynesian legends. But the approach is so vague, drawing on individual elements and throwing them into a melting pot, that ultimately each distinct culture starts to feel homogenised with the others. Though the studio absolutely had the best intentions, their approach to each culture – particularly the transposing of these cultures into a new, completely fictional world entirely separate from our own – means that individual philosophies and indicators are lost. The unique cultural heritage of countries like Laos, Vietnam, Cambodia and Malaysia are appropriated without their wider context. We see this all the time with British culture – each year brings a new direct-to-streaming Christmas romance set in the royal household of a non-distinct European micronation where everybody sounds like Hugh Grant. But British culture is already well-represented in cinema. Hollywood spends much less time in Southeast Asia, and the individual cultural markers of each nation are difficult for international audiences to appreciate when they are all presented as belonging to fictional tribes. Critics and audiences across Southeast Asia were also frustrated that, except for Tran, most of the main cast came from East Asian backgrounds – further diluting the meaningfulness of the region's representation in the film.

It's symptomatic of Disney's recent approach towards their filmmaking. Everything appears to be designed by committee to appeal to the broadest audience. Laudable efforts towards inclusivity are hampered by decision-making that veers so safe that it becomes ineffective and, in doing so, pleases no one. In *Lilo & Stitch*, the film's representation of Hawaiian culture was so well received not because the crew had attempted to build a story around the best possible representation of it but instead because they had created a compelling story and then asked how the nuances of Hawaiian life would impact, or be impacted by the central plot.

By comparison, *Raya* appears to build itself upon the foundation of Southeast Asian culture. Like *Lilo & Stitch*, the plot isn't intrinsically linked to its setting – it would be relatively simple to transpose it to any number of locations and times, from mediaeval England to a long time ago in a galaxy far, far away. But the balance is wrong – much time has been put into creating a mystical world that draws on Southeast Asian cultures, but the story doesn't match the energy with its distinctly universal theme: the importance of trust.

At least, I think that's what the message is. It's hard to tell because, for a story that wants to teach that suspicion harms everyone, there is *so much* vindication of every suspicious thought in the film. Raya doesn't trust the other tribes not to steal the magical gem. They trick her, break the gem, steal the pieces, and cause a minor apocalypse. Raya doesn't trust the people of the floating market town of Talon: a toddler steals the gem fragments, and the chief attempts to kill Sisu. Raya finally takes a risk by bringing Sisu and Namaari together, and Namaari instantly betrays her. The message here seems to be, 'Trust is important! It'll come through for you once for every five to eight times that it almost kills you!'

And while we're on the dual subjects of trust and killing, *Raya* represents perhaps the most egregious example of Disney's much-loved trope: the fake character death.

By my count, of the sixty-two animated classics covered in this book, over a quarter make a point of appearing to kill off a major character in the final act, only for that character to be revived, saved, or (in my favourite versions) just having a little rest.

Though the studio started this practice in its earliest films (Snow White is technically excluded but covers the same ground. Pinocchio definitely seems dead until the Blue Fairy pops up to transform him into a real boy), the greatest example of all fake character deaths is surely *The Jungle Book*'s Baloo. He takes a hit to the head during the climactic battle with Shere Khan, and once the big cat has retreated, audiences are drawn into one of the most moving and bleak moments in the Disney canon. Baloo lies on the ground, still. Mowgli tries to wake him, but it's no use. And so the stately Bagheera delivers a noble soliloquy in which he champions his former sparring partner.

Even now, I remember the overwhelming sadness the scene instilled in me as a child. The screen-time-to-emotional-impact ratio of Baloo's seemingly lifeless body is remarkable. Obviously – *obviously* – the permanence of Mufasa's death makes it ultimately more devastating than the fifty-nine seconds for which Baloo lies unconscious. But at that moment – in that brief minute – *The Jungle Book* stands on equal footing with *The Lion King*.

It was impactful enough to see the fake Disney death find its way into a dozen more animated classics in the years that followed. *Robin Hood* repeated the trick just two films later, appearing to kill off its title star by drowning. Another titular protagonist is seemingly taken down in *Oliver & Company*. *The Black Cauldron* somehow pulls off the emotional reverse – pretending to kill off that rug-rat Gollum rip-off, Gurgi, before reviving him in the film's final moments. It's a decision that infuriates me more every time I see it.

By the beginning of the Renaissance era, the trope had been used so much that the studio needed to justify the false death of a character. More frequently, the solution to a seemingly permanent death has been tied intrinsically to the magic of the plot. The prince in *Beauty and the Beast* and Anna in *Frozen* are saved by the love of another. Flynn Rider only survives *Tangled* because Rapunzel is willing to sacrifice her magical hair.

Raya and the Last Dragon offers perhaps the logical conclusion to the trend: not only does it appear to kill off the dragon in question, Sisu – it then continues to wipe out the entirety of humankind, finishing with the film's central characters.

It is, of course, all a temporary problem. The inherent magic of 'trust' revives everybody. In a sense, I suppose, this might give hope to Disney fans: if we continue to trust in the studio, sooner or later, their sense of creativity will be brought back to life.

Chapter 60

The First Rule of Bruno is...

Encanto • *2021* • *Jared Bush, Byron Howard, Charise Castro Smith*

Family can often be found at the heart of the conflict in Disney's animated classics. In both *The Lion King* and *Hercules*, our hero faces off against an uncle who is tired of being relegated to the sidelines. Snow White and Cinderella were victims of evil stepmothers, while *The Hunchback of Notre Dame* and *Tangled* each deal with adoptive parents who lie to their children and keep them locked away from the world.

But each of these films offers a more or less binary approach to morality. Hades, Frollo and Mother Gothel are bad. Hercules, Quasimodo and Rapunzel are good. There are heroes, and there are villains, and those in between are simply passive onlookers who either have no role at all or serve to quietly encourage someone else to do the heavy lifting on their behalf.

Over the last decade, though, there has been something of a sea change in Disney's animated output. Without warning, the villains have disappeared off to some distant mountain lair, and we have seen a flurry of films in which the real enemy is the most insidious thing of all: generational trauma.

For me, the first steps towards the Generational Trauma Cinematic Universe were made in 2015, when Pixar released *Inside Out*. It was a film devoid of a clear villain – instead, the characters faced a problem of their own making. Joy, Sadness, Anger, Fear and Disgust were not technically family members – but they were a unit that needed to work together, whether they liked it or not. And what is that, if not a family?

Four years later, *Frozen II* moved beyond the first film's message of self-acceptance, offering instead a story about facing up to the damage done by those who came before you. In 2022, Disney and Pixar released *Strange World* and *Turning Red*, respectively, each film about the expectations parents place upon their children.[1]

Encanto is perhaps the most challenging and complex of the lot, though. It's a film that achieves something particularly special, capturing unique family dynamics that

1. In the same year, this premise leapt beyond the confines of the Disney studios, with Academy Award-winning action film *Everything Everywhere All At Once* covering broadly similar themes, only much more violently.

are recognisable to Latinx audiences while delivering broadly relatable characters among whom audiences can see their own experiences.

It is easy to recognise both ourselves and our loved ones in the characters of the film. You may identify as a Mirabel, seemingly unremarkable among a family of borderline superheroes. Perhaps your siblings remind you of Isabela, who can do no wrong, or Luisa, who seems to have the strength of a small army.

But *Encanto* is a film about perspectives, and our understanding of each character shifts as the plot develops. Isabela is drowning under the weight of her family's expectations – particularly those of her quietly controlling Abuela (the Spanish word for 'grandmother'). In one scene, Isabela, whose power is to create verdant blooms of flowers wherever she goes, spawns a garland of beautiful pink flowers; Abuela takes a moment to pick an errant white blossom from the mix. It is, in itself, a perfect specimen. But because it differs slightly from the others, it isn't perfect *enough*. Luisa, too, is suffering. She might not struggle under the weight of half a dozen donkeys, but the expectation that she will use her strength at every conceivable opportunity is a burden in itself.

Disney has often placed an underlying moral at the heart of their films, but never has that message been so universal or so nuanced as it is in *Encanto*. The character of Abuela is one of the most complex in the Disney canon. A refugee from an unknown conflict, we are able to understand that Abuela's quiet determination and stoic fortitude stem from the suffering she has seen. She has been persecuted, has had her husband stolen from her by violent forces, and has worked hard to create security for those around her. But these trials do not absolve her, or excuse her behaviour as she controls her family, has them take on wartime duties in a period of peace and, at her worst, diminishes the value of those who cannot fit into her singular vision. Instead, she, too, must learn to evolve.

As far back as *Pinocchio*, Disney has been telling us stories about growing up and accepting that your place in the world might require compromise on your part. Too often, this story has been told to younger generations by their elders. In *Melody Time*, Little Toot must put his childish desire to play behind him. In *Peter Pan*, Wendy must accept that she has outgrown the nursery. But this need for compromise has, for too long, been a one-way street. A demand made by animators and writers; Abuelas who themselves refuse to shift as the world moves around them. In *Encanto*, we are at last encouraged to see the story from every angle. To acknowledge the way that each character's actions impact those around them.

It is no coincidence that Mirabel's family are called the Madrigals. Yes, it is a very neat rhyme for 'magical', which is particularly handy for the dazzling (and borderline impossible to follow) opening musical number, a song that bears all the flourishes of songwriter Lin-Manuel Miranda. But it also has a deeper relevance within the film. A madrigal is a type of vocal song popular in Europe across the Renaissance and early Baroque periods. Importantly, it is a song performed by a number of different voices, each singing in counterpoint to one another. Different voices, singing different tunes in a way that somehow comes together to create something entirely unique and beautiful. If that's difficult to conceive, take a moment to listen to the film's break-out hit, 'We Don't Talk About Bruno'. The song builds to an exhilarating climax, during which each family member sings a different refrain. It is a Madrigal madrigal, and it is so overwhelmingly irresistible that it became Disney's most successful charting song of all time, outperforming 'Let It Go', 'Can You Feel the Love Tonight' and 'A Whole New World'.

The secret to family, then, has been hidden in the character's names all along. They are the Madrigals, and perfect harmony was never meant to be the end goal. Instead, like all families, the key is finding a balance that works for everyone.

Encanto came out in the heart of the pandemic, releasing in cinemas just as a new variant of COVID-19 hit the United States. And yet, more than any other film from the Streaming Era, *Encanto* seems to have struck a chord with audiences. The broad and pliable character archetypes have enabled viewers to connect more deeply with a film that otherwise eschews much of what we expect from a Disney movie. There is no real villain nor any significant love interest. Instead, there are characters we recognise from our own lives. Siblings that harbour a mutual jealousy, each thinking the other has the better deal. Grandparents who refuse to make an effort for those they understand the least. Parents who insist on controlling everyone and everything around them. But also siblings that play together, who hide under the bed, or gleefully make a mess that they have no intention of cleaning up. Grandparents who can change, who can accept that the generations that succeed them will have different needs, and are happy to find new ways to support their family. And parents who feed, who nourish, who defend, and who know when to let go.

There is a photo of my family, taken around my sister's 18th birthday. Most of our closest relatives are present – our grandparents, our parents, our aunt and our uncle. My father, like so many millions of fathers before him, decided to capture the moment. He set up his camera on the patio, arranged us all so that we would be visible, instructed us all to smile, and set the automatic timer so that he could take his place among us. I am certain that the picture my father intended to take would have been very nice. Very obviously staged, our smiles a little too rigid to be believable, but a very nice photo all the same.

Unfortunately for my father, but to the undeniable benefit of the photo, our patio was filled with little obstacles. As he rushed to beat the camera's timer and take his place among us, he tripped on a plant pot and fell loudly to the ground behind us all.

If you want the truest picture of my family, you need look no further than the one we ended up with that day. A brief moment was captured in which everyone was their truest self. In which the conventions of family portraiture were, much like my father, completely upended. *Encanto* is a success not because of its canny representation of Latinx culture or its insights into the impacts of generational trauma. It's a success because it captures the same thing that my sister's birthday photo does: that families are at their very best when everyone is free to be themselves.

Chapter 61

Journey to the Self-Centred of the Earth

Strange World • 2022 • Don Hall

You wouldn't think it necessary in a book about Disney films, and we almost made it through to the end without needing to do this, but here is a short etymology lesson on the word 'woke'. African-Americans have been using the word since the 1930s, initially as part of the phrase 'stay woke'. In this setting, 'woke' is a state of active attention – awareness of (and an implied reaction to) the facts and issues impacting a matter. And, generally speaking, the issue at hand has been related to racial or social justice. In a sense, 'wokeness' is about empathy. It is about being engaged with reality – not just yours, but the lived reality of those around you – and considering the impact of your actions within this context.

There is, of course, a very different sort of meaning to 'woke'. A definition that has been hijacked by the very people least engaged with the concept – usually far-right politicians and media commentators but also, and this is always fun come Christmas, your least favourite uncle. For these people, 'wokeness' is a cynical action. It is empathy, yes – but *performative* empathy, committed not because it matters but because it earns kudos. It's a silly sort of idea that says more about the people making such a claim than anything else. I don't always boil things down to 'he who smelt it dealt it', but it seems to me that suggesting somebody is only being performatively empathetic is exactly the sort of thing that you'd do if you yourself were the sort of self-centred person whose every action was made for solely their own benefit; an idea cradled by individuals who themselves had only ever pretended to care about others.[1]

It is, annoyingly, this second definition that we turn to for *Strange World*, a relatively lightweight Disney cartoon about explorers and families that nevertheless angered all sorts of people.[2] Some commentators were upset about a plotline that touched upon environmentalist themes and the idea that parents are fallible. Most were just hung up on the fact that Ethan Clade, the youngest of the heroic dynasty at the centre of the film, is queer.

1. Also, the idea of performative empathy being the worst thing in the world is very funny to me. 'How awful it is when people do nice things that have a real and consequential impact, but don't *mean* it'.
2. Well, *one* sort of person – but they were the very loudest sort.

For the small but vocal minority for whom this sort of thing matters, it *really* matters. The film's moral critics were clear that Ethan's inclusion in *Strange World* was the latest strike in a war against American values that Disney had been waging for some time. And it's certainly *some sort* of argument. Ethan Clade is an *absolutely abhorrent* example for young children. In one scene – and you may wish to stop reading now, just in case you consider yourself extra-prone to indoctrination – in one scene, Ethan *flirts harmlessly* with his crush.

Strange World was far from the first time Disney had come up against disgruntled opposition. The same future-shocked lemmings had leapt into action just a few years earlier when they noticed that *Frozen II* featured a black character in 19th-century Scandinavia. They simply could not get their heads around it. The film's magical fire lizard and eighty-foot-tall earth giants they have no problem with, sure, but send Sterling K. Brown anywhere that might require a scarf, and their world collapses in on itself.

In *Strange World*, the lone scene in which Ethan and his crush, Diazo, share the screen features nothing more than gentle flirtation. Elsewhere in the film, Diazo gets just two mentions during conversations with older family members in which nobody bats an eyelid at the teenager's affection for another male. But even this was too much for many – Disney decided not to release the film in international markets where homophobia was a matter of policy. And even in America, Disney's choices were blamed for the film's financial failings.

Strange World was released almost twenty years to the day after the debut of the reigning champion for the biggest box office bomb across Disney's animated output. Like *Treasure Planet*, the film was another science-fiction epic filled with curious creatures and absent fathers. And like *Treasure Planet*, it promptly set new records in the world of Disney failures.

'Go woke, go broke' has been a catchphrase among some of America's more empathy-challenged residents since around 2018. Disney's social media accounts were inundated with comments to the same effect in 2022, when *Strange World* was released. It was not the only Disney film that triggered America's homophobes that year. In June, Pixar had put out their first cinematic release since before the COVID-19 pandemic, the *Toy Story* spin-off *Lightyear*. This, too, was considered 'woke' – partly for featuring a brief kiss between two women, and partly due to the casting of Chris Evans as Buzz Lightyear. The latter complaint centred on the conservative-leaning comedian Tim Allen seemingly being replaced in the role that he had originated. Nobody seemed to care that the character was intended to be 'the inspiration behind' Buzz Lightyear, and thus a different character. Nor did they notice that Allen had already been announced for another Disney project due out that winter, so hadn't exactly been ostracised for his beliefs.

As it turned out, 2022 was a pivotal year for Disney's involvement in the culture wars – both on and off the big screen. In March, the governor of Florida, Ron DeSantis, signed into law a controversial act that banned schools in the state from discussing sexual orientation or gender identity with any child in the third grade or below. This restriction was later expanded to include all grades up to and including high school. The law was quickly nicknamed 'Don't Say Gay' and was widely criticised by students, teachers, psychologists and paediatricians. It was championed by Republican politicians, far-right religious groups, and other folks who list their primary hobby as 'shaking their fist at the sky'.

Notably, for a while, there was no word from Disney on the 'Don't Say Gay' law – a silence that increasingly upset both fans and staff members who supported the LGBTQ+ cause. After all, the Disney World theme park complex covers an area of central Florida that is bigger than Miami, and the company had previously donated tens of thousands of dollars to DeSantis (Disney has a habit of donating to the campaigns of politicians on both sides of the political divide). Faced with mounting criticism and a choice to make, the relatively new CEO of Disney, Bob Chapek, announced $5 million of donations to LGBTQ+ causes and an intention for the company to help support repealing the act. DeSantis struck back with what appeared to be vengeful and economically ill-conceived moves against the company's enterprises in the state. After decades of carefully playing up to both political parties, Disney had finally found itself in the middle of the culture war minefield.[3]

It was in this environment that braying mobs began boycotting Disney's products. There were pickets outside Disney World in which 'Make America Great Again' slogan-wearing Republicans protested side-by-side with men waving swastika flags. Staunch conservative families refused to take their children to see the two recent Disney releases that happened to feature queer characters. Fox News reported that the studio's SEC filings were proof of the 'go woke, go broke' mantra.

In just one of the many egregious examples of rampant homophobia, Florida teacher Jenna Barbee was investigated by the state's education department for 'indoctrination' for showing her 10-year-old students *Strange World* as a treat after exams. The class had been learning about Earth science and ecosystems (and spoiler alert: the film makes a *far* bigger political statement around ecosystems than it does about homosexuality).

But there is another factor behind the box office failings of *Strange World*. In 2022, Disney was in the middle of a prolonged assault on the established giants of the digital streaming world. It had been just three years since the company had launched Disney Plus. After an initial boost to numbers brought about by locked-down families looking for ways to entertain children amid a global pandemic, Disney was still looking for ways to cement their place in the market.

The three Pixar films released prior to *Lightyear* had all skipped cinemas entirely, premiering on Disney Plus. The previous two animated classics had each enjoyed

3. In March 2023 the stand-off between Ron DeSantis and Disney quietly came to an end. DeSantis drastically toned down plans to interfere with Disney's longstanding 'special district' that covered the Disney World complex. The agreement came shortly after DeSantis ended a campaign to run for the presidency of the United States. In the same month the 'Don't Say Gay' law was also severely dampened, allowing for discussions around gender identity and sexual orientation to take place outside of formal instruction.

only brief theatrical runs before appearing online. *Encanto* was available to stream just one month after it opened in cinemas. *Raya*, released during the third wave of COVID, was released in theatres and on Disney Plus simultaneously, with home audiences able to pay for access for the first six months until the film was made available for all. By the time *Strange World* was released, it seemed inevitable that a home streaming release was so close it barely warranted a trip to the cinema – especially given the tepid reviews.

The embarrassing fact of the matter for the 'go woke, go broke' brigade is that they didn't really have much of an impact at all. They claimed that their activism had led to a 17 million subscriber exodus from Disney Plus between the summer of 2022 and the spring of 2023. But even this doesn't ring true – more or less that entire figure was lost specifically in India, where the streaming service had lost the rights to show live cricket.[4] There had, in fact, been an increase of 800,000 subscribers around the rest of the world.

Ultimately, there is no denying that *Strange World* is a flawed film and that those flaws would have had some impact on box office numbers during its theatrical release. The movie lacks much of the finesse that we've come to associate with Disney, but it wasn't devoid of enjoyable elements. As the characters descend into a vibrant underworld that even Barbie might baulk at for being a little too zealous with the pink, we discover a dazzling spectrum of creatures unlike anything we've seen before. Children will relish the Flubber-esque Splat and three-legged sheepdog, Legend. Adults – some adults[5] – will take joy from realising that this is the second film in which Dennis Quaid and Jake Gyllenhaal play a father and son caught up in a major climate incident.[6]

Nevertheless, as many suspected (and perhaps hastened by the underwhelming figures), *Strange World* debuted on Disney Plus just one month after its US cinema release. But here is where it finally had a chance to shine. *Strange World* was the most streamed film on the site during its first week, and the eighth most-streamed film in the whole of the United States in the week leading up to Christmas, despite having only been available for two days in that period.

There is the *Strange World* in which rolling pink landscapes are filled with families learning how better to love one another, and there is the strange world in which people are determined to tear each other apart because one cartoon character flirted with another. The former might not be perfect, but I choose it over the latter any day.

4. I don't know what I find harder to get my head around: the sheer numbers of viewers that Indian streaming services are dealing with, or the idea that 17 million people care more about cricket than, say, regular access to *Lilo & Stitch*.
5. This adult. Me.
6. See also: *The Day After Tomorrow*

Chapter 62

Seeking Happily Ever After

Wish • 2023 • Chris Buck, Fawn Veerasunthorn

It's so easy to forget that, in the grand scheme of mankind's cultural history, that cinema – moving pictures – is among the newest of art forms. The most recent, of course, is terrifying pictures of crustacean Jesuses forged in the soulless pits of AI render engines. Before that, I suppose, we had bullet journalling, and a little earlier still, somebody worked out how to put olives in gelatine and for a brief period in the 1970s everybody seemed to agree that this was the pinnacle of humanity's aesthetic inventions to date. But just a little further back: cinema.

2023 marked the centenary of The Walt Disney Company. Anyone who expected the occasion to pass without note clearly had not been paying attention to the mythologising of the brand that had begun before Walt had even conceived of his first animated feature. Nowadays Disney is less the name of a Hollywood studio than it is an idea, a *feeling*. Disney – the company, or the name, it doesn't really matter – is a sort of active nostalgia. A memory of an implacable point in time, one that very possibly never existed. It is the pop culture equivalent of the good old days that we remember fondly, not because they were the true peak of our existence (for every *Beauty and the Beast,* there is a *Black Cauldron*; for every meet and greet with Mickey Mouse, there is a fundamentally terrifying experience with a talking bin), but because they are intimately connected to a time when our worries were few, our joy so easy to spark.

As adults our love for Disney, however powerful it might be, is complex. It is an intricate web of emotions that weaves in and out of our lives. The quality of the films matters – of course it does – but it isn't the only factor in play. There are terrific movies we never connected with because they escaped us during a pivotal period of self-discovery or arrived in our lives a little too early to have the necessary impact. And there are poorer films that we will defend passionately against all who would stand against them, because nostalgia flies as high as any flag. Because they belong to a version of ourselves that we need to hold on to in whichever way we can.

The 'Disney 100' celebrations reflected this. The studio put out television specials that looked back on its illustrious history and re-released some of its animated classics into cinemas, including *Snow White*, *Beauty and the Beast* and *Frozen*. But there were also a few fumbles during the celebration, giving fans a sense that the studio misunderstood both what audiences wanted from Disney and what had made them such a success in the first place.

The biggest of these misjudgments came in the form of the 62nd animated classic, *Wish*, a film that seeks to catalogue one hundred years of history and, in doing so, accidentally makes itself the villain of its own story.

Wish is deeply inspired by the look and feel of Disney's fairy tale princess movies, with *Snow White* and *Sleeping Beauty* both being cited as significant influences on the aesthetics of the fictional Mediterranean island of Rosa. Crucially, though, the story is an original one, and the film's heroine, Asha, is not a princess. Instead, she is a teenage girl who starts the film seeking employment in the royal castle as – and give me a little wave if you can see what they've done here – a sorcerer's apprentice.

The sorcerer in question is humbly named Magnifico, and he is also the king of Rosa. It becomes apparent early on that despite being well-loved by his subjects, he is actually a fairly straightforward Disney villain. Magnifico has the power to grant the wishes of Rosa's citizens. He separates individuals from their heart's desire on their 18th birthday and keeps these wishes secure in his castle. Lucky citizens have their wishes granted, though Asha quickly realises that many will never be so fortunate.

And so the film's entire premise is built around celebrating that most Disney of ideas – the wish. And this isn't the only way the studio weaves its history into the very fabric of the movie. A deer in the woods is revealed to be Bambi. A bear is named John, in reference to Robin Hood's sidekick. There are townsfolk cosplaying as Peter Pan and Wendy, and the studio's modern-day mascot, Alan Tudyk, puts on a surprisingly annoying voice to play a talking goat who, at one point, describes the world of *Zootopia* pretty succinctly.

The problem is that these nods don't feel organic – instead, they are forcefully wedged into the plot, leaving little room for important things like motivation or character development. Magnifico is fleetingly shown to be vain about his appearance, but only in order to set up some allusions to *Snow White*'s magic mirror in the final act.

The most obvious of these nostalgic invasions comes in the form of Asha's seven closest friends, who all seem to spend their entire lives hanging out in the castle's kitchens, where only one of them actually does any work. And you might be thinking: "Seven? That sounds like an awful lot of characters to fit into a ninety-five-minute film. Why on earth would they do that?" The answer, unfortunately, has nothing to do with the film's narrative. It doesn't even have anything to do with the film. It is, once again, solely regarding that first animated classic, sixty-one films earlier.

Asha's friends each represent a different one of *Snow White*'s seven dwarfs. Leader Dahlia is smart and wears little round spectacles, like Doc. Safi has allergies and is always sneezing. Dario is distinctly dopier than the others, and Bazeema is so shy she often simply goes missing. It isn't subtle – during the film's final moments, the diminutive Gabo even shouts, "I'm grumpy!"

These seven characters exist solely as a wry nod for an audience who would rather have a coherent screenplay and characters who are given more depth – something that simply isn't possible when you have seven people filling a role that could just as easily have been filled by two.

One gets the sense that in *Wish*, Disney sees itself as Asha – trying to free people to be the best version of themselves, hoping that inspiration and good feelings will fill their hearts. Instead, the studio more closely reflects King Magnifico by repackaging nostalgia and cynically presenting us with glimpses of what we desire packaged within elaborate vanity projects. It is commercialising our fantasies and delivering them back to us in a branded plastic bag.

It doesn't have to be like this; thankfully, it won't be forever.

The Walt Disney Company has come a long way in the one-hundred-plus years since two brothers came together and founded a small studio in Los Angeles. The journey has created one of the biggest entertainment companies in the world, and Disney has done so off the back of its remarkable catalogue of animated classics. But how often have we seen this canon almost come to a shuddering halt along the way?

One hundred years is an awfully long time to keep any creative endeavour going. The world changes significantly over a period like that. Walt's first animated features were ornate masterpieces that transcended anything the world had thought possible within the medium of cartoon. In the short but magnificent run from *Snow White* to *Bambi*, the studio offered the world five of the most influential films of all time. But war came, and the only way Disney could survive was to adapt their approach to filmmaking. The Package Era may have temporarily offered salvation to the studio, but soon there was a need to reinvent the medium once again.

There is no run of films in cinema history like the animated canon, and we have seen it adapt and evolve, run creatively dry and then revive itself time and time again. By my count, there are at least seven films in this book that offered last-minute redemption to an animation department that was on the verge of closure. After Michael Eisner and Frank Wells joined the company in the 1980s, this uncertainty came to an end. The studio made leaps and bounds, and the canon itself took on new meaning within pop culture. It's almost impossible now to imagine the death of the Disney animated feature. But that doesn't make it immune from sickness.

In the early 2000s, several factors led to a slump in the quality of the studio's classics. Infighting among Disney's leadership begat a period of creative complacency, while old-fashioned storytellers struggled to adapt to changing techniques and the irreverence of new films like *Shrek*. There were glimmers of hope, as there always are in the studio's fallow periods. I've rewatched every one of the animated classics in the process of writing this book, and I honestly think *Lilo & Stitch* may be the most perfect film the studio ever made. But Disney wasn't able to wholly break free from its slump until it recognised what was at the heart of all its biggest successes: a pioneering spirit, and some of the greatest creative talent on the planet.

The last eight years or so have seen the world once again evolve in ways that threaten the very foundations upon which the animated canon has been built. The global pandemic coincided with Disney's belated adoption of the streaming phenomenon, taking audiences out of cinemas and disrupting a century's worth of movie-watching tradition. The problem isn't unique to Disney. The tentpole blockbuster releases that Hollywood could historically rely on to do big numbers are falling at the first hurdle, with audiences expecting an imminent home release. Streaming services like Netflix and Amazon Prime Video are pushing out bland, forgettable films that are driven by algorithms and the need for continual growth for shareholders.

The creatives at the heart of Disney's latest films aren't necessarily to blame for their failings. This is simply another period of change, and story artists and animators alike are looking for ways to adapt and find their next *Cinderella*, their next *Little Mermaid*.

In *Wish*, though, the studio made the wrong call. It attempted to create a Disney film by formula, picking and choosing elements from a century of animation but missing the point entirely along the way.

Because while the studio is right to see 'Disney' as a concept, as a feeling that is held deep within the collective consciousness, they've misunderstood what the source of that feeling actually is. 'Disney' isn't defined by the seven dwarfs or the hopeful melody of 'When You Wish Upon a Star'. It isn't defined by talking animals or 'I want' songs. 'Disney' isn't a formula but rather the culmination of the creativity of tens of thousands of individuals, working collectively over one hundred years to introduce children to the world, and reintroduce adults to their childhood. In *Wish*, Disney accidentally captures the true cause of their success, portraying a victory that is only won when the hearts and spirits of hundreds of people align in collective action.

Walt Disney started something wonderful, but it only flourished because of the artists and writers and musicians and actors and inkers and technicians and heck, even the key grips who all worked so hard to bring something magical to our screens. The Sherman Brothers and Ashman and Menken. Voice actors like Sterling Holloway, Verna Felton, and David Ogden Stiers. The directors whose names appear so often throughout these pages: Clyde Geronimi, Hamilton Luske, Wolfgang Reitherman. Clements, Musker, Trousdale, Wise.

Their work has not been without faults – but by god, they still tried. More often than not, they succeeded. And so we are left not only with the existing animated canon and all of the unmatched classics it holds, but also with an unfettered hope. A knowledge that given time and opportunity, another Disney Golden Age, another Disney Renaissance, is only ever a few brave creative decisions away.

Chapter 63

A Waterlogged Epilogue

Moana 2 • 2024 • David G. Derrick Jr., Jason Hand, Dana Ledoux Miller

When I first pitched this book to my publisher, I had a perfectly structured plan in place. We'd start with *Snow White*, and run right up to *Wish*, which had been out for just a month or so, the tentpole release of the 'Disney 100' anniversary year. It was the perfect finale: a film that looked back on all those that came before it, positioned tidily as the very last chapter in the book.

And then, two days after I signed my contract, Disney announced *Moana 2*, surprising absolutely everybody. And I mean that: *everybody*. The Kiwi comedian Rose Matafeo, one of the film's main actors, didn't realise she was going to be in a Disney movie until someone shared the trailer with her on Instagram. Up until that point, Matafeo was expecting to be among the cast of a new *Moana* TV series that was set to debut on Disney Plus some time in 2024. The show, thrillingly titled *Moana: The Series*, had been in production since 2020, and was going to run to just five episodes – a positive sign, at the time, that it had a well-formed plot, and producers who were willing to give it exactly the amount of time needed to tell the story. It wasn't until January 2024 that studio president Alan Bergman made the decision to pivot to a feature length theatrical release. There was a lot of work to do – just a month later the change was announced publicly, with the film set for release in November of that same year.

There was a mixed reception to the news. Parents whose children had been watching the original film on loop rejoiced at the idea of a slight deviation to their daily screentime. Many saw reasons for concern, though, remembering the TV sequels that Disney had attempted to turn into feature length films in the past: *Beauty and the Beast: Belle's Magical World* and *Atlantis: Milo's Return*. Others noted that while the studio were bringing back the film's biggest stars, Auli'i Cravalho and Dwayne Johnson, as well as composers Mark Mancina and Opetaia Foa'i, there was to be no input from Lin-Manuel Miranda, whose inimitable songwriting style had played a major part in the success of *Moana* the first time around. The decision to make the film at all seemed odd, given that a live action remake of the original movie was already slated for release in the summer of 2025, just eight months after the release of this sequel.[1]

---

1. The release date for the film has since been pushed back a year. Johnson is set to reprise his role as Maui, perhaps because – and I say this with all the love in the world for the silly big

And so, as November rolled around, all eyes were on *Moana 2*. Could it live up to the standard of the first film, or at least shake off the albatross of its television origins? Currently – and I write this in late January 2025, with the film is still playing in some cinemas – the consensus depends entirely on whether or not you are employed by Disney's accounting department. Because while critics were underwhelmed and fans were frustrated by both a plot and a soundtrack that seemed content to faintly echo those of the original, *Moana 2* managed to make over a billion dollars at the global box office – a feat matched by only two other films in 2024.[2]

What I find most interesting about the film isn't really about the film at all, but rather about the corporate juggernaut that Disney has morphed into over the last forty years since Eisner, Wells and Katzenberg first joined the company. Disney's animated releases have always had their peaks and troughs. In a sense, the studio's output broadly resembles the water cycle. Plenty of Disney's films are indistinguishable from everything else in the vast ocean of animated cinema – they are enjoyable but ultimately a little generic. Over time, though, the quality rises and rises until the films reach new heights. These masterpieces appear to float effortlessly miles above their competition.[3] They are minor miracles, but the studio only ever manages a short run before the weight of expectation pulls them back down to earth again. From there, we can only hope that the decline is mercifully brief. It's a sad truth that we have seen play out repeatedly over the course of this book; sometimes, in order to make it back to the ocean, you've got to be put through the shitter.

That's not where *Moana 2* lies, though. We're still in the earliest moments of reaction to the film, where discourse is led by the loudest and least nuanced voices. In time, I suspect that we'll come to see the film has more to offer than its strange journey to the screen, or its curious soundtrack that manages both to ape the music of Lin-Manuel Miranda while also featuring the most forgettable songs in almost ninety years of the animated canon. Because there's still a lot to love in *Moana 2*, from the return of Alan Tudyk's spectacularly lucky, incomprehensibly stupid chicken, Heihei, to the deeply charming relationship between Moana and new character Simea, her little sister.[4] It's notable, too, that in order to address the change in Cravalho's voice (she was just fourteen when first cast in the role, and twenty-three when the sequel was announced), Moana herself has been allowed to visibly age – possibly the first time a female lead has done so within the Disney canon.

It would have been comforting if, after I wrote the final sentiment in my chapter on *Wish*, Disney had proven me right and released another film that truly earned the title of 'animated classic'. A film that could stand tall alongside the likes of *Snow White*, *The Lion King* and, yes, maybe even *Moana*. But this isn't the case.

---

man with his expressive eyebrows and dancing tits – *Moana* might be the only truly great film that Dwayne 'The Rock' Johnson has ever been in.

2. *Inside Out 2* and *Deadpool & Wolverine*, both of which are also Disney sequels.
3. It's clouds, lads. The laboured metaphor I'm attempting here is *clouds*.
4. Simea is voiced by the first actor in a Disney movie to have been named after a character (or rather, a title) in *Game of Thrones*, Khaleesi Lambert-Tsuda.

At least we aren't ending on a dud – *Moana 2* easily outshines *Wish*. Yes, the film fumbles the move from streaming TV show to blockbuster movie, the five biggest songs noticeably spaced out as though they would appear at a rate of one per episode. And admittedly it's frustrating to see the studio's ongoing interest in building franchises within their animated canon.[5] But while *Snow White* and *The Lion King* look effortless in their final forms, we know that their productions were endless challenges built upon a tremendous collective effort to try something new and make it work. In *Moana 2*, we can see the studio still trying to push boundaries and try new things.

When I wrote the final words of my chapter on *Wish*, I thought I had finished this book. It's a neat ending, I thought. A tidy closing statement. But there is no finishing a book about an ongoing artistic endeavour. There is only telling the story so far, and hoping it won't be the last opportunity you get. I suspect it won't be. Whether it's a *Moana* sequel, or a follow-up to *Zootopia*, or something completely new, still fermenting in the mind of a writer, there is always another story to tell.

---

5. Where *Frozen II* attempted to organically build the foundations for a future franchise, *Moana 2* opts for a far more cynical approach, replicating the Marvel Cinematic Universe template of introducing a future villain in a mid-credit sequence. In fact, even the villain himself appears to be stolen wholesale from the MCU here: the entire scene appears to be a shot-for-shot rehash of the introduction of Thanos in the end credits of *The Avengers*.

Acknowledgements

Reading through my manuscript one final time before sending this book over to my publishers, I realised that I had accidentally stumbled upon a theme during the writing process: that all art – be it film, music, or non-fiction books about the animated feature output of a specific Hollywood studio – is a collaborative effort built upon the input and labour of dozens – if not hundreds or thousands of people. And with that in mind, I can't help but ask where the hell they've all been these last eight months.

This book took bloody ages to write, and I had to do it all myself. Outrageous.

That said, I can probably muster up a few thanks. First and foremost, to everyone at White Owl Publishing. Writing is the easy part. The hard part is finding people willing to put their time and faith in what you've done, and help you get it out into the world. To Jon, Charlotte, Mélanie, and everyone else who gave up their time to help this book get into the readers' hands: you are my favourites.

I'm also just about smart enough to accept I don't know everything. Kelcey Anyá, Jen Brough and Fran Vaney were instrumental in making sure I was informed in those areas I'm not so familiar with. Nat Guest was my regular sounding board for the stupid chapter titles found throughout the book. Kirsten Parnell helped me get my head around occasional stumbling blocks. You, also, are all my favourites.

Chris Riddell was born with an artistic talent that should, frankly, make him unbearably cocky. Instead, he is one of the kindest people on the planet, and provided the stunning cover illustration for this book. Chris, *you* are my favourite.

A wealth of friends and family have supported me both in the writing of this book, and through years of other creative endeavours (of varying quality). Julia Barber was my first reader for years, and I once promised to kill off a character named Julia in every book I wrote. So, *of course*, the first one to get published is non-fiction. Sorry for killing you off in my dedication, Julia. It was the only way. Marc Burrows got me this gig, and I'll never forget that. Go read his books. Mark, Nat, Josh, Kirsty, Sam, Louis, Frances, Hannah and the rest of the people who cheered me on during the writing process: you're my favourites too.

I've been running gigs for the best part of fifteen years as Folkroom. We've even put on a couple of Disney cover nights in our time. To Ben, Katie and Michelle, and to everyone who has ever played or supported a Folkroom night: you are my favourites, but also, I've spent fifteen years buying your albums and EPs. You better all be buying my damn book.

I signed my book deal in early 2024, during the middle of a prolonged house move. A *really* prolonged house move. In fact, as I write this, I'm still waiting on the keys for the damn thing. Which means all but the final chapter of this book was written between permanent residencies, from my parents' home in Norfolk. Mum, Dad: thank you. Not just for the temporary housing arrangements, but for everything that came before it. And to my sister, Claire: I'm sorry I told the bin story. You are all my favourites.

And finally, a thank you to my wife, Bruna. You aren't even really a fan of Disney, but you let me read every single chapter of this book aloud to you so that I could hear it for myself and see how it landed. You have been on the receiving end of any number of weird little facts that are so niche and boring that they didn't even come close to warranting a footnote. And you're still here. I'll count that as a victory. You are my *real* favourite.

Oh, and actually, one more: thank you, Disney. Thank you for the films, and the music, and most of all, thank you for not suing me.[1]

1. Now that I've said, you'll look like real pricks if you actually do sue me. So please, please don't.

Bibliography

Books

Barbera, Joseph: 'My Life in 'Toons: From Flatbush to Bedrock in Under a Century', Turner, 1994

Barrier, Michael: 'Hollywood Cartoons: American Animation in its Golden Age', Oxford University Press, 1999

Baxter, John: 'Disney During World War II: How the Walt Disney Studio Contributed to Victory in the War', Disney Editions, 2014

Bell, Elizabeth, Haas, Lynda and Sells, Laura: 'From Mouse to Mermaid: The Politics of Film, Gender, and Culture', Indiana University Press, 1995

Bluth, Don: 'Somewhere Out There: My Animated Life', Smart Pop, 2022

Byrne, Eleanor & McQuillan, Martin: 'Deconstructing Disney', Pluto Press, 1999

Canemaker, John: 'Walt Disney's Nine Old Men and the Art of Animation', Disney Editions, 2001

Culhane, Shamus: 'Animation: From Script to Screen', St. Martin's Griffin, 1988

Dorfman, Ariel, Mattelart, Armand: 'How to Read Donald Duck: Imperialist Ideology in the Disney Comic', Siglo Veintíuno Argentina Editores, 1972 (Edition used: Pluto Press, 2019)

Eliot, Marc: 'Walt Disney: Hollywood's Dark Prince', Birch Lane Press, 1993

Finch, Christopher: 'Disney's Winnie the Pooh: A Celebration of the Silly Old Bear', Disney Editions, 2002

Fleischer, Richard: 'Out of the Inkwell: Mac Fleischer and the animation revolution', The University Press of Kentucky, 2005

Ghez, Didier: 'They Drew as The Pleased: The Hidden Art of Disney's Golden Age', Chronicle Books, 2015

Ghez, Didier: 'They Drew as They Pleased: The Hidden Art of Disney's Musical Years', Chronicle Books, 2016

Ghez, Didier: 'They Drew as They Pleased: The Hidden Art of Disney's Late Golden Age', Chronicle Books, 2017

Ghez, Didier: 'They Drew as They Pleased: The Hidden Art of Disney's Mid-Century Era', Chronicle Books, 2018

Ghez, Didier: 'They Drew as They Pleased: The Hidden Art of Disney's Early Renaissance', Chronicle Books, 2019

Ghez, Didier: 'They Drew as They Pleased: The Hidden Art of Disney's New Golden Age", Chronicle Books, 2020

Girveau, Bruno (edited by): 'Once Upon a Time Walt Disney: The sources of inspiration for the Disney Studios', Prestal Verlag, 2008

Green, Howard E.: 'The Tarzan Chronicles', Hyperion, 1999

Hischak, Thomas S., Robinson, Mark A.: 'The Disney Song Encyclopedia', Scarecrow Press, 2009

Holliss, Richard and Sibley, Brian: 'The Disney Studio Story', Octopus, 1988
Holt, Nathalia: 'The Queens of Animation: The Untold Story of the Women Who Transformed the World of Disney and Made Cinematic History', Little, Brown & Company, 2019
Iger, Bob: 'The Ride of a Lifetime', Bantam Press, 2019
Johnson, Mindy: 'Ink & Paint: The Women of Walt Disney's Animation', Hyperion, 2017
Kimball, Ward: 'Art Afterpieces', Magnum Books, 1979
King, C. Richard, Lugo-Lugo, Carmen R. & Bloodsworth-Lugo, Mary K.: 'Animating Difference', Rowman & Littlefield Publishers, Inc., 2010
Maltin, Leonard: 'The Disney Films', Hyperion, 1973 (3rd Edition, Hyperion, 1995)
Norman, Floyd: 'Animated Life: A Lifetime of tips, tricks, techniques and stories from a Disney Legend', Taylor & Francis, 2013
Osmond, Andrew: '100 Animated Feature Films', BFI/Palgrave Macmillan, 2010
Roberts, Shearon: 'Recasting the Disney Princess in an Era of New Media and Social Movements', Lexington Books, 2020
Schweizer, Peter & Schweizer, Rochelle: 'Disney: The Mouse Betrayed', Regnery Publishing, 1998
Shale, Donald: 'Donald Duck Joins Up: The Walt Disney Studio during World War II', UMI Research Press, 1982
Sherman, Robert B. and Sherman, Richard M.: 'Walt's Time: From Before to Beyond', Camphor Tree Publishers, 1998
Smith, Dave: 'Disney A to Z: The Official Encyclopedia', Disney Editions, 2006
Solomon, Charles: 'Once Upon A Dream: From Perrault's Sleeping Beauty to Disney's Maleficent', Disney Book Publishing Inc., 2014
Thomas, Bob: 'Walt Disney: An American Original', Simon & Schuster, 1976
Wasko, Janet: 'Understanding Disney: The Manufacture of Fantasy', Polity Press, 2001

Papers and articles

Armstrong, Stephen: 'Nazis at the gates: inside 'woke' Disney's culture wars', The Telegraph, May 28th, 2022 (https://www.telegraph.co.uk/films/0/nazis-gates-inside-woke-disneys-culture-wars/)
Bahr, Sarah: "Lilo & Stitch' at 20: How It Broke the Mold Long Before 'Moana'', New York Times, June 21st, 2022 (https://www.nytimes.com/2022/06/21/movies/lilo-and-stitch-20th-anniversary.html)
Bevan, Henry: 'Have Disney movies always had poor LGBTQ+ representation?', Little White Lies, March 16th, 2017 (https://lwlies.com/articles/disney-animation-queer-coding-lgbt-subtext/)
Buchwald, Elisabeth and Delouya, Samantha: 'Disney and DeSantis have settled their yearslong dispute', CNN.com, March 27th, 2024 (https://edition.cnn.com/2024/03/27/business/desantis-disney-fight-reaches-settlement/index.html)
Callen, April: 'Almost There, Indeed: Disney Misses the Mark on Modernizing Black Womanhood and Subverting the Princess Tradition in The Princess and the Frog', College of Communication Master Arts Theses. 1., 2012 (https://via.library.depaul.edu/cmnt/1)
Chase, Marilyn: 'How Disney Propaganda Shaped Life on the Home Front During WWII', Smithsonian Magazine, July 11, 2022
Dickson, EJ: 'How 'Disney Adults' Became the Most Hated Group on the Internet', RollingStone.com, June 21, 2022 (https://www.rollingstone.com/culture/culture-features/disney-adults-tiktok-hated-internet-1370226/)

Doherty, Thomas: 'When Leni Riefenstahl Came to Hollywood', The Hollywood Reporter, August 23rd, 2021 (https://www.hollywoodreporter.com/movies/movie-features/leni-riefenstahl-hollywood-1235001606/)

Ebiri, Bilge: ''Let's Make the *Dumbo* of Our Generation' An oral history of *Lilo & Stitch*, the Disney movie that almost brought hand-drawn animation back', vulture.com, October 19th, 2022 (https://web.archive.org/web/20221019144402/https://www.vulture.com/2022/10/an-oral-history-of-lilo-and-stitch-a-hand-drawn-miracle.html)

Fisher, Timmy: 'Life of a Song: When You Wish Upon a Star – the Disney song taps into a need for escapism', Financial Times, September 19th, 2022 (https://ig.ft.com/life-of-a-song/wish-upon-a-star.html)

Flood, Brian: 'Disney admitted foray into politics, culture wars hurt its bottom line in SEC filing: Jonathan Turley', foxnews.com, November 27th, 2023 (https://www.foxnews.com/media/disney-admitted-foray-politics-culture-wars-hurt-bottom-line-sec-filing-jonathan-turley)

Giardina, Henry: 'How Howard Ashman Forced Disney to Tell Queer Stories', intomore.com, August 11th, 2021 (https://www.intomore.com/entertainment/film/howard-ashman-forced-disney-tell-queer-stories/)

Johnson, Lisa: 'The Disney Strike of 1941: From the Animator's Perspective', Rhode Island College, 2008

Kadlec, Jeanna: 'Deconstructing Disney: The Princess Problem of 'Frozen II', longreads.com, January 2nd, 2020 (https://longreads.com/2020/01/02/princess-problem-of-frozen-ii/)

King, Susan: 'New 'Winnie the Pooh' movie goes back to its Hundred Acre Wood roots', Los Angeles Times, July 13th, 2011 (https://www.latimes.com/entertainment/la-xpm-2011-jul-13-la-et-winnie-the-pooh-20110713-story.html)

Laemle, Jessica L.: 'Trapped in the Mouse House: How Disney has Portrayed Racism and Sexism in its Princess Films', Student Publications. 692, 2018 (https://cupola.gettysburg.edu/student_scholarship/692)

Lodge, Guy: 'Why Beauty and the Beast isn't the first Disney movie for LGBT audiences', Guardian, March 3rd, 2017 (https://www.theguardian.com/film/2017/mar/03/beauty-and-the-beast-gay-disney-movie)

Norman, Floyd: 'Black Crows and Other PC Nonsense', floydnorman.com, April 27th, 2019 (https://web.archive.org/web/20200629121250/https://floydnormancom.squarespace.com/blog/2019/4/27/black-crows-and-other-pc-nonsense)

Parks, Kristine: 'Disney's 'stunning' financial statements show company has risked profits for woke politics: Ted Cruz', foxnews.com, November 28th, 2023 (https://www.foxnews.com/media/disneys-stunning-financial-statements-show-company-risked-profits-woke-politics-ted-cruz)

Prater, Nia: 'The Disney-DeSantis Feud Ends With a Whimper', New York Magazine, March 27th, 2024 (https://nymag.com/intelligencer/article/the-disney-desantis-feud-ends-with-a-whimper.html)

Radloff, Jessica: 'Why Most Disney Heroines Don't Have Mothers and So Many More Secrets From The Disney Archives', Glamour.com, September 10th, 2014 (https://www.glamour.com/story/disney-secrets-beauty-and-the-beast)

Radulovic, Petrana: ''We're going to hide it': How Lilo & Stitch succeeded by staying off Disney's radar', polygon.com, September 16th, 2021 (https://www.polygon.com/features/22675483/lilo-and-stitch-disney-animation-chris-sanders-dean-deblois)

Rose, Steve: 'Cotton plantations and non-consensual kisses: how Disney became embroiled in the culture wars', Guardian, June 16th, 2021 (https://www.theguardian.com/film/2021/jun/16/how-disney-became-embroiled-in-the-culture-wars)

Stanley, Tim: 'From conservative to 'woke': the truth about Disney's politics', The Telegraph, September 11th, 2023 (https://www.telegraph.co.uk/films/0/the-truth-about-disneys-woke-politics/)

Tait, Amelia: 'The "Disney adult" industrial complex', NewStatesmen.com, February 24th 2024 (https://www.newstatesman.com/culture/2024/02/disney-adult-superfan-industrial-complex)

Taylor, Drew: ''The Rescuers Down Under': The Untold Story of How the Sequel Changed Disney Forever', collider.com, December 16th, 2020 (https://collider.com/disney-rescuers-down-under-history-explained/)

VanHooker, Brian: 'Why the hell did straight-to-VHS Disney sequels ever exist?', melmagazine.com, January 21st, 2020 (https://melmagazine.com/en-us/story/why-the-hell-did-straight-to-vhs-disney-sequels-ever-exist)

Wabuke, Hope: 'Disney's Disembodied Black Characters', LA Review of Books, March 23rd, 2021 (https://lareviewofbooks.org/article/disneys-disembodied-black-characters/)

Films

The Boys: The Sherman Brothers' Story (dir. Gregory V Sherman, Jeffrey C. Sherman, Walt Disney Pictures, 2009)

Frank and Ollie (dir. Theodore Thomas, Walt Disney Pictures, 1995)

Growing Up with Nine Old Men (dir. Theodore Thomas, Walt Disney Studios Home Entertainment, 2013)

Howard (dir. Don Hahn, Stone Circle Pictures, 2018)

The Many Adventures of Winnie the Pooh: The Story Behind the Masterpiece (dir. Harry Arends, Walt Disney Home Video, 1996)

Mickey: The Story of a Mouse (dir. Jeff Malmberg, Disney Original Documentary, Tremolo Productions, 2022)

Pencils Vs. Pixels (dir. Barry Dariz, Phil Earnest, Hideout Pictures, 2023)

Picture Perfect: The Making of Sleeping Beauty (dir. Les Perkins, Walt Disney Studios Home Entertainment, 2008)

The Sweatbox (dir. John-Paul Davidson, Trudie Styler, Buena Vista Pictures, 2002)

Waking Sleeping Beauty (dir. Don Hahn, Stone Circle Pictures, 2009)

Short films

Four Methods of Flush Riveting (Disney, 1942)

Chicken Little (Disney, 1943)

Picture Credits

Picture 1: Wikimedia Commons, photographer unknown

Pictures 2, 9–11, 13–37, 39: moviestillsdb.com, copyright by Walt Disney Pictures and other relevant production studios and distributors.

Pictures 3–8: moviestillsdb.com, copyright by Walt Disney Pictures, RKO Radio Pictures and other relevant production studios and distributors.

Picture 12: moviestillsdb.com, copyright by Metro-Goldwyn-Mayer and other relevant production studios and distributors.

Picture 38: Author's personal collection, copyright by Michael Thomas

Index

9/11 *see* World Trade Center
101 Dalmatians (1996), 73

A Bug's Life, 168, 181
A Goofy Movie, 35, 84, 117
ABBA, 131
Academy Award Review of Walt Disney Cartoons, 3
Academy Awards:
 76th Academy Awards, 176–9
 Best Animated Feature, 171, 176–9
 Best Animated Short Film, 3, 4, 37
 Best Picture, 176, 238
 Best Score, 91, 114, 132
 Best Screenplay, 127
 Best Song, 91, 114, 132, 149
 Honorary Award, 176
Adventures of Ichabod and Mr. Toad, The, 46–8, 192
Aguilera, Christina, 43
Aids crisis, 114
Aladdin (1992), **125–8**
 Aladdin (character), 88, 125
 Aladdin and the King of Thieves, 117
 animated series, 117
 Disney Renaissance, place in, 134, 172
 Genie, 126–7
 Goofy cameo, 34
 Iago, 125, 192
 pitch by Howard Ashman, 114, 120
 Princess Jasmine, 88, 125, 192, 217, 227
 Return of Jafar, The, 117, 127
 Robin Williams feud, 126–8
 soundtrack, 115, 120, 222
Alcohol, representation of, 18–20, 60–61
Alice in Wonderland (1951), **54–7**,
 influence of Mary Blair, 56, 64
 production, 53, 54–7
 recycled animation, 48
 remake, 74, 99
 rotoscope, use of, 38
 voice actors, 84
Alice in Wonderland (2010), 74, 99
Aliens, 228
Altman, Robert, 126
Anastasia, 228
Anderson-Lopez, Kristen, 207, 211, 213
Andrews Sisters, The, 43–4
Animator's strike of 1941, 63, 77
Antz, 168, 181
Aristocats, The, **83–6**,
 alcohol in, 18
 Marie, 83, 169, 171
 original story, 131, 181
 proposed sequel, 118
 racism in, 182, 198
 recycled animation, 47
 soundtrack, 92
 talking animals, 192
 Thomas O'Malley, 83, 109
 voice actors, 83–6
Ashman, Howard:
 Aladdin, influence on, 114
 Beauty and the Beast, influence on, 123
 death, 115
 early career, 113
 Howard, 115, 123
 illness, 114–5, 123
 legacy, 115, 222, 248
 Menken, work with, 113–5
 soundtrack work:
  Aladdin, 114, 125
  Beauty and the Beast, 114, 120, 121
  Little Mermaid, The, 113
  Oliver & Company, 113
Atlantis: The Lost Empire, **165–8**,
 Atlantean language, 166
 Atlantis: Milo's Return, 249

box office performance, 181
deaths relating to, 146, 165, 217
Princess Kida, 228
plagiarism claims, 165–8
voice actors, 85

Babbitt, Art, 5, 63
Bambi, **21–3**,
Bambi, a Life in the Woods, 4, 23, 217
death in, 21, 217
emotional impact, 21, 132
influence of, 22, 167, 246, 247
recycled animation, 48
Barbera, Joseph, 51
Beauty and the Beast (1991), **120–4**,
awards nominations, 176
Beast, 88, 237
Belle, 217, 120, 122, 124, 227
Belle's Magical World, 117, 249
box office success, 148
death in, 146
influence of earlier films, 10, 121
influence on later films, 141, 211
queer readings of, 122–4
recycled animation, 48
remake, 123–4
soundtrack, 114, 115, 120–1
stage musical, 115, 121, 143
success of, 125, 134, 138, 245
voice actors, 85
Beauty and the Beast (2017), 123–4
Bedknobs and Broomsticks, 92
Bergen, Edgar, 40–1
Big Hero 6, 19, 85, **215–8**, 226
Bird, Brad, 61, 97–9
Black Cauldron, The, **100–102**,
animators, 97, 100
author's hatred of, ix, 100–2, 146, 174, 237
box office failure, 100–1, 105, 165, 188
death in, 146, 237
Gurgi, 101, 165, 237
Princess Eilonwy, 228
production, 100–2, 105, 107
Blair, Mary, 56, 64, 68
Blessed, Brian, 148, 149
Bluth, Don, 97, 104, 109, 158, 173
Bolt, **190–3**, 203
Brave, 228
Broderick, Matthew, 75, 89, 199
Bronze Age, ix, 47, 105, 215
Brother Bear, **176–9**, 181
Brothers Grimm, 4, 52, 134–5, 136, 202, 208
Bugs Bunny, 18, 34
Burton, Tim, 34, 74, 98–9
Buttram, Pat, 84, 96

Callen, April, 199–200
Cars, 118, 168, 220
Castellaneta, Dan, 127
CGI:
early experimentation with, 98
impact on animation industry, 181, 182, 190–1
scepticism of, 98
transition to, 181, 182
use in *Dinosaur*, 158, 177
use in Disney animated classics:
Bronze Age, 105, 107
Disney Renaissance, 118, 132, 141
Post-Renaissance, 154, 173, 177
Revival Era, 203–4
use in live-action Disney films, 159
use in *The Lion King* (2019), 202
Chapek, Bob, 243
Chicken Little, **182–6**,
author's hatred of, 182, 186, 193
critical derision, 191
death relating to, 217
early *Chicken Little* short, 29–30
use of *Raiders of the Lost Ark*, 42, 193
Chinese Communist Party, 145
Christianity:
complaints made in the name of, 95, 139–40, 185–6, 243
Pocahontas' conversion to, 136
representation of, 12, 14, 43, 139–40
Cinderella (1950), **51–3**,
absent parents in, 217
box office success, 53
Cinderella (character):
animation of, 59, 61
Disney Princess, 227
role in film, 51–3, 70, 216, 238
wishes, relationship to, 11

early film adaptations, 52
family in, 217, 238
Goofy holler, 35
history of, 52, 135
Mary Blair's influence on, 64
production, 52–5, 59, 61
remake, 229
Clark, Buddy, 42–3
Clark, Les, 59
Clements and Musker:
Aladdin, 125, 126, 172, 199
Great Mouse Detective, The, 103
Hercules, 142, 144, 172
legacy, 248
Little Mermaid, The, 113, 172, 199
Moana, 200–1, 223–4
Princess and the Frog, The, 199, 200–1
Treasure Planet, 172–3, 175
Clements, Ron, *see* Clements and Musker
Coco, 22
Collins, Phil, 149
Colvig, Pinto, 3, 7
Computer Generated Imagery *see* CGI
COVID-19, 235, 240, 242, 244, 247
Cristiani, Quirino, 3
Cruella de Vil, 75
Cruise, Tom, 125, 171
Cummings, Jim, 85

Daisy Duck, 34
Dark Age *see* Bronze Age
Davis, Mark, 59
Day, Dennis, 43
Death:
fake character death, 237
of protagonist's parents, 216–8
representation of, 22–3, 96, 146–7, 216–7
Deja, Andreas, 144
Destino, 156
DeVito, Danny, 132, 143
Dinosaur, **157–60**, 165, 193
'Disney 100', 245, 249
Disney Adults, 182–6
Disney Channel, 116, 175, 198
Disney MovieToons *see* Disneytoon Studios
Disney Plus:
availability of films, ix, 156, 189, 215
cost of, 184
exclusives, 215
impact on box office, 243–4
sensitivity warnings, 67
Disney Princesses, 156, 215, 224, 226–8, 230
Disney Renaissance, The:
fake deaths, 237
flops within, 116
inclusivity, efforts at, 198
place in animated canon, ix, 103, 125
quality of films during, 129, 134, 248
Disney, Roy, 8, 103, 104, 216–7
Disney, Roy E.:
Chairman of Animation Department, work as, 104, 107, 153, 156
role in company management, 104, 180–1, 227
Disney theme parks:
Disney Adults and, 183–4
Disney-MGM Studios, 131
Disneyland California, 60, 116, 188, 201
Disney World, 77, 243
'Gay days', 140
Imagineers, 188
influences on, 65–6
Magic Kingdom, Florida, 77, 183, 201
Tokyo Disneyland, 188
Disney, Walt:
anti-union stance, 63
childhood, influence of, 54, 58, 65
death of, 76–7, 79
death of parents, 216–7
early work, 3–4, 52, 54–5
futurist, 67
hands-on approach of, 53, 69, 77
legacy, 248
pioneering spirit, 3, 4, 10, 14–5, 187–9
profligacy, 8, 14, 15–6
rotoscoping, views on, 38
Disney's Sing-Along Songs, 37, 150
Disneytoon Studios, 117–118, 190, 206
Donald Duck:
Brazil, adventures in, 28, 34, 44
Fantasia 2000, 154
Mathmagic Land, adventures in, 34
Nazi Party, brief stint in, 30

popularity of, 13, 30–1, 33
sexual attraction to human women, 34
Dreamworks, 159, 163, 173, 181, 182, 203
DuckTales, 34, 116, 117, 208, 223
Dumbo (1941), **17–20**,
influence of, 92, 170
length, 28
production, 17–8, 20, 63
remake, 74, 99
representation of alcohol in, 18–20, 92
VHS release, 174
voice actors, 84–5
Dumbo (2019), 74, 99

Earle, Eyvind, 68–9
Eisner, Michael:
CEO of Walt Disney Company:
success as, 106, 180, 247, 250, 215
takeover as, 101, 104–5, 106
corporate responsibility, thoughts on, 201
editorial input of, 101, 105, 126
Fantasia 2000, thoughts on, 155
Jeffrey Katzenberg, feud with, 180
Jeffrey Katzenberg, work with, 104, 106
Pixar, refusal to buy, 190
Robin Williams, feud with, 127–8, 176, 178
Steve Jobs, feud with, 178, 179
Emperor's New Groove, The, **161–4**, 180, 192, 235
Encanto, 181, 192, 223, **238–40**, 244
Enchanted, 35, 203, 228
Endings, changed by Disney, 134–135

Fantasia, **13–6**,
dancers, 38
deleted scenes, 36
Fantasia 2000, gap between, 229
Fantasound, 15, 188
financial fallout, 15–6
influence of, 141, 153–6
marketing, 56
proposed sequels, 153–4
racism in, 197
Rite of Spring, The, 14
roadshow performances, 15, 155
Sorcerer's Apprentice, The, see *Sorcerer's Apprentice, The*
Fantasia 2000, **153–6**,
Culhane, John, 93
Donald Duck in, 34
Hunt, Pixote, 197
live action in, 42
musical choices, 154–6
sequel, role as, 117, 153–6, 229
Sorcerer's Apprentice, The, see *Sorcerer's Apprentice, The*
Felix the Cat, 5, 54–5
Finding Nemo, 22, 159, 168, 177–9
Fleischer, Max, 37, 38, 54
Florida:
culture war involvement, 242–3
Disneyworld Florida, *see* Disney theme parks
'Florida Project' *see* Disney theme parks
Florida studios, 131, 170
Fox, Michael J., 125
Fox and the Hound, The, **96–9**,
animators, 61, 96–9
death in, 22, 96
original ending, divergence from, 135
production, 96–7
recycled animation, 48
voice actors, 84
Frozen, **211–4**,
Academy Award win, 179
Anna, 180, 212, 227, 237
death in, 217
Disney 100 re-release, 245
Elsa, 123, 180, 227
influences, 115, 211, 212, 213
references in later films, 221, 227
sequels, 123, 229–31, 230
soundtrack, 211–4, 222
'Let It Go', 213, 229, 240
stage musical, 211
voice actors, 212, 213–4
Frozen II, **229–31**,
flaws, 229–31, 235
generational trauma, representation of, 238
inclusivity in, 230–1, 242
queer representation, lack thereof, 229–30
sequel, role as, 117, 221, 227, 229–31

Frozen III, 123, 230
Fun and Fancy Free, 34, **39–41**,

Gabor, Eva, 83, 85, 119
Garity, William, 187–8, 189
Gen Z, 173–4, 183
Generational trauma, 238–40
Geronimi, Clyde, 69, 248
'Go woke, go broke', 242–3
Golden Age, ix, 17, 248
Good Neighbor Policy, 27
Goofy:
  early shorts, 33, 46
  film roles, 34–5
  Goofy holler, 35, 139
  popularity of, 13, 31, 185
  Saludos Amigos, 29, 47
  voice actor, 7
Great Mouse Detective, The, **103–6**,
  animators, 58, 61
  death in, 146
  production, 103, 105, 107, 193

Hall, Don, 206, 215, 216
Hamlet, 117, 118, 130
Hamilton, 114, 222–3
Hanna, William, 51
Harris, Phil, 83–4, 88
Henry IV, 130
Hercules, **142–4**,
  family affairs of, 217, 238
  influenced by, 143–4
  Meg, 88, 143
  Muses, the, 198
  mythological inaccuracies, 142–3, 217
  production, 143, 172
  voice actors, 143
Historical liberties, 135–7, 145
Hitler, Adolf, 12, 30, 31
Holloway, Sterling, 36, 84–5, 248
Home on the Range, 35, 115, **180–1**, 182, 217
Hunchback of Notre Dame, The, **138–41**,
  Christian themes, 138
  dark themes, 138–41, 238
  Esmeralda, 135, 139, 140, 227, 198
  Frollo, 138–40
  'Hellfire', 139, 141
  influence of earlier films, 10
  original ending, divergence from, 135
  Quasimodo, 135, 138–40, 198, 206, 217
  soundtrack, 222
  stage musical, 141
  voice actors, 85
Hundred Acre Wood *see* Ashdown Forest
Huxley, Aldous, 55–6

IMAX, 153, 155
Incredibles, The, 61, 97
Indiana Jones:
  Chicken Little cameo, 42, 193
  Disney reboot, 215
  Indiana Jones and the Last Crusade, 35, 146, 165
  Indiana Jones and the Temple of Doom, 101
  pop culture references, 208–9
  Raiders of the Lost Ark, 42, 104, 193, 209
Inside Out, 22, 132, 238
Inside Out 2, 133, 250
Iron Giant, The, 61, 97, 132
It's A Small World, 60, 91
Iwerks, Ub, 4, 32, 51, 54, 187

Jiminy Cricket, 9, 10, 12, 31, 40
Jobs, Steve, 98, 178, 179
Joel, Billy, 11, 108–109, 186
John, Elton, 45, 131–2, 149
Johnston, Ollie, 60–1, 96
Jones, James Earl, 74, 198
José Carioca, 29, 34, 44
Judaism, 23
Jungle Emperor, 166–7
Jungle Book, The, **78–80**,
  a night out with the characters from, 19
  animators, 61, 62, 79
  Baloo, 19, 47, 79, 84, 88, 192, 237
  box office success, 79–80
  missing parents, 217
  production of, 77, 78–9
  re-releases of, 34, 78, 80
  recycled animation, 47, 48
  references in, 208
  soundtrack, 79, 92, 212
  talking animals in, 192
  voice actors, 84
Jurassic Park, 132, 158

Kahl, Milt, 8, 61, 97
Katzenberg, Jeffrey:
  Ashman, Howard, work with, 113, 115
  CEO of Dreamworks, 163, 181
  Chairman of Walt Disney Studios:
    departure as, 127, 180–1
    films commissioned as, 107, 113, 157, 172
    success as, 106, 250
    takeover as, 101, 104–5, 106
  early career of, 101
  editorial input of, 101, 120, 122, 129–32,
Keane, Glen, 148, 202, 203
Kimba the White Lion see *Jungle Emperor*
Kimball, Ward, 60, 62–3
Kitt, Eartha, 161,162, 180

Lady and the Tramp, **65–7**, 83, 84, 109, 192, 198
Land Before Time, The, 97, 109, 158
Larson, Eric, 8, 61
Lasseter, John, 98–9, 118, 188, 190–1, 203
Laugh-O-Gram Studios, 52, 54
Laurel and Hardy, 33–4
Lebo M., 117, 131, 158
Lewis, Huey, 108, 113
Lightyear, 124, 242, 244
Lilo & Stitch, **169–71**,
  author's love of, 164, 247
  awards nominations, 176–7
  box office success, 171
  ending, 107
  Hawaiian culture in, 236
  hidden Mickey, 95
  influence of earlier films, 22
  merchandising, 169, 171
  Presley, Elvis, 42
  production, 169–71
  voice actors, 85
Lion King, The, **129–33**,
  adult images, rumours of, 95
  box office success, 132–3, 134, 161
  influence on future films, 141, 161–2
  influences, 130–1
  Lion King 1 ½, The, 118
  Lion King II: Simba's Pride, The, 117
  marketing, 129
  Mufasa, death of, 22–3, 217, 237
  original story, 131, 181
  plagiarism claims, 166–8
  popularity of, 129, 250–1
  production, 129–33
  remake, 74–5, 133, 202
  Scar:
    cameo in Hercules, 144
    'Be Prepared', 131
    role in early versions of film, 130
    queer coding of, 122, 229
    villainy of, 134, 238
  Simba, 88, 89, 166–7, 217
  talking animals, 193
  soundtrack, 115, 131–2, 158, 212
  voice actors, 74–5, 85, 89, 198–9
Lion King, The (2019), 74–5, 133, 202
Little Mermaid, The, **113–5**,
  adult images, rumours of, 95
  Ariel, 217, 227
  cameos in, 34
  influence of earlier films, 10
  Miranda, Lin-Manuel, 224
  original ending, 135
  production, 113–5, 172
  remake, 223–4
  Sebastian, 198, 224
  significance of success, 103, 125
  soundtrack, 113–5, 222, 224
  Ursula, 114, 146
Little Shop of Horrors, 113, 114
Live-action remakes, 73–5, 223–4
Lopez, Robert, 207, 211–3, 222
Lord of the Rings, The (1978), 100
Lounsbery, John, 61–2

Madagascar, 158
Make Mine Music, ix, 28, **36–8**, 42, 44, 48, 153
Many Adventures of Winnie the Pooh, The *see* Winnie the Pooh
Marvel:
  Big Hero 6, 215
  Disney films, appearances in, 226
  Disney ownership of, 183, 215
  Marvel Cinematic Universe, 202, 250, 251
  rotoscope, use of, 38
Mary Poppins, 91, 92, 209, 223, 230

McCartney, Linda, 43
Meet the Robinsons, **187–9**, 217
Melody Time, 28, **42–5**, 153, 239
Menken, Alan:
  Ashman, work with, 113–5, 120–1, 222, 248
  Egan, Susan, 143
  Miranda, Lin-Manuel, 224
  Post-Ashman work for Disney, 125, 141, 143, 224
Mickey Mouse:
  development of, 14, 32–3, 187
  film roles of, 33–4, 154
  hidden Mickeys, 95
Midler, Better, 109, 155
Millennials, 108, 129, 183, 203
Miller, Ron, 97, 98, 104, 126
Milne, AA, 90, 205
Miniature railways, 58
Minnie Mouse, 10, 34, 184
Miranda, Lin-Manuel, 222–4, 239, 249, 250
Misogyny, examples of, 59
Miyazaki, Hayao, 166
Moana, **222–4**,
  cultural sensitivity and, 201
  impact of, 230, 235
  Moana, 227
  original story, 181
  soundtrack, 222–4
  voice actors, 86, 249
  Zootopia, referenced in, 221
Moana 2, 86, 117, **249–51**
Monsters Inc., 176, 177
Mufasa, 22–3, 132, 237
Mulan, **145–7**,
  death in, 145–7, 165
  Disney Renaissance, role in, 125, 181, 198
  Mulan, 123, 145, 146, 165, 198, 217, 227
  production, 145–6
  queer readings of, 123
Multiplane, 10, 187
Muppets, The, 172, 183, 215, 226
Musker, John, *see* Clements and Musker

Nadia: The Secret of Blue Water, 165, 166
Nazi Party, The, 12, 23, 30, 131, 146
Ne Zha 2, 133
Nightmare Before Christmas, The, 99
Nine Old Men, the, 58–64, 96, 97, 153
Norman, Floyd, 197

Oh My Disney, 226
Okrand, Marc, 166
Oliver & Company, **107–109**, 113, 212, 237
One Hundred and One Dalmatians, **73–5**,
  animators, 60, 61
  box office success, 73
  Oliver & Company, reference in, 109
  remake, 73–5
  rotoscope, use of, 38
  Starlight Barking, The, 75
  talking animals, 191–2
Oswald the Lucky Rabbit, 5, 7, 32, 55

Package Era, ix, 28, 42, 53, 247
Parnell, Kirsten, 122
Patten, Luana, 40–1, 45
Peet, Bill, 79
Peter Pan, **58–64**,
  alcohol, representation of, 19
  animators, 58–64
  production, 53
  racism in, 59, 74, 182
  remake, 74
  soundtrack, 57, 58–9
  voice actors, 84
  Wendy, 239, 246
Peter Pan and Wendy, 74
Pinocchio, **9–12**,
  allegorical readings, 12
  animators, 13, 62, 63
  impact of World War II, 28
  original novel, 9–10
  Pinocchio (character), 9–12, 40, 177, 237, 239
  rotoscope, use of, 38
  soundtrack, 11, 40
  talking animals, 192
  VHS release, 174
  voice actors, 12, 84
  'When You Wish Upon A Star', 11, 211, 248
Pixar:
  impact on animation, 177–8, 182, 190–1

cameos in the animated canon, 226
CAPS technology, 118
collaborations with former Disney animators, 98
emotional response to, 22
falling out with, 178
founding of, 98
'gone woke', 242
production of *Toy Story 2*, 235
purchase by Disney, 98, 179, 190, 215
Pocahontas, **134–7**,
critical reception of, 134
historical inaccuracies, 135–7
Pocahontas (character), 198, 217, 227
Pocahontas II: Journey to a New World, 117
production, 131
rotoscope, use of, 38
soundtrack, 134, 222
voice actors, 85
Post-Renaissance Era, ix
Price, Vincent, 106
Princess and the Frog, The, **197–201**,
Blackness in, 197–201
death in, 217
Disney Renaissance, role in, 202, 204
recycled animation, 48
Tiana, 192, 199, 227
Princesses *see* Disney Princess
Propaganda films, 29–30

Queer readings, 122–4
Queer representation, 123–4, 229–30, 241–3
Queer-coding in Disney villains, 122, 229

Racism:
among audience members, 74
attempts to address, 74–5, 198–201
examples of:
Aladdin, 125
Aristocats, The, 83, 85, 198
Dumbo, 197–8
Fantasia, 197
Lady and the Tramp, 67, 74, 83, 198
Peter Pan, 59, 74
Princess and the Frog, The, 199–200
Rescuers, The, 94
Song of the South, 198, 201
Superman, 37
Ralph Breaks the Internet, 115, 117, **225–8**, 229
Ratatouille, 97
Ravenscroft, Thurl, 84
Raya and the Last Dragon, 85–6, 200, 227, **235–7**, 244
Recycled animation, 47–8, 62, 77
Reitherman, Wolfgang:
cost-cutting techniques, 47, 77, 104
Musicana, 153
nepotistic tendencies, 77
Nine Old Men, role among, 62, 96
Remakes *see* Live-action remakes
Renaissance *see* Disney Renaissance, The
Rescuers, The, **93–5**,
animators, 62
Goofy holler, 35
hidden Mickey, 95
International Rescue Aid Society, incompetence of, 93–5
later releases, 34, 94
reception, 93
recycled animation, 48
sequel, 116–9, 229
talking animals, 192
VHS scandal, 94
voice actors, 84
Rescuers Down Under, The, **116–9**, 120, 144, 217, 229
Return of Jafar, The see *Aladdin*
Revival Era, ix, 203, 221
Rice, Tim, 125, 131, 149
Riefenstahl, Leni, 131
Robin Hood, **87–9**,
animators, 61–62
raw sex appeal of, 87–9
recycled animation, 47
Robin Hood (character), 87–9, 237, 246
talking animals, 193
voice actors, 84, 88–89
Rogers, Roy, 45
Rotoscoping, 7, 36–7

Salten, Felix, 4, 23
Sanders, Chris, 169–71
Saludos Amigos, **27–31**, 33, 34, 64

Scarfe, Gerald, 144
Schafer, Sam, 103
Schumacher, Thomas, 148, 150, 170, 177
Schwartz, Stephen, 141, 222
Second Anglo-Afghan War, 106
Second World War *see* World War II
Selick, Henry, 99
Sequels, 116–9, 229, 230, 249
Sexual awakenings, 87–9, 116
Shaggy Dog, The, 23
Shakespearean influences, 117, 118, 130, 168
Sherman Brothers, the, 44, 79, 91–92, 207, 248
Shrek,
  Best Animated Feature, 176
  impact of, 173, 181, 203, 247
  references, 209
Silver Age, ix
Simpsons, The, 97, 127, 215
Sleeping Beauty, **68–70**,
  alcohol, representation of, 19
  animators, 59, 197
  art design, 68–69
  Aurora, 70, 199, 227
  earlier versions, 136
  influence on later films, 100, 246
  Maleficent, 69–70
  recycled animation, 47
Smith, Dodie, 73, 75
Smith, Ethel, 44–5
Snow White and the Seven Dwarfs, **3–8**,
  Academy Awards, 176
  Animators, 8, 58–9, 61, 63
  box office success, 8, 28, 53
  death in, 146, 216–7, 237
  Dopey, 6, 13
  dwarfs, 6–7, 84
  Evil Queen, 7, 88, 134–5, 146, 238
  financial incentive, 4, 16
  influence on later films, 246, 247, 250–1
  later releases, 245
  marketing, 185
  production, 4–8, 77, 187
  recycled animation, 47
  rotoscope, use of, 37–8
  Snow White (character), 7, 227, 237, 238
  voice actors, 6, 7, 84
Song of the South, 40, 198, 200, 201
Sorcerer's Apprentice, The, 8, 13, 34, 154
South America:
  representation of, 28–9, 34, 44
  studio tour of, 28–9
Spielberg, Steven, 97, 104, 171, 181, 223
Sporting prowess, the author's complete lack thereof, 17, 27
Star Trek, 166, 172
Star Wars,
  Disney ownership, 183, 215, 226
  'hero's journey', 168
  Lucasfilm, 98
  Princess Leia, 228
  rotoscope, use of, 38
Starlight Barking, The, 75
Steamboat Willie, 4, 32–3
Stewart, James, 43, 143
Stiers, David Ogden, 85, 248
Sting, 161–3
Stockholm Syndrome, 121–2
Stokowski, Leopold, 13–4
Studio Ghibli, 166, 171, 177, 178
Strange World, 123, 238, **241–4**
Streaming Era, ix, 240
Styler, Trudi, 161–3
Sweatbox, The, 162–4
Swift, Taylor, 182–3
Sword in the Stone, The, **76–77**,
  absent parents, 217
  animators, 61, 77
  Archimedes (owl), 192
  recylced animation, 47, 48
  soundtrack, 92
  voice actors, 62, 77

Talking animals, 191–3, 248
Tangled, 146, **202–4**, 212, 227, 237, 238
Tarzan, 146, **148–150**, 158, 192, 217
Taylor, Deems, 14, 154
Thomas, Frank, 60–1, 96
Thompson, Bill, 84
Three Caballeros, The, 29, **32–5**, 48
Tinker Bell, 19, 59, 60, 227
Tippett, Phil, 157–8
Touchstone Pictures, 126, 145
Toy Story, 98, 177, 190, 242
Toy Story 2, 22, 235

Toy Story 3, 22
Toy Story 4, 230
Transition Era, ix, 47
Treasure Planet, **172–5**, 177, 182, 242
Trigger (horse), 45
Triplettes de Belleville, Les, 178–9
Tripping college students, 34, 56
Trousdale and Wise,
  Atlantis: The Lost Empire, 165
  Beauty and the Beast, 120, 165
  Hunchback of Notre Dame, The, 138, 139, 141, 165
  influence, 248
  Rescuers Down Under, The, 120
Trousdale, Gary, *see* Trousdale and Wise
Turning Red, 124, 238
Twin Towers *see* World Trade Center
Tudyk, Alan, 85–6, 224, 246, 250
Tytla, Bill, 5, 7, 14

Up, 22, 132

Verhoeven, Paul, 157–8

WALL•E, 191
'We Don't Talk About Bruno', 240
Wells, Frank, 104, 132, 180, 215, 247, 250
Who Framed Roger Rabbit, 34, 84
Wild, The, 157–60
Williams, Robin,
  Academy Awards, 176, 178, 179
  Aladdin, 126–8, 208
  collaborations with Disney, 126–7
  fued with Disney, 127–8, 176, 178
  voice acting, 117, 126
Wilson, Owen, 161

Winnie the Pooh:
  Christopher Robin, 230
  Many Adventures of Winnie the Pooh, The, **90–2**,
    animators, 62
    recycled animation, 47
    relationship to sequel, 206, 229
    soundtrack, 91–2
  voice actors, 84, 85, 207
  Welcome to Pooh Corner, 116
  Winnie the Pooh, **205–7**,
    runtime, 28
    sequel, role as, 117, 206, 207, 229
    soundtrack, 207, 211
    suitability for young children, 78
  Winnie the Pooh and the Blustery Day, 91
  Winnie the Pooh and the Honey Tree, 90
Wise, Kirk, *see* Trousdale and Wise
Wish, 11, 85, **245–8**, 249
Wishing, the concept of, 11, 12, 256
World Trade Center, 107–108
World War II,
  impact,
    on European box office, 15, 53, 77, 153
    on studio output, 29–31, 55, 156
    on US foreign policy, 27
  military insignia, design of, 30–31, 185
  military service in, 31, 42, 43
Wreck-It Ralph, 85, 146, **208–10**, 225, 227
Wreck-It Ralph 2 see *Ralph Breaks the Internet*

Zimmer, Hans, 132
Zootopia, 123, 184, 193, **219–21**, 246
Zootopia 2, 86